HTML
WEB Magic

HTML
WEB Magic

BY ARDITH IBAÑEZ AND NATALIE ZEE

Hayden
Books

HTML Web Magic

Library of Congress Catalog Number: 96-78281
ISBN: 1-56830-335-1

Printed in the United States of America 1 2 3 4 5 6 7 8 9 0

Warning and Disclaimer

Trademark Acknowledgments

Associate Publisher
John Pierce

Publishing Manager
Laurie Petrycki

Managing Editor
Lisa Wilson

Marketing Manager
Stacey Oldham

Acquisitions Editor
Michelle Reed

Development Editors
Robyn Holtzman, Laurie McGuire

Copy/Production Editor
Terrie Deemer

Technical Editor
George Pytlik

Editorial Contributor
Tim Webster

Publishing Coordinator
Karen Flowers

Cover Designer
Aren Howell

Book Designer
Gary Adair

Manufacturing Coordinator
Brook Farling

Production Team Supervisors
Laurie Casey, Regina Rexrode, Joe Millay

Production Team
Trina Brown, Dan Caparo, Christopher Morris,
Scott Tullis, Pamela Woolf

v

About the Authors

Currently working as a designer for Macromedia's award-winning Web site, **Ardith Ibañez** has amassed experiences as a graphic designer, illustrator, painter, and photographer. She received a Bachelor of Arts in Design from Stanford University where she earned various grants and awards to create an interdisciplinary design project examining urban culture in Manila, Philippines. You can find examples of her artwork throughout the book. In her spare time, Ardith is designing and helping to maintain the "Global Collage" art project—a Web site that displays artwork from all over the world, from all walks of life, projected on the exterior wall of a public San Francisco building. Through the Collage, Ardith and fellow project coordinators hope to bring the Internet and art appreciation into the everyday lives of everyday people.

Natalie Zee has been a Web designer for Macromedia's award-winning Web site for the past year and a half. She received her Bachelor of Arts degree from the University of California at Berkeley in Communications and Technology where she focused her study on the social and cultural implications of the Internet on society. In the days before Netscape, she and her classmates were some of the first to experiment with the Web by creating a class Web site containing student home pages, papers, assignments, and class discussions. That pioneering Web site took hold as the model for future classes, eventually becoming a meeting place for the first distance learning class between U.C. Berkeley and the University of Michigan. While attending Berkeley, Natalie worked as a research assistant for Howard Besser, a leading professor in information technology, assisting him in his Web research and teaching HTML to students.

Dedication

This book is dedicated to anyone who appreciates design in all forms, enjoys pumpkin pie, and is kind to children.

—Ardith

This book is dedicated to the Web designers of the world.

—Natalie

Acknowledgments

I am eternally grateful to my soul man, Ben, for his love, support, patience, programming smarts, goofy antics, and smiling face. Responsible for introducing me to the World Wide Web, he has also contributed amazing JavaScript examples to this book. Thanks, also, to friends and colleagues for their inspiration, ideas, and work contributions—Jason Wolf, Elliot Loh, Joanie McCollom, Michael Merrill, Olivia Ongpin and the Macromedia Web team. I also appreciate the companies and organizations who agreed to serve as examples—Macromedia, The Main Quad, Trilogy, Toad the Wet Sprocket, c|net, and Barbell Web Design. Thanks to my dear friends and family who had to deal with me falling off the face of the earth, especially my sister, Arlene, Freda Koblik, Chris Han, Katie Geib, Claudia Gonzalez, Julie Jo Bousman, and Cindy Ramirez. Special thanks go out to my parents (and Ben's), Dan, Gloria, Gerry, and Helen, who kept me going by sending care packages, writing letters, or calling—constantly reminding me how great I am. I couldn't have written this book without you. Finally, I would also like to salute my partner, Natalie Zee. By writing this book, we have become better friends and better Web designers.
— Ardith

Thanks to my parents, Edward and Jennie, for their love and support, especially to my dad who let me break his computer when I was 12. Also thanks to Howard Besser for introducing me to the Web and for his wisdom and guidance. I would like to thank Jason Wolf for everything he has done for me, without him this book would not be possible. I must also thank Ardith Ibañez. Thanks to the original IMPACT crew at Berkeley who in addition to being great friends, taught me all about HTML and Web design: Brian Hoshi, Larry Shein, David Stazer, and Alex Sutton. To the entire Web team at Macromedia, it is great to be part of such an awesome group! I would especially like to thank Victoria Dawson, Christine Mc Carthy, Susan Harris, John Petersen, Jorge Arriola and Matt Connors. Finally, to my dear friends Karen Vigna, Maggie Peng, Kate Martin, Eli Baker, and Paul Suto, thanks for understanding and putting up with me in the book writing process. Long live HTML!
—Natalie

Hayden Books

The staff of Hayden Books is committed to bringing you the best computer books. What our readers think of Hayden is important to our ability to serve our customers. If you have any comments, no matter how great or how small, we'd appreciate your taking the time to send us a note.

You can reach Hayden Books at the following:

Hayden Books
201 West 103rd Street
Indianapolis, IN 46290
317-581-3833

Email addresses:

America Online: Hayden Bks
Internet: hayden@hayden.com

Visit the Hayden Books Web site at http://www.hayden.com

Contents

Before You Begin

We decided to write *HTML Web Magic* to address the need for a comprehensive reference guide incorporating artistic and technological concerns. We wanted to help others realize that everyone is capable of good design if every aspect of their Web projects follows these basic rules:

- Be concise
- Be consistent
- Stick to your main objective
- Have fun with your ideas

The techniques mapped out in this book provide the tools for taking your Web site to the next level. We hope to inspire you to combine the techniques and apply them to your site as you see fit.

Welcome

If you're reading this book, you know that the World Wide Web is a highly dynamic medium giving you great potential to interact with people all over the world. As a Web designer, you must deal with issues that range from the technical—server impact, bandwidth, download time—to the practical—clear navigation, compelling, comprehensible content, interactivity with user—to the creative—graphics, movies, and sound.

By synthesizing techniques and tips for content organization, HTML (HyperText Markup Language) coding and graphics production, this book provides the tools and framework to build a well designed Web site. We focus on the fundamentals of good design on the Web so that the fast-growing Web technology will not outdate the information in this book. As we teach the importance of presenting information clearly and intelligently, we will also emphasize the necessity of fun and interactivity in a Web site.

1

Our Audience

We designed this book for those who want to create fun and well designed Web sites that strike a balance between great graphics and great information organization. Suggested prerequisites include basic familiarity with the Web, digital graphics, and general knowledge of HTML.

Conventions Used in This Book

Ellipses (...) are used in some techniques to denote abbreviated text.

The code continuation character (➡) is used in some techniques to show a continuous line of code split into 2 or more lines due to its length. ■

HTML Basics

How to Use this Section

This section offers some general guidelines and quick reference materials for writing HTML code. For basic reference guides, we have provided a comprehensive chart for all the HTML tags to build your Web pages, and table layout examples.

Web Design Basics

Here are a list of things we think you should keep in mind as you develop your content for the Web:

Images

1 **Bandwidth**—Who is your audience? How fast is your readers' connection to the Internet? What can they handle? What can your server handle? You must keep the size of your page proportional to the size of the network that carries it.

2 **High-resolution versus low-resolution images**—Consider the purpose of the graphics. Are you creating a portfolio (that requires high-quality, and hence high-resolution, images) or an informational site, where it might be appropriate to settle for slightly lower image quality for the sake of speed?

3 **File Sizes**—Keep them down! Try reducing the number of colors and gradients. Flatten your colors by erasing any stray dots or pixelation.

4 **Palettes**—Do you know what platform your audience uses? If not, we recommend using the "browser-safe" CLUT included on the CD to save your Web graphics with the 216 colors common to both Macintosh and Windows machines.

5 **Window Size**—Keep as much of your image as possible within a standard 640×480 window to avoid any unnecessary scrolling.

6 **Copyright Infringement**—Be original. You can't just "grab" images from other people's sites.

7 **Test Images**—Use samples to visualize concepts for your layout prototypes.

8 **Significance**—Use images to express your message clearly and powerfully. Gratuitous graphics just take extra time to download and view.

9 **Original Files**—Keep the original image files with layers intact for future editing and manipulation.

HTML Code

1 **Style**—You might want to write your tags in all caps to distinguish them from the rest of the page. Regardless of your style preference, be consistent! (HTML isn't case sensititve, but using the same style throughout makes it easier for you to read and "debug" your code later.)

2 **Tag Hierarchy**—It's a good idea to have consistent order for writing your tags. For the Macromedia site, font attributes are coded as follows:

```
<CODE><B><FONT SIZE=X COLOR=Y>text</FONT></B></CODE>
```

Image tag attributes look like this:

```
<IMG SRC="" WIDTH=X HEIGHT=Y BORDER=0 ALT="TEXT HERE">
```

With a consistent coding style, you can understand your code much easier and edit it much more quickly.

3 **Image Dimensions**—Including dimensions in your image tags means that your browser doesn't have to ask your server how large your image is. You have a better chance of faster download time.

4 **Alt Text**—Using alt text in your image tags provides necessary information to your audience that turns their images off. If you have a link described by a graphic, but fail to replicate the link in text form, alt text provides the necessary information.

5 **Table Border**—When using a table where you want the table items to align flush against the border, you must set the table border equal to zero or an invisible gutter will show up.

6 **Table Columns**—Browsers do not download tables as they scan the HTML code; they wait for the closing table tag before the table data shows up. You can expedite the download time by adding the COLSPEC=x in the main table tag, where x represents the number of columns in your table.

4

Quick Reference Chart

This is a handy chart of HTML tags organized to keep as a reference tool next to your computer. These are not ALL the HTML tags that exist, but the ones that are discussed in this book and the ones most frequently used by Web designers.

HTML Reference Chart-Main Tags

Element	Description
<HTML></HTML>	Start/End tags of the HTML document
<HEAD></HEAD>	Identifies the document head

Element	Description
`<META>`	Meta-info about document (must be in head)
`<META HTTP=EQUIV="name">`	Binds element to HTTP response header
`<META HTTP=EQUIV="Refresh"` `➥CONTENT=n>`	Refresh page every n seconds
`<META HTTP=EQUIV="Refresh"` `➥CONTENT=n; URL>`	Refesh page in n seconds by jumping to URL
`<TITLE></TITLE>`	Denotes title of HTML page (must be in head)
`<BODY></BODY>`	Specifies body of document
`<BODY BACKGROUND="URL">`	Background texture
`<BODY BGCOLOR=="#RRGGBB"` `➥or "colorname" ></BODY>`	Background color
`<BODY TEXT="#RRGGBB"` `➥or "colorname"> </BODY>`	Text Color
`<BODY LINK="#RRGGBB"` `➥or "colorname" ></BODY>`	Link Color
`<BODY VLINK="#RRGGBB"` `➥or "colorname" ></BODY>`	Visited Link Color
`<BODY ALINK="#RRGGBBî` `➥or "colorname" ></BODY>`	Active Link Color

Type Related	Description
`<Hn></Hn>`	Heading (n=1-6 with 1 as the largest heading)
`<Hn ALIGN=LEFT¦CENTER¦` `➥RIGHT¦NOWRAP¦CLEAR></Hn>`	Align heading 3.0
`<CODE></CODE>`	Text in monospace computer code
`<TT></TT>`	Teletype font
`<FONT SIZE=n></FONT>`	Font Size (n ranges from 1-7; default is 3)
`<FONT COLOR=="#RRGGBB"` `➥or "colorname"></FONT>`	Font Color
`<FONT FACE="fontname">` `➥</FONT>`	Specify Font (ususally common system fonts)
`<BASEFONT SIZE="n">`	Changes the base font value (where default basefont is 3) n=1-7
`<B></B>`	Bold

continues

HTML Reference Chart-Main Tags

Type Related	Description
<I></I>	Italic
<U></U>	Underline text
<S></S>	Strikeout text
	Subscript text
	Superscript text

Layout	Description
<BLOCKQUOTE></BLOCKQUOTE>	Block indent
 	Line break
<BR CLEAR=LEFT¦RIGHT¦ALL>	Clearing line break
<CENTER></CENTER>	Center
<DIV>	Division of a document
<HR>	Horizontal rule
<HR ALIGN=LEFT¦RIGHT¦ ➡CENTER>	Aligns horizontal rule
<HR SIZE=n>	Thickness of horizontal rule (n=number in pixels)
<HR WIDTH=n>	Width of horizontal rule (n=number in pixels)
<HR WIDTH=n%>	Width of horizontal rule defined by percentage of page
<HR NOSHADE>	Solid black horizontal rule
<NOBR>	Prevents line break
<P>	Paragraph return
<P ALIGN=LEFT¦CENTER¦RIGHT>	Align paragraph
<PRE></PRE>	Preformatted (displayed with browser default font, usually Courier)

Links	Description
<A HREF="url"></a>	Hypertext link
<A HREF="url" TARGET= ➡"window">	Link opens a new browser window

6

Links	Description
`<A HREF="url" TARGET=` `➡"framename">`	Link loads in a frame specified by frame name
`<A HREF="url" TARGET=` `➡"_self">`	For Frames: link loads in frame where the link was clicked
`<A HREF="url" TARGET=` `➡"_parent">`	For Frames: link loads in the immediate FRAMESET parent of document
`<A HREF="url" TARGET=` `➡"_top">`	For Frames: link loads in the full body of the window

Images	Description
`<IMG SRC="URL">`	Display image
`<IMG SRC="URL" ALIGN=TOP¦` `➡BOTTOM¦MIDDLE>`	Align image relative to text baseline
`<IMG SRC="URL" ALIGN=` `➡LEFT¦RIGHT>`	Align image relative to page
`<IMG SRC="URL" ALT=` `➡"alttext">`	Alternative/Descriptive Text—displayed when images are turned off
`<IMG SRC="URL" ISMAP>`	Image is an image map
`<IMG SRC="URL" USEMAP>`	Image is a client-side image map
`<IMG SRC="URL" WIDTH="n"` `➡HEIGHT="n">`	Image dimensions (in pixels)
`<IMG SRC="URL" BORDER=n>`	Image border (in pixels)
`<IMG SRC="URL" HSPACE=n` `➡VSPACE=n>`	Specifies horizontal or vertical spacing (in pixels)
`<IMG LOWSRC="URL" SRC=` `➡"URL">`	Specifies low-resolution load of image

Lists	Description
`<DL></DL>`	Definition title
`<DD>`	Definition
`<DT>`	Definition term
`<LI>`	List item (bullet when used with `<UL>`, numbered list with `<OL>`
`<OL></OL>`	Ordered list

continues

7

HTML Reference Chart-Main Tags

Lists	Description
`<OL COMPACT></OL>`	Compact ordered list
`<OL TYPE=A¦a¦I¦i¦1>`	Format of list items (caps, small, numerical, roman, or default)
`<LI TYPE=A¦a¦I¦i¦1>`	Controls format of list item
`<UL></UL>`	Unordered list
`<UL COMPACT></UL>`	Compact version of unordered list
`<UL TYPE=DISC¦CIRCLE¦` `➡SQUARE>`	Specifies bullet style

Forms	Description
`<FORM ACTION="URL"` `➡METHOD=GET¦POST></FORM>`	Define form

`<INPUT TYPE="TEXT¦`
`➡PASSWORD¦CHECKBOX¦RADIO¦`
`➡SUBMIT¦RESET">`
	Input field for HTML form

`<INPUT NAME="fieldname">`	Field name forms
`<INPUT CHECKED>`	Checked checkboxes or radio boxes forms
`<INPUT SIZE=n>`	Field size (in characters)
`<INPUT MAXLENGTH=n>`	Maximum length (in characters)
`<OPTION>`	Option (items that can be selected forms)
`<SELECT></SELECT>`	Selection list forms
`<SELECT NAME="listname">` `➡</SELECT>`	Name of list forms
`<SELECT SIZE=n></SELECT>`	n=number of options
`<TEXTAREA ROWS=n COLS=n>` `➡</TEXTAREA>`	Input box size
`<TEXTAREA NAME="boxname">` `➡</TEXTAREA>`	Name of box forms

Tables	Description
`<TABLE></TABLE>`	Defines table
`<TABLE BORDER></TABLE>`	Table border (on or off)

Tables	Description
`<TABLE BORDER=n></TABLE>`	Table border (width of table border)
`<TABLE CELLSPACING=n>`	Spacing between cells
`<TABLE CELLPADDING=n>`	Thickness of cell borders
`<TABLE WIDTH=n>`	Desired width (in pixels)
`<TABLE WIDTH=%>`	Width percent (percentage of page)
`<TD></TD>`	Table cell (must appear within table rows)
`<TD ALIGN=LEFT¦RIGHT¦CENTER` ➡`VALIGN=TOP¦MIDDLE¦BOTTOM>`	Alignment
`<TD NOWRAP>`	No linebreaks
`<TD COLSPAN=n>`	Columns to span
`<TD ROWSPAN=n>`	Rows to span
`<TD WIDTH=n>`	Desired width (in pixels)
`<TD WIDTH=n%>`	Width percent (percentage of table)
`<TH></TH>`	Table header
`<TH ALIGN=LEFT¦RIGHT¦CENTER` ➡`VALIGN=TOP¦MIDDLE¦BOTTOM>`	Alignment
`<TH NOWRAP>`	No linebreaks
`<TH COLSPAN=n>`	Columns to span
`<TH ROWSPAN=n>`	Rows to span
`<TH WIDTH=n>`	Desired width (in pixels)
`<TH WIDTH=n%>`	Width percent (percentage of table)
`<TR></TR>`	Table row
`<TR ALIGN=LEFT¦RIGHT¦CENTER` ➡`VALIGN=TOP¦MIDDLE¦BOTTOM>`	Alignment
`<CAPTION ALIGN=TOP¦BOTTOM>` ➡`</CAPTION>`	Specifies table caption

9

Frames	Description
`<FRAMESET></FRAMESET>`	Hosts the frame elements (must be placed in the header)
`<FRAMESET COLS=n>`	Column Widths

continues

HTML Reference Chart-Main Tags

Frames	Description
`<FRAMESET ROWS=`*`n`*`>`	Row height
`<FRAMESET SPACING=1¦0>`	Frame Spacing adds additional space between frames
`<FRAME SRC="`*`URL`*`">`	Single frame
`<IFRAME SRC="URL">`	Floating frame

Frame Attributes	Description
`<FRAME ALIGN=left¦center¦` ➡`right>`	Frame alignment
`<FRAME FRAMEBORDER=1¦0>`	Frame border (1 is default, 0 is no border)
`<FRAME NAME="`*`name`*`">`	Frame name
`<FRAME NORESIZE>`	Prevents resizing of frame
`<FRAME SCROLLING=yes¦no>`	Scrolling frame
`<FRAME MARGINHEIGHT="`*`n`*`">`	Frame height (in pixels)
`<FRAME MARGINWIDTH="`*`n`*`">`	Frame width (in pixels)

Multimedia	Description
`<EMBED SRC="`*`url`*`" WIDTH=` ➡`HEIGHT=`*`n`*`>`	Indicates an embedded object (used for *n* Shockwave)

Style Sheets	Description
`<STYLE TYPE="text/css">` ➡`</STYLE>`	Start and closing tags for the style element (must live in the head of the document)

Paragraph Style Properties	Description
`P{ color: color name }`	Text color of paragraph
`P{ background: color }`	Background color of paragraph
`P{ padding: length, %,` ➡`auto }`	Controls spacing between text and border of paragraph; can specify up to four values in order of padding for top, right, bottom, left
`P{ font-size: size in` ➡`points or pixels }`	Font size of text in paragraph (must have pt or px suffix)

10

HTML Reference Chart-Main Tags

Paragraph Style Properties	Description
`P{ font-family: font name }`	Specifies font
`P{ letter-spacing: }`	Controls spacing of letters
`P{ text-align: left¦` `➥right¦center¦justify }`	Alignment of paragraph
`P{ text-indent:length` `➥or % }`	Controls indent of first line of paragraph
`P{ border-color: color }`	Specifies color of border
`P{ border-width: thin¦` `➥medium¦thick }`	Specifies width of paragraph border

Link Style Properties	Description
`A:link {color: color name}`	Link color
`A:link {font-size: size in` `➥points or pixels}`	Size of font (must have pt or px suffix)
`A: link {font-family:` `➥font name}`	Specifies font

HTML Table Examples

Because HTML tables are such valuable layout tools for Web page design, we have provided some code examples and graphics of some basic table variations. We used table data background colors in the code to illustrate clearly the different cells, rows and columns. Remember you can set your own alignment and dimensions for table data to fit your needs.

1 Table 1 is a regular table with no border specified.

| Table Data Cell 1 | Table Data Cell 2 | Table Data Cell 3 | Table Data Cell 4 | Table Data Cell 5 |

```
<table>
     <tr>
          <td bgcolor=003333><font color=white>Table Data Cell
➥1</font></td>
```

11

```
            <td bgcolor=336666><font color=white>Table Data Cell
➥2</font></td>
            <td bgcolor=669999>Table Data Cell 3</td>
            <td bgcolor=99cccc>Table Data Cell 4</td>
            <td bgcolor=ccffff>Table Data Cell 5</td>
        </tr>
</table>
```

2 Table 2 is a regular table with border=0. Notice that this specification brings the table data cells closer together.

| Table Data Cell 1 | Table Data Cell 2 | Table Data Cell 3 | Table Data Cell 4 | Table Data Cell 5 |

```
<table border=0>
    <tr>
            <td bgcolor=003333><font color=white>Table Data Cell
➥1</font></td>
            <td bgcolor=336666><font color=white>Table Data Cell
➥2</font></td>
            <td bgcolor=669999>Table Data Cell 3</td>
            <td bgcolor=99cccc>Table Data Cell 4</td>
            <td bgcolor=ccffff>Table Data Cell 5</td>
        </tr>
</table>
```

3 Table 3 shows cellpadding used to create a buffer within the table data cells.

| Table Data Cell 1 | Table Data Cell 2 | Table Data Cell 3 | Table Data Cell 4 | Table Data Cell 5 |

```
<table border=0 cellpadding=10>
    <tr>
            <td bgcolor=003333><font color=white>Table Data Cell
➥1</font></td>
            <td bgcolor=336666><font color=white>Table Data Cell
➥2</font></td>
            <td bgcolor=669999>Table Data Cell 3</td>
            <td bgcolor=99cccc>Table Data Cell 4</td>
            <td bgcolor=ccffff>Table Data Cell 5</td>
        </tr>
</table>
```

4 Table 4 shows cellspacing used to create a buffer between the cells.

| Table Data Cell 1 | Table Data Cell 2 | Table Data Cell 3 | Table Data Cell 4 | Table Data Cell 5 |

```
<table border=0 cellspacing=10>
     <tr>
          <td bgcolor=003333><font color=white>Table Data Cell
➥1</font></td>
          <td bgcolor=336666><font color=white>Table Data Cell
➥2</font></td>
          <td bgcolor=669999>Table Data Cell 3</td>
          <td bgcolor=99cccc>Table Data Cell 4</td>
          <td bgcolor=ccffff>Table Data Cell 5</td>
     </tr>
</table>
```

5 Table 5 shows a cellpadding and cellspacing combination.

| Table Data Cell 1 | Table Data Cell 2 | Table Data Cell 3 | Table Data Cell 4 | Table Data Cell 5 |

```
<table border=0 cellpadding=10 cellspacing=10>
     <tr>
          <td bgcolor=003333><font color=white>Table Data Cell
➥1</font></td>
          <td bgcolor=336666><font color=white>Table Data Cell
➥2</font></td>
          <td bgcolor=669999>Table Data Cell 3</td>
          <td bgcolor=99cccc>Table Data Cell 4</td>
          <td bgcolor=ccffff>Table Data Cell 5</td>
     </tr>
</table>
```

6 In Table 6 Width=100%

| Table Data Cell 1 | Table Data Cell 2 | Table Data Cell 3 | Table Data Cell 4 | Table Data Cell 5 |

```
<table border=0 width=100%>
     <tr>
          <td bgcolor=003333><font color=white>Table Data Cell
➥1</font></td>
          <td bgcolor=336666><font color=white>Table Data Cell
➥2</font></td>
          <td bgcolor=669999>Table Data Cell 3</td>
          <td bgcolor=99cccc>Table Data Cell 4</td>
          <td bgcolor=ccffff>Table Data Cell 5</td>
     </tr>
</table>
```

7 Table 7 shows a specific width set for the whole table.

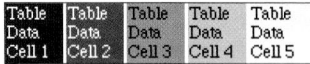

```
<table border=0 width=200>
     <tr>
          <td bgcolor=003333><font color=white>Table Data Cell
➡1</font></td>
          <td bgcolor=336666><font color=white>Table Data Cell
➡2</font></td>
          <td bgcolor=669999>Table Data Cell 3</td>
          <td bgcolor=99cccc>Table Data Cell 4</td>
          <td bgcolor=ccffff>Table Data Cell 5</td>
     </tr>
</table>
```

8 Table 8 is an example of two rows.

Table Data Cell 1	Table Data Cell 2	Table Data Cell 3	Table Data Cell 4	Table Data Cell 5
Table Data Cell 1	Table Data Cell 2	Table Data Cell 3	Table Data Cell 4	Table Data Cell 5

```
<table border=0 cellpadding=10 cellspacing=10>

     <tr>
          <td bgcolor=ff0000><font color=white>Table Data Cell
➡1</font></td>
          <td bgcolor=ff3333><font color=white>Table Data Cell
➡2</font></td>
          <td bgcolor=ff6666>Table Data Cell 3</td>
          <td bgcolor=ff9999>Table Data Cell 4</td>
          <td bgcolor=ffcccc>Table Data Cell 5</td>
     </tr>

     <tr>
          <td bgcolor=003333><font color=white>Table Data Cell
➡1</font></td>
          <td bgcolor=336666><font color=white>Table Data Cell
➡2</font></td>
          <td bgcolor=669999>Table Data Cell 3</td>
          <td bgcolor=99cccc>Table Data Cell 4</td>
          <td bgcolor=ccffff>Table Data Cell 5</td>
     </tr>

</table>
```

9 Table 9 shows one long <TD> using colspan.

Table Data Cell 1				
Table Data Cell 1	Table Data Cell 2	Table Data Cell 3	Table Data Cell 4	Table Data Cell 5

```
<table border=0 cellpadding=10 cellspacing=10>

     <tr>
          <td colspan=5 bgcolor=ff0000><font color=white>Table Data Cell
➥1</font></td>
     </tr>

     <tr>
          <td bgcolor=003333><font color=white>Table Data Cell
➥1</font></td>
          <td bgcolor=336666><font color=white>Table Data Cell
➥2</font></td>
          <td bgcolor=669999>Table Data Cell 3</td>
          <td bgcolor=99cccc>Table Data Cell 4</td>
          <td bgcolor=ccffff>Table Data Cell 5</td>
     </tr>
</table>
```

10 Table 10 is an example of shorter colspan.

Table Data Cell 1			Table Data Cell 2	Table Data Cell 3
Table Data Cell 1	Table Data Cell 2	Table Data Cell 3	Table Data Cell 4	Table Data Cell 5

```
<table border=0 cellpadding=10 cellspacing=10>

     <tr>
          <td colspan=3 bgcolor=ff0000><font color=white>Table Data Cell
➥1</font></td>
          <td bgcolor=ff3333><font color=white>Table Data Cell
➥2</font></td>
          <td bgcolor=ff6666>Table Data Cell 3</td>
     </tr>

     <tr>
          <td bgcolor=003333><font color=white>Table Data Cell
➥1</font></td>
```

```
        <td bgcolor=336666><font color=white>Table Data Cell
➥2</font></td>
        <td bgcolor=669999>Table Data Cell 3</td>
        <td bgcolor=99cccc>Table Data Cell 4</td>
        <td bgcolor=ccffff>Table Data Cell 5</td>
    </tr>
</table>
```

11 Table 11 is an example of tall <td> using rowspan.

```
<table border=0 cellpadding=10 cellspacing=10>

    <tr>
        <td rowspan=2 bgcolor=ff0000><font color=white>Table Data Cell
➥1</font></td>
        <td bgcolor=ff3333><font color=white>Table Data Cell
➥2</font></td>
        <td bgcolor=ff6666>Table Data Cell 3</td>
        <td bgcolor=ff9999>Table Data Cell 4</td>
        <td bgcolor=ffcccc>Table Data Cell 5</td>
    </tr>

    <tr>
        <td bgcolor=003333><font color=white>Table Data Cell
➥1</font></td>
        <td bgcolor=336666><font color=white>Table Data Cell
➥2</font></td>
        <td bgcolor=669999>Table Data Cell 3</td>
        <td bgcolor=99cccc>Table Data Cell 4</td>
    </tr>
</table>  ■
```

Creating Client-Side Image Maps

Use this technique to:

- **Achieve faster page loading.** By having the image coordinates in the HTML, client-side image maps provide faster connections to pages. This bypasses the standard map file calling on the server for the coordinates.

- **URLs on the page.** Client-side image maps enable the browser to display complete URLs, instead of the annoying arbitrary image coordinates, so users know to what pages they are jumping.

- **Local Web pages can have image maps.** Because the hot zone coordinates are directly on the HTML page, you can have image maps work in local Web pages.

Image maps are graphical "hot links" where users can click certain areas on an image and the Web browser jumps to the referenced HTML page for that area. Best used for navigational purposes, image maps are easily created by using shareware image map programs such as WebMap for the Macintosh or MapThis! For Windows 95. (Both programs are included on the CD.) These image map editors create .map files that contain all the coordinates and URLs for the hot areas of the graphic. The .map file must be on the server; therefore, image maps are a server-side application. When a user clicks on an area, the server searches and calls upon the .map file to find the correct URL for the area.

Client-side image maps, on the other hand, are directly in the HTML page and require no server-side lag time. To create client-side image maps, you can use your shareware programs to make .map files and then transform the data into your HTML pages. With a few added steps you can create image maps that enable better viewing of URLs and faster processing of HTML pages!

Writing the HTML

```
<MAPNAME="nameofmap">  start of client-side map tag

<AREA SHAPE="rect" COORDS="#,#,#,#" HREF="page.html">   Hot area -
➥rectangular (4 coordinates)

<AREA SHAPE="circle" COORDS="#,#,#," HREF="page.html">   Hot area - circle
➥(3 coordinates)

<AREA SHAPE="rect" COORDS="#,#,#,#,#,#" HREF="page.html">   Hot area -
➥polygon (multiple coordinates)

</map> closing map tag

<IMG SRC="image.gif" USEMAP="#nameofmap">  Client-side imagemap reference
➥(must have # sign, name must be same as specified in <MAPNAME>

<A HREF="file.map"><IMG SRC="image.gif" ISMAP></a>  Server-side imagemap
➥reference
```

1 Select the graphic you want to use for your image map and open it in your selected image map application. Begin to mark out your hot areas and insert the URLs.

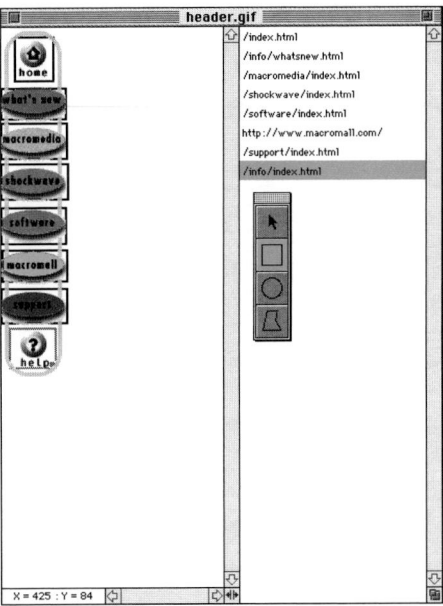

2 After all eight hot areas are recorded, export the .map file. Depending on your server you can export the file as NCSA or as CERN.

3 Begin by setting up the client-side map HTML tags. These tags can go any-where within the HTML document but it is easier to place them above the IMG SRC tag of the graphic. Because there are eight hot areas; there are eight area COORDS tags.

```
<MAPNAME="navigation">
<AREA SHAPE="rect" COORDS=" " HREF=" ">
<AREA SHAPE="rect" COORDS=" " HREF=" ">
<AREA SHAPE="rect" COORDS=" " HREF=" ">
<AREA SHAPE="rect" COORDS=" " HREF=" ">
<AREA SHAPE="rect" COORDS=" " HREF=" ">
<AREA SHAPE="rect" COORDS=" " HREF=" ">
<AREA SHAPE="rect" COORDS=" " HREF=" ">
<AREA SHAPE="rect" COORDS=" " HREF=" ">
</MAP>
```

4 Now open the .map file created earlier. Cut and paste the coordinates from the .map file into the area COORDS tags. Make sure there are commas between all coordinates. Some browsers need this to work so it is a good idea to always add them.

19

```
                              header.map
# Created by WebMap 1.0.1
# Format: NCSA
#

default
rect / 9,14 54,47
rect /info/whatsnew.html 0,51 55,84
rect /macromedia/ 1,92 55,121
rect /shockwave/ 1,132 57,161
rect /software/ 0,173 55,199
rect http://www.macromall.com/ 0,209 56,240
rect /support/ 0,250 55,276
rect /info/ 8,280 48,316
```

```
<MAPNAME="navigation">
<AREA SHAPE="rect" COORDS="9,14,54,47" HREF=" ">
<AREA SHAPE="rect" COORDS="0,51,55,84" HREF=" ">
<AREA SHAPE="rect" COORDS="1,92,55,121" HREF=" ">
<AREA SHAPE="rect" COORDS="1,132,57,161" HREF=" ">
<AREA SHAPE="rect" COORDS="0,173,55,199" HREF=" ">
<AREA SHAPE="rect" COORDS="0,209,56,240" HREF=" ">
<AREA SHAPE="rect" COORDS="0,250,55,276" HREF=" ">
<AREA SHAPE="rect" COORDS=" 8,280,48,316" HREF=" ">
</MAP>
```

5 Supply the corresponding URLs to each coordinate.

```
<MAPNAME="navigation">
<AREA SHAPE="rect" COORDS="9,14,54,47" HREF="/">
<AREA SHAPE="rect" COORDS="0,51,55,84" HREF="/info/whatsnew.html">
<AREA SHAPE="rect" COORDS="1,92,55,121" HREF="/macromedia/">
<AREA SHAPE="rect" COORDS="1,132,57,161" HREF="shockwave">
<AREA SHAPE="rect" COORDS="0,173,55,199" HREF="software">
<AREA SHAPE="rect" COORDS="0,209,56,240" HREF="http://
➥www.macromall.com">
<AREA SHAPE="rect" COORDS="0,250,55,276" HREF="/support/">
<AREA SHAPE="rect" COORDS=" 8,280,48,316" HREF="/info/">
</MAP>
```

6 With the USEMAP tag, add the client-side image map reference to the graphic. Make sure the USEMAP has a "#" symbol and the correct map name in quotes.

```
<A HREF="images/header.map">
<IMG SRC="images/header.gif" WIDTH=64 HEIGHT=329 BORDER=0
➥USEMAP="#navigation" ISMAP alt="navigation bar"></A>
```

> **TIP** Adding the image map references in addition to the client-side image map is a good idea as a backup for other browsers that do not support client-side image maps.

7 Here are all the HTML tags when complete.

```
<MAPNAME="navigation">
<AREA SHAPE="rect" COORDS="9,14,54,47" HREF="/">
<AREA SHAPE="rect" COORDS="0,51,55,84" HREF="/info/whatsnew.html">
<AREA SHAPE="rect" COORDS="1,92,55,121" HREF="/macromedia/">
<AREA SHAPE="rect" COORDS="1,132,57,161" HREF="shockwave">
<AREA SHAPE="rect" COORDS="0,173,55,199" HREF="software">
<AREA SHAPE="rect" COORDS="0,209,56,240" HREF="http://www.macromall.com">
<AREA SHAPE="rect" COORDS="0,250,55,276" HREF="/support/">
<AREA SHAPE="rect" COORDS=" 8,280,48,316" HREF="/info/">
</MAP>
<A HREF="images/header.map">
<IMG SRC="images/header.gif" WIDTH=64 HEIGHT=329 BORDER=0 USEMAP="#navi-
gation" ISMAP alt="navigation bar"></A>
```

8 Now you can add the content to your page. Upload the HTML page, graphic and .map file in their correct directories, and test this in your browser.

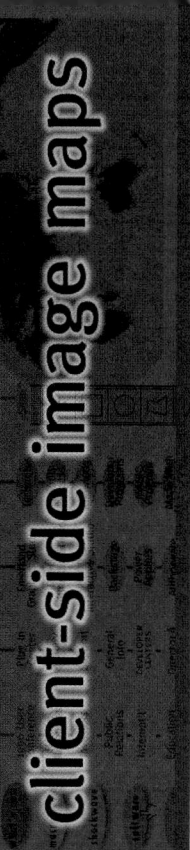

When creating large image maps, such as this site map for Macromedia, having the client-side references allows better viewing of URLs—especially in this example where there are so many.

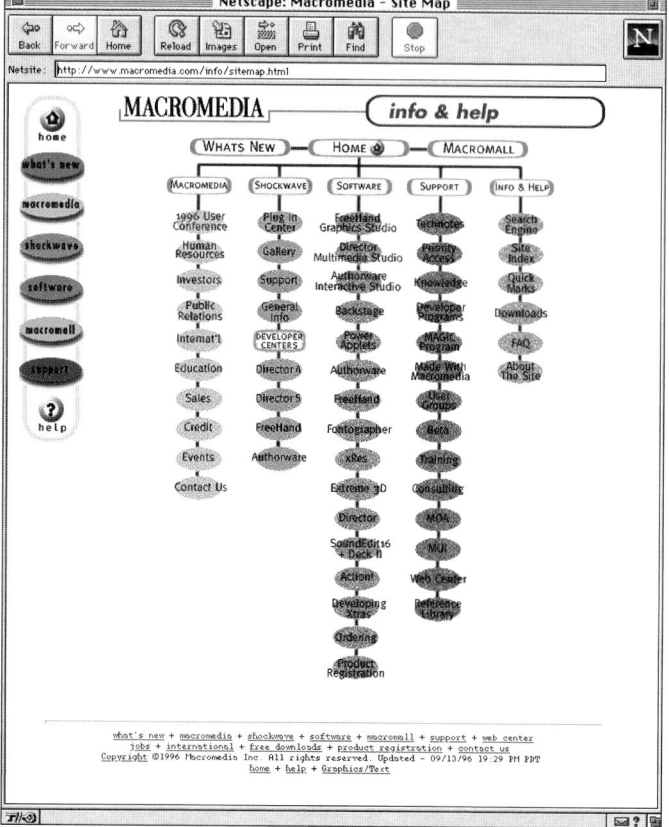

This also works for unusual shapes, such as this international world map. The different polygon shapes are hard to find with server-side image maps, but with the added client-side capability you can see instantaneous links as the mouse is rolled over them.

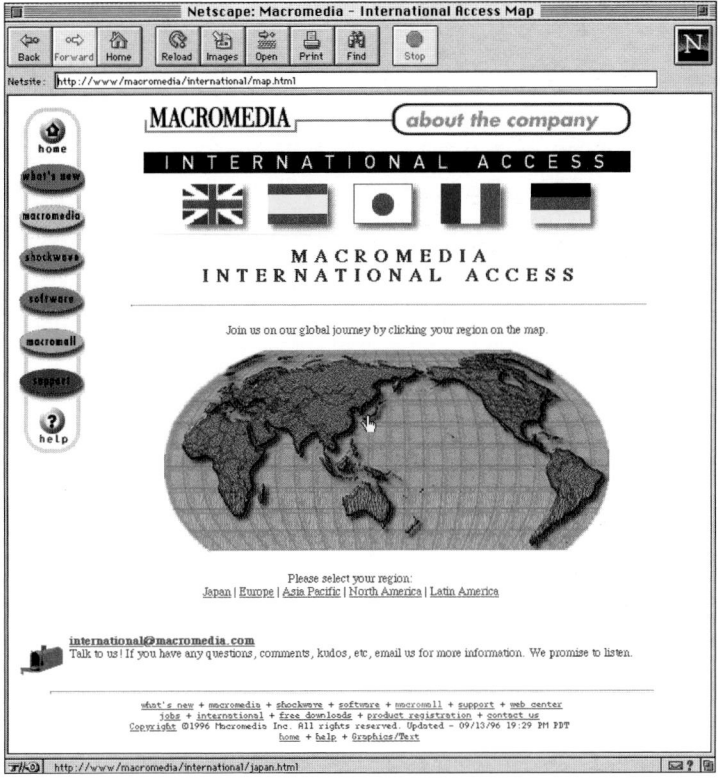

Browser Watch

Netscape 2.0 and higher

Internet Explorer 3.0 ■

Creating Descriptive Links

Use this technique to:

- **Signal to your audience what selection they are about to make when they rollover a link.** This technique deals with a more immediate and intuitive way to provide signals to your audience to help them make decisions about how to navigate through your site.

- **Provide detailed text descriptions about a link.** Whereas a window status bar provides only one line of text, HTML form text fields in this example enable you to furnish your reader with paragraphs of information.

Ideal for dealing with linked graphics and image maps, this technique illustrates a method for better communication with your user. Use this technique to emphasize graphics without putting too much text on the page to describe the images; therefore text appears only when the user's mouse passes over an image.

This example involves a series of thumbnails describing two different types of entrées. When the mouse cursor "rolls over" a thumbnail, the name of the entrée pops into a text field while the detailed text description pops into a separate scrolling text area. The "Chicken Teriyaki" thumbnail has its own title and description. Similarly, the "Seafood Brochettes" rollover event displays a title and description unique to that item.

Normally when you roll over an image, a message appears in the window status bar as personalized text or as the URL path to the next destination, but displaying link information in text fields within the page brings information into the viewer's normal field of vision. With a larger text area, you can display more information to your viewer than you could in a status bar.

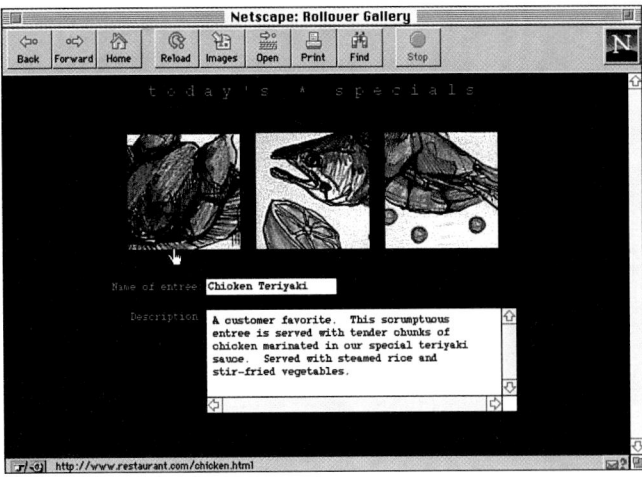

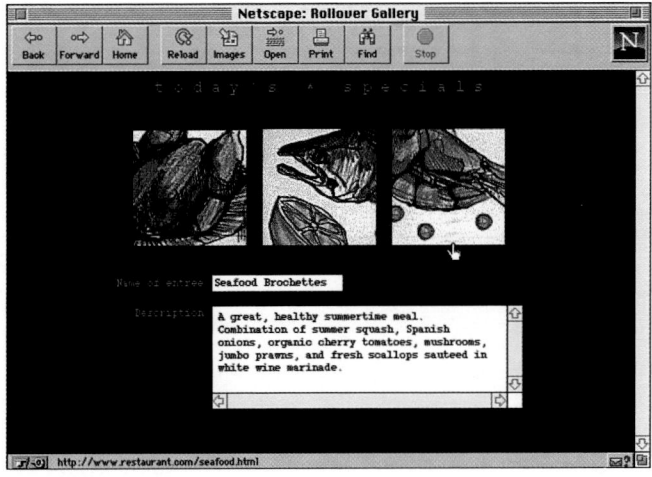

Writing the HTML

Three areas within your HTML code operate together to create this descriptive link effect. First, you must deal with the clickable image, then the text fields, and finally, the back-end JavaScript function that makes it all happen.

Prepare the <a href> Tag

You must add the onMouseOver event handler within the <a href> tag surrounding the clickable image to create the roll-over effect. Using onMouseOver calls upon a function fillDescriptionBox in order to fill the description boxes with two parameters—the entrée title and the text description. These parameters are found between the paran-theses following fillDescriptionBox and are marked with single quotes and separated by a comma.

```
<a href="http://www.restaurant.com/chicken.html" onMouseOver=
"fillDescriptionBox('Chicken Teriyaki','A customer favorite. This scrumptuous
entree is served with tender chunks of chicken marinated in our special teriyaki
sauce. Served with steamed rice and stir-fried vegetables.')">
```

Create the Form

Creating the fields to display the roll-over text involves creating a form. The code for a form is listed below. The names you see within the tags relate to the function discus-sed in the next section. The text areas of HTML forms are usually used for input fields, and single-line text fields, <input type=text>, are commonly used for letting users type their names, addresses, and so on. In surveys, you can use this same type of input field to display text. The first field is used to display the entrée title, such as "Chicken Teriyaki," taken from the first parameter described within fillDescriptionBox. Another type of input/output field enables more text to display as you set the number of rows

and columns within the <TEXTAREA> tag. You can also activate a text wrap with wrap=yes so that the information does not show up only as one line of text cut off by the right-hand side of the text area.

```
<FORM NAME="info">
<pre>
Name of entree:<INPUT TYPE=TEXT NAME="titleBox"><BR>
  Description:<TEXTAREA NAME="descriptionBox" WRAP=YES ROWS=6 COLS=45>
➡</TEXTAREA>
</pre>
</FORM>
```

Define the Function

The function, fillDescriptionBox, called upon in the onMouseOver event handler, is defined between the <HEAD> tags. Here, the function reads the parameters specific to each graphic and fills them into the corresponding boxes named within the HTML form. The function takes the value of the parameters, marked by the variables, title and description and writes them out within the text fields in the form. For example, the command document.info.titleBox. value=title recognizes the title parameter and writes it out in the single-line text field called titleBox.

```
function fillDescriptionBox(title,description){
    document.info.titleBox.value=title;
    document.info.descriptionBox.value=description;
}
```

Put It All Together

Here is the code that combines the thumbnail images and the form with the rollover functionality:

```
<HTML>
<HEAD>
<SCRIPT LANGUAGE="JavaScript">
function fillDescriptionBox(title,description){
    document.info.titleBox.value=title;
    document.info.descriptionBox.value=description;
}
</SCRIPT>
<TITLE>Rollover Gallery</TITLE>
 </HEAD>
 <BODY BGCOLOR="black" TEXT="green">
<p align=center>
<code><font size=5>t o d a y ' s   *   s p e c i a l
➡s</font></code>
<hr>
<p>
```

```
<!-- the images that will be rolled over -->
<center>
<table border=0 cellpadding=5>
<tr>
    <td><a href="http://www.restaurant.com/chicken.html"
onMouseOver="fillDescriptionBox('Chicken Teriyaki','A customer favorite. This
scrumptuous entree is served with tender chunks of chicken marinated in our spe-
cial teriyaki sauce. Served with steamed rice and stir-fried vegetables.')"><IMG
SRC="images/thumb1.jpeg" WIDTH=109 HEIGHT=109 BORDER=0 ALT="Chicken
Teriyaki"></A>
    </td>
    <td><a href="http://www.restaurant.com/salmon.html"
onMouseOver="fillDescriptionBox('Salmon Steak','Fresh Catch of the Day. Fresh
herbs, grilled scallions over a juicy salmon fillet. Served with California wild
rice and mango tomato salsa.')"><IMG SRC="images/thumb3.jpeg" WIDTH=109
HEIGHT=109 BORDER=0 ALT="Salmon Steak"></A>
    </td>
    <td><a href="http://www.restaurant.com/seafood.html"
onMouseOver="fillDescriptionBox('Seafood Brochettes','A great, healthy summertime
meal. Combination of summer squash, Spanish onions, organic cherry tomatoes,
mushrooms, jumbo prawns, and fresh scallops sauteed in white wine mari-
nade.')"><IMG SRC="images/thumb2.jpeg" WIDTH=109 HEIGHT=109 BORDER=0
ALT="Seafood Brochettes"></A>
    </td>
</tr>
</table>
</center>
<!-- the form that will house the descriptions -->
<center>
<table>
<tr>
    <td>
<FORM NAME="info">
<pre>
Name of entree:<INPUT TYPE=TEXT NAME="titleBox"><BR>
  Description:<TEXTAREA NAME="descriptionBox" WRAP=YES ROWS=6 COLS=45>
➥</TEXTAREA>
</pre>
</FORM>
    </td>
</tr>
</table>
</center>
</BODY>
</HTML>
```

This technique helps your users make more informed decisions about how they navigate within your site. You eliminate a substantial amount of guesswork and frustration for your audience, and besides, roll-overs are so cool! ■

Pull-Down Icon Illusion

Use this technique to:

- ■ **Provide links to all of the main sections of your Web site.** This compact format enables you to reveal and hide all of your key links with a click of the mouse.

- ■ **Provide comprehensive navigation similar to your computer's file and folder management.** You can create navigation based on viewing files and folders on a Macintosh or Windows machine.

Most Web surfers are used to clicking on basic text or graphic links. You can take your navigation a step further by creating the illusion of pull-down icons based on the file management system familiar to Macintosh and Windows users where an arrow next to an item indicates that more subcategories lie within it.

Say your Web site has four main sections with three subsections within each of those sections. If you showed links for all 12 sections, not only do you overwhelm your visitors, but you have too many links to monitor on each page.

Instead of listing all 12 links, you could list the four main sections with some kind of arrow icon next to each section, indicating further subsections within them. If someone clicks on an arrow icon, the list of links shows up below it. A user can close that section by clicking on the icon again and open other sections by clicking on their respective icons; thus this technique offers a simple solution for providing a substantial list of links at a glance. Visitors have a choice between viewing all of the links or just a specific set. Now, how do you do it?

Writing the HTML

The basic strategy in this technique is to create pages for every possible configuration of the outlines. There's a page that shows all of the outline heading collapsed; a page that shows only one heading expanded; a page that shows the first and third headings expanded; and so on, with one page for each permutation.

 Pay special attention to the naming scheme of the HTML files. Each file is named for the first outline section that's revealed, with the numbers of subsequent expanded sections appended to the basic name. The page, for instance, that reveals the expanded "Drawings," "Paintings," and "Design" sections is named Drawings124.html because "Drawings" is the first expanded section, "Paintings" is the second section, and "Design" is the fourth section. This makes it easier to follow the intricate inter-linking between pages.

Text Links

Because this technique requires separate HTML pages for each stage of the navigation, a frames layout with a vertical frame for the navigation provides the best results. This way, you can dedicate one specific frame for navigation where new HTML pages must load or reload. A whole window reloading each time a small part of the page changed is extremely obnoxious.

Here are some of the HTML pages you can construct based on the scenario described above. This technique is a bit labor-intensive, but you achieve a great deal without any fancy scripting.

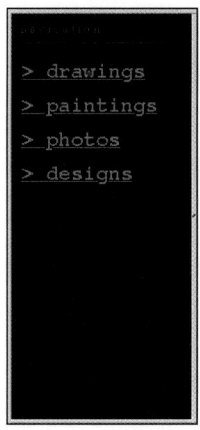

1 Build the Main Navigation page. This page should look like a collapsed outline; each link on the page represents an outline section head.

```
<html>
<head>
<title>pulldown icon examples</title>
</head>
<body bgcolor="black" text="red" link="4090d0"
➥alink="white" vlink="gray">
n a v i g a t i o n
<hr>
<p>
<code><b><font size=+3><a href="drawings.html">&gt;
➥drawings</a></font></b></code>
<p>
<code><b><font size=+3><a href="paintings.html">&gt;
➥paintings</a></font></b></code>
<p>
<code><b><font size=+3><a href="photos.html">&gt;
➥photos</a></font></b></code>
<p>
<code><b><font size=+3><a href="designs.html">&gt;
➥designs</a></font></b></code>
<p>
</body>
</html>
```

2 Create a new HTML file called "paintings.html." (It's called "paintings.html" because that's the file specified in the paintings collapsed outline head in Step 1.) Make sure that the file is properly named and resides in the same directory as the Main Navigation page, or this technique won't work.

The paintings.html creates the page that shows the paintings outline header expanded. Here's the listing:

29

```html
<html>
<head>
<title>pulldown icon examples</title>
</head>
<body bgcolor="black" text="red" link="4090d0"
➥alink="white" vlink="gray">
n a v i g a t i o n
<hr>
<p>
<code><b><font size=+3><a href="drawings12.html">&gt;
➥drawings</a></font></b></code>
<p>
<nobr><code><b><font size=+3><a
➥href="main_navigation.html"><font face=helvetica,
➥arial>V</font> paintings</a></font></b></code>
<dl>
<dd><a href="" target="main">painting 1</a>
<dd><a href="" target="main">painting 2</a>
<dd><a href="" target="main">painting 3</a>
</dl>
<p>
<nobr><code><b><font size=+3><a href="paintings23.html">&gt;
➥photos</a></font></b></code>
<p>
<nobr><code><b><font size=+3><a href="paintings24.html">&gt;
➥designs</a></font></b></code>
</body>
</html>
```

3 Create Drawings13.html. Here is what the code looks like for the first and third sections revealed:

```html
<html>
<head>
<title>pulldown icon examples</title>
</head>
<body bgcolor="black" text="red" link="4090d0"
➥alink="white" vlink="gray">
n a v i g a t i o n
<hr>
<p>
<code><b><font size=+3><a href="photos.html"><font
➥face=helvetica, arial>V</font>
➥drawings</a></font></b></code>
<dl>
<dd><a href="" target="main">drawing 1</a>
<dd><a href="" target="main">drawing 2</a>
<dd><a href="" target="main">drawing 3</a>
</dl>
<p>
```

```
<nobr><code><b><font size=+3><a href="drawings123.html">&gt;
➥paintings</a></font></b></code>
<p>
<nobr><code><b><font size=+3><a href="drawings.html"><font face=helvetica,
➥arial>V</font> photos</a></font></b></code>
<dl>
<dd><a href="" target="main">photo 1</a>
<dd><a href="" target="main">photo 2</a>
<dd><a href="" target="main">photo 3</a>
</dl>
<p>
<nobr><code><b><font size=+3><a href="drawings134.html">&gt;
➥designs</a></font></b></code>
</body>
</html>
```

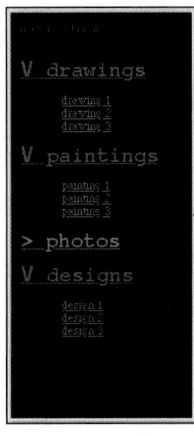

4 Create Drawings124.html. Here is what the code looks like for the first, second, and fourth sections revealed:

```
<html>
<head>
<title>pulldown icon examples</title>
</head>
<body bgcolor="black" text="red" link="4090d0"
➥alink="white" vlink="gray">
n a v i g a t i o n
<hr>
<p>
<code><b><font size=+3><a href="paintings24.html"><font
➥face=helvetica, arial>V</font>
➥drawings</a></font></b></code>
<dl>
<dd><a href="" target="main">drawing 1</a>
<dd><a href="" target="main">drawing 2</a>
<dd><a href="" target="main">drawing 3</a>
</dl>
<p>
<nobr><code><b><font size=+3><a href="drawings14.html"><font face=
➥helvetica, arial>V</font> paintings</a></font></b></code>
<dl>
<dd><a href="" target="main">painting 1</a>
<dd><a href="" target="main">painting 2</a>
<dd><a href="" target="main">painting 3</a>
</dl>
<p>
<nobr><code><b><font size=+3><a href="drawings1234.html">&gt;
➥photos</a></font></b></code>
<p>
<nobr><code><b><font size=+3><a href="drawings12.html"><font face=
➥helvetica, arial>V</font> designs</a></font></b></code>
```

```
<dl>
<dd><a href="" target="main">design 1</a>
<dd><a href="" target="main">design 2</a>
<dd><a href="" target="main">design 3</a>
</dl>
</body>
</html>
```

5 Create Drawings1234.html. Here is what the code looks like for all of the sections revealed:

```
<html>
<head>
<title>pulldown icon examples</title>
</head>
<body bgcolor="black" text="red" link="4090d0"
➥alink="white" vlink="gray">
n a v i g a t i o n
<hr>
<p>
<code><b><font size=+3><a
➥href="paintings234.html"><font face=helvetica,
➥arial>V</font> drawings</a></font></b></code>
<dl>
<dd><a href="" target="main">drawing 1</a>
<dd><a href="" target="main">drawing 2</a>
<dd><a href="" target="main">drawing 3</a>
</dl>
<p>
<nobr><code><b><font size=+3><a href="drawings134.html"><font
➥face=helvetica, arial>V</font> paintings</a></font></b></code>
<dl>
<dd><a href="" target="main">painting 1</a>
<dd><a href="" target="main">painting 2</a>
<dd><a href="" target="main">painting 3</a>
</dl>
<p>
<nobr><code><b><font size=+3><a href="drawings124.html"><font
➥face=helvetica, arial>V</font> photos</a></font></b></code>
<dl>
<dd><a href="" target="main">photo 1</a>
<dd><a href="" target="main">photo 2</a>
<dd><a href="" target="main">photo 3</a>
</dl>
<p>
<nobr><code><b><font size=+3><a href="drawings123.html"><font
➥face=helvetica, arial>V</font> designs</a></font></b></code>
<dl>
<dd><a href="" target="main">design 1</a>
```

```
<dd><a href="" target="main">design 2</a>
<dd><a href="" target="main">design 3</a>
</dl>
</body>
</html>
```

6 Make sure that all of the HTML files are in the same directory. Load the main navigation page that you built in Step 1 into your browser, and test the links. ∎

Providing No-Frames Options

Use this technique to:

- **Provide pages to browsers that do not support frames.** Providing simplified, no-frames versions of your pages allows users with older browsers to access your site.

Remember when designing for the Web that not everyone who surfs the Web has the latest browsers available; therefore, when providing content, it is important that everyone out there can see it. Frames become an issue because they are slowly becoming a layout standard for creating and organizing Web pages, but some older browsers do not support them. So what do you do when some of your users are still on Netscape 1.1? By using the <NO FRAMES> container, you ensure that any browser not supporting frames still recognizes this and displays your page. You can safely use <NO FRAMES> because all browsers support it.

Writing the HTML

In this section, you create a second version of the page for users of older browsers. The second page is wrapped up between a <NOFRAMES> </NOFRAMES> pair. Older browsers ignore the <FRAMESET> tags and display the backup page; newer browsers display the frames and discard the backup page.

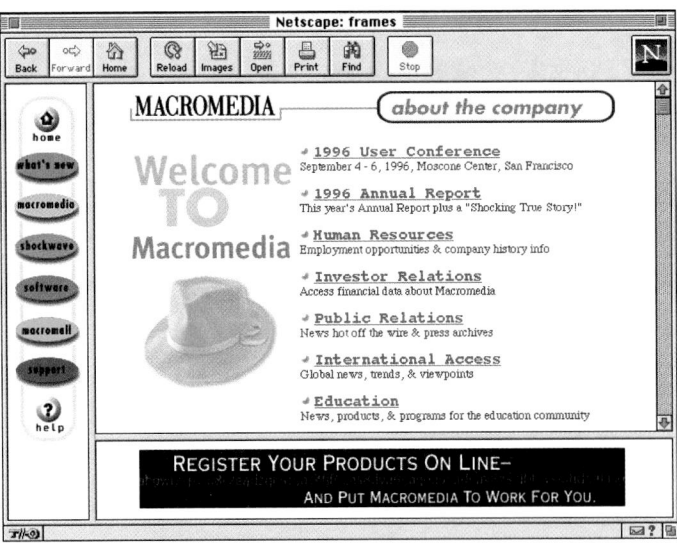

The frame example you are converting is in a nested frame. To provide a no frame option, you must include all three panels in one page.

1 Open the HTML page containing the FRAMESET codes. After the last closing </FRAMESET> tag, type **<NOFRAMES></NOFRAMES>**.

```
<HTML>
<HEAD>
<TITLE>frames</TITLE>
</HEAD>
<FRAMESET COLS="85,*">
    <FRAME SRC="navbar.html"NAME="sidebar" SCROLLING="no">
            <FRAMESET rows="*,80">
        <FRAME SRC="main.html" NAME="main" SCROLLING="Auto">
            <FRAME SRC="ad.html" NAME="adspace" SCROLLING=No
➥NORESIZE>
        </FRAMESET>
</FRAMESET>
<NOFRAMES>
<!-- Insert backup page here --!>
</NOFRAMES>
</HTML>
```

2 Open the three HTML files that represent each of the frames: navbar.html, main.html, and ad.html.

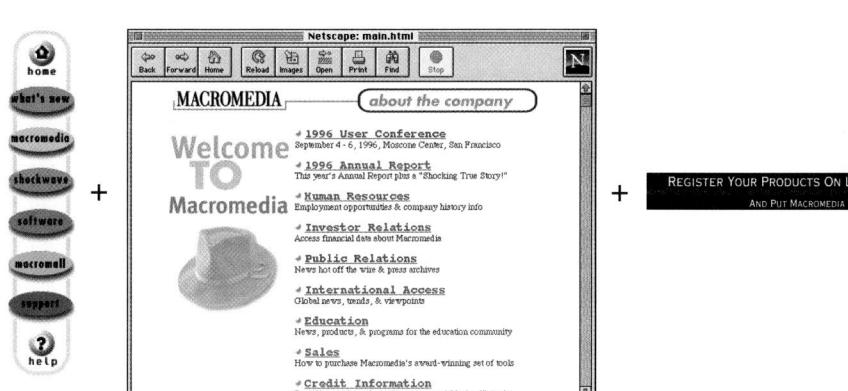

35

3 Cut the contents from the navbar.html file and paste them into main.html making sure that the contents fit in relatively the same area as they do in the frame layout. Because this graphic was centered on its own page in the navbar.html file, remove the <CENTER></CENTER> tags from the graphic and add ALIGN= LEFT to the IMG SRC in order for it to have the same effect as the frame. Save this file as main2.html. Here is the code:

```
<html><head>
<title>About Macromedia</title>
</head>
<body bgcolor="#FFFFFF" TEXT="#595959" LINK="#337299"
➥ALINK="#000000" VLINK="#B24C00">
<MAP NAME="headermap">
<AREA SHAPE="RECT" COORDS="9,14,54,47" HREF="main.html"
➥target="main">
<AREA SHAPE="RECT" COORDS="0,51,55,84" HREF="whatsnew.html"
➥target="main">
<AREA SHAPE="RECT" COORDS="1,92,55,121" HREF="macromedia.html"
➥target="main">
<AREA SHAPE="RECT" COORDS="1,132,57,161" HREF="shockwave.html"
➥target="main">
<AREA SHAPE="RECT" COORDS="0,173,55,199" HREF="software.html"
➥target="main">
<AREA SHAPE="RECT" COORDS="0,209,56,240" HREF="http://www.macromall.
➥com/" target="mm_window">
<AREA SHAPE="RECT" COORDS="0,250,55,276" HREF="support.html"
➥target="main">
<AREA SHAPE="RECT" COORDS="8,280,48,316" HREF="info.html"
➥target="main">
</MAP>
<IMG SRC="images/navigation.gif" WIDTH=64 HEIGHT=329 ALIGN= LEFT
➥BORDER=0 USEMAP="#headermap" ALT="[ navigation icons turn on
➥graphics or reload please ]">
<P ALIGN=center>
<IMG SRC="/macromedia/images/macromedia.gif" WIDTH=468 HEIGHT=30
➥ALT="Macromedia">
<P>
<center>
<table WIDTH=100%>
<tr>
<td valign=top align=right><IMG SRC="/macromedia/images/
➥welcomemm.gif" WIDTH=155 HEIGHT=235
ALT="Welcome to Info about Macromedia"></td>
<td>
<dl>
<dt><IMG SRC="/images/dot.gif" WIDTH=10 HEIGHT=10 ALT="[o]">
<CODE><B><FONT SIZE=5><A HREF="/macromedia/ucon/index.html" \
➥TARGET="main">1996 User Conference</A></FONT></B></CODE><br>
September 4 - 6, 1996, Moscone Center, San Francisco
<P>
```

4 Cut and paste the contents of the ad.html file into the main2.html file, placing the contents at the bottom of the document.

```
<P>
<dt><IMG SRC="/images/dot.gif" WIDTH=10 HEIGHT=10 ALT="[o]">
<CODE><B><FONT SIZE=5><A HREF="/macromedia/contact.html"
➥TARGET="main">Contact Us</A></FONT></B></CODE><br>
Important addresses & telephone numbers
</DL>
</TD></TR>
</TABLE>
<IMG SRC="images/ad.gif" WIDTH=468 HEIGHT=55 ALT="Register Products
➥Online">
</center>
```

5 Test the main2.html file in your browser to see if the page looks good on its own.

6 Cut the entire contents of main2.html file from the first <BODY> tag to the closing </BODY> tag and paste them into your frames page between the <NOFRAMES> </NOFRAMES> tags in place of the "put backup page here" comment. ∎

37

Replicating Frames Layout with Tables

Use this technique to:

- **Create the illusion of a side navigation frame without all the headache.**
- **Keep navigation in one area for easy reference.**

Although frames can be a great way to navigate around a site, they can be frustrating to some users whose browsers don't support frames or those who aren't used to the dividing screen layout. Perhaps as a designer you are worried about the high maintenance that frames require. A great solution to this problem is to replicate the frames layout with tables instead.

Writing the HTML

The key to creating this look is to have a great background tile that looks like the page is separated in a "frame." The whole page actually is one big table with the side navigation and middle content nested within tables.

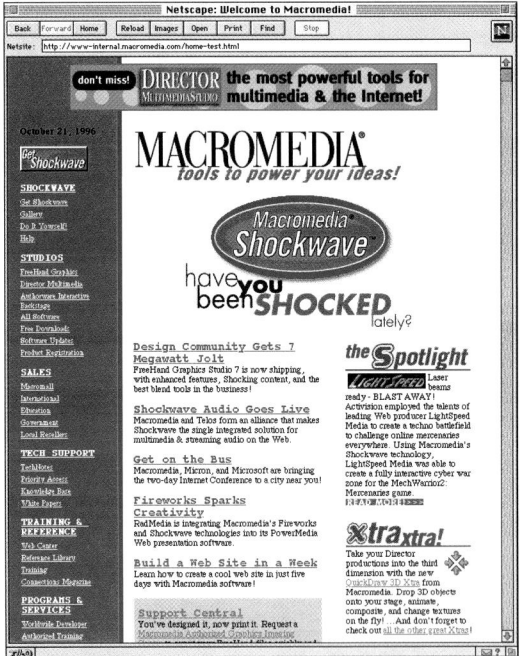

1 Create the main table layout. Start by dividing the table widths for each area. Because our side bar will be 120 pixels in width, our main area will be 500 pixels in width. This seems to be a great size that works well on Windows and Macintosh browsers. Lay out the tables with one table row <TR> and two table data cells <td> for our two areas. The two table data

cells should be aligned to the top with <td VALIGN=top> so that they are even in the final layout despite their differences in length.

```
<TABLE WIDTH="620">
<TR>
        <td VALIGN=top>
        side bar content goes here
        </td>
        <td VALIGN=top>
        homepage content goes here
        </td>
</TABLE>
```

TIP With nested tables, it's a good idea to cascade your table HTML so that you can keep better track of each table and its contents.

2 Set the width for the first table data cell. This is where your side bar will go. This will be a narrow table that is quite long. Make the TABLE WIDTH=125 and add your navigation links. Keep in mind your limited space and try to be concise.

To better view how the side bar works you can create a dummy graphic with a width of 125 so that you can measure how the text will all fit.

```
<table cols=1 border=4>
<tr>
<td valign=top width=124>
<img src="red.gif">
</td>
<td nowrap valign=top width=440></td>
</tr>
</table>
```

Now you can try it with the text links.

```
<TABLE WIDTH=620>
<TR>
    <td VALIGN=top>
    <table>
    <tr>
        <td valign=top width=124>
        <b>Wednesday<br>October 2, 1996</b>
        <p>
        <a href="javascript:dashBoard()"><b><font
color =white>Customize Your Environment</font></b></a>
            <p>
    <img src="/shockwave/images/get.shockwave.gif" alt="Get
Shockwave">
            <p>
        <a href="/shockwave/"><b><font size=4 color=white
size=-
    1><tt>SHOCKWAVE</tt></font></b></a><br>
        <img vspace=1 src="/images/pixel.gif"><br>
        <a href="/shockwave/download/"><font color=white size=-
1>Get    Shockwave</font></a><font
        size=+1> </font><br>
        <a href="/shockwave/epicenter/"><font color=white
size=-
    1>Gallery</font></a><font
        size=+1> </font><br>
        <a href="/shockwave/developer.html"><font color=white
size=-
        1>Create Shocked
        Content</font></a><font size=+1> </font><br>
. [HTML omitted due to length]
.
.
.
.
        <a href="/macromedia/contact.html"><font color=white
size=-
        1>Contact Us</font><font size=+1> </font></a>
        </font>
        <p>
        <img src="images/help3.gif" width=85 height=20
align=center
        alt="help and info"><br>
        <img src="images/home2.gif" width=85 height=20 align=center
        border=0 alt="Macromedia home">
        <p>
        </td>
    </tr>
    </table>
    </td>
```

3 Add the main table to the home page by making another table in the second `<td>` tag of the larger table. Because there is so much content, you want to add NOWRAP and WIDTH=440 to the `<td>` tag.

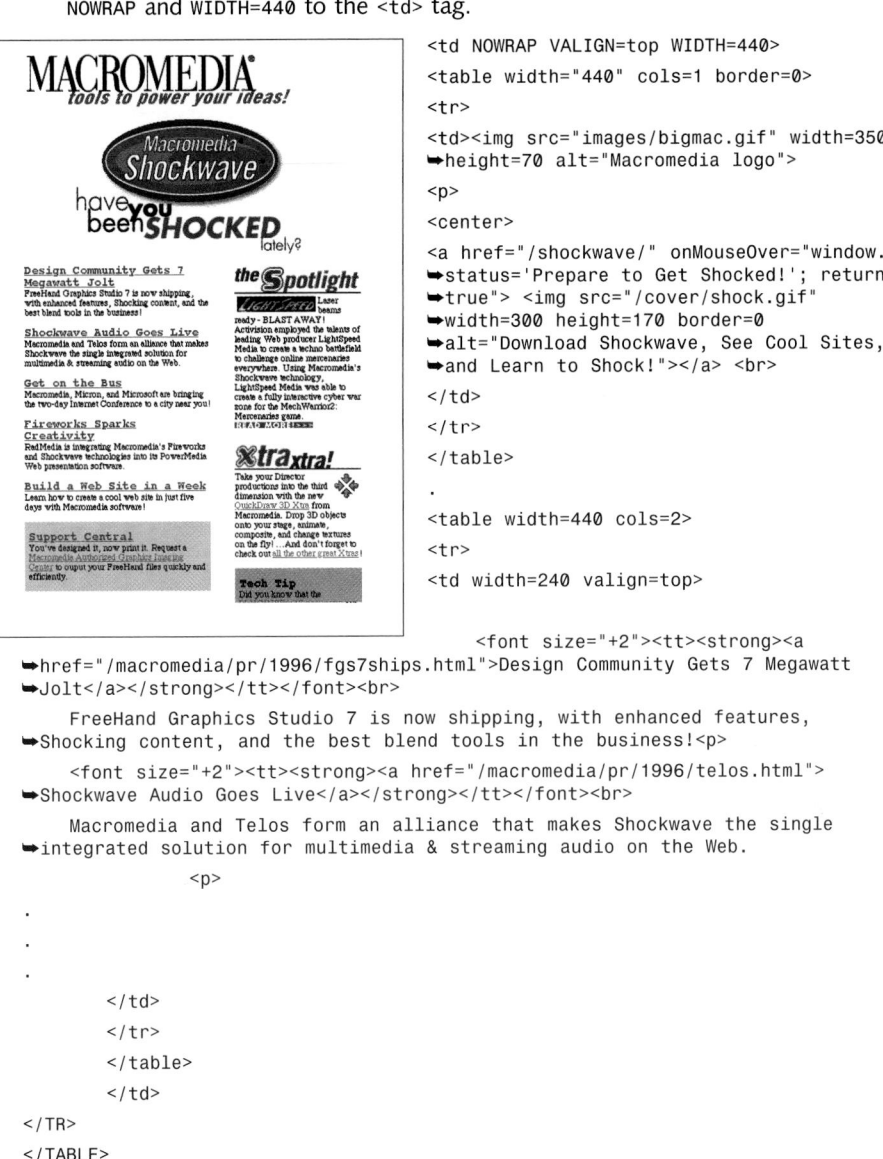

```
<td NOWRAP VALIGN=top WIDTH=440>
<table width="440" cols=1 border=0>
<tr>
<td><img src="images/bigmac.gif" width=350
➥height=70 alt="Macromedia logo">
<p>
<center>
<a href="/shockwave/" onMouseOver="window.
➥status='Prepare to Get Shocked!'; return
➥true"> <img src="/cover/shock.gif"
➥width=300 height=170 border=0
➥alt="Download Shockwave, See Cool Sites,
➥and Learn to Shock!"></a> <br>
</td>
</tr>
</table>

.

<table width=440 cols=2>
<tr>
<td width=240 valign=top>
```

```
        <font size="+2"><tt><strong><a
➥href="/macromedia/pr/1996/fgs7ships.html">Design Community Gets 7 Megawatt
➥Jolt</a></strong></tt></font><br>
    FreeHand Graphics Studio 7 is now shipping, with enhanced features,
➥Shocking content, and the best blend tools in the business!<p>
        <font size="+2"><tt><strong><a href="/macromedia/pr/1996/telos.html">
➥Shockwave Audio Goes Live</a></strong></tt></font><br>
    Macromedia and Telos form an alliance that makes Shockwave the single
➥integrated solution for multimedia & streaming audio on the Web.
            <p>
.
.
.
    </td>
    </tr>
    </table>
    </td>
</TR>
</TABLE>
```

4 Tweak your tables as you see fit. It is easy to cut and paste the HTML for the navigation side bar to all your pages or you might want to include them on one HTML file and reference them on the page as a virtual header.

TIP You can use the comment tags `<!- -` and `- ->` to place notes for yourself so that you can keep track of your nested tables (for example, `<!- - This table is your side navigation bar- ->`) ■

41

Pull-Down Menus

Use this technique to:

- **Provide a compact list of navigation choices.** Although the "Pull-Down Icon Illusion" technique (p.28) offers the same compactness, this technique offers more flexibility and ease-of-change. All you need are a few HTML changes as opposed to multiple separate files.

- **Highlight options.** Sometimes text links can get lost in the sea of text you already have on your Web page. Using pull-down menus delivers a distinct look for clickable options for your audience.

When you read a book, you have a table of contents, page numbers, and the book cover to orient your position within the realm of the narrative or instructional text. On a Web page, you can enable your "readers" to jump back to your home page that might contain a table of contents, or you can provide your table-of-contents links on every page! Usually giving your audience choices makes them happier customers, but at the same time, providing too many options might overwhelm and confuse them. Pull-down menus enable you to display all your navigational choices at once, but only when selected. In the past, you had to write a CGI program to make use of pull-down menus, but now you can use some simple JavaScript.

Writing the HTML

Using the `<select>` tag within a `form` results in a pull-down menu with various selections, each indicated by an `<option>` tag. With the help of JavaScript functions, you can have the menu operate with or without buttons in order to navigate through a site.

Basic Pull-Down Menu with Button

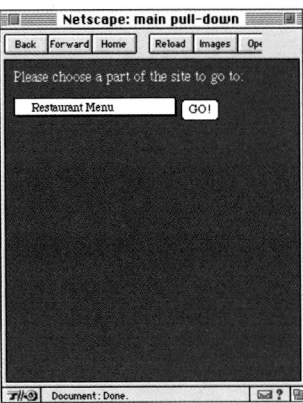

To use a basic pull-down menu, press it to reveal the options, click on your choice, that then appears at the top of the menu, and then click an extra form button to generate a certain action, based on your selection. Having to use this button helps to create some extra time for a user to consider and confirm the selected destination.

Creating the Menu

1 Start your form with the opening tag, `<FORM NAME="info">`. Give the form a name of your choice to be used later in a JavaScript function.

2 Start your pull-down window with the opening tag, `<select NAME="jumpMenu">`, giving it a name to be used later in a JavaScript function.

3 List each selection to be displayed in the pull-down menu with an `<OPTION>` tag.

4 Close the pull-down menu area with `</select>`.

5 Add a button with `<INPUT TYPE=BUTTON VALUE="GO!" onClick="jump()">`. The `TYPE=BUTTON` creates a standard HTML button form, while the `VALUE` attribute enables you to determine the text that appears on the button. The event handler, "`onClick`," calls upon the function "jump" to perform a certain action.

6 Close the form with the closing tag, `</FORM>`. Here is what the isolated code for the pull-down looks like:

```
<FORM NAME="info">
<select NAME="jumpMenu">
<OPTION> Restaurant Menu
<OPTION> Breakfast
<OPTION> Lunch
<OPTION> Dinner
<OPTION> Feedback
<OPTION> About
</select>
<INPUT TYPE=BUTTON VALUE="GO!" onClick="jump()">
</FORM>
```

Defining the Function

1 Define the function within the `<head>` tags.

2 The `function jump()` begins the function definition.

3 The function finds out what the user selected with `var loc=document.info.`
➥`jumpMenu.options[document.info.jumpMenu.selectedIndex].text`

4 Then the function goes through a series of tests. If the user selects "Breakfast" JavaScript tells the browser to go to breakfast.html, if the user selects "Lunch," JavaScript tells the browser to go to lunch.html, and so on. Here is what the code looks like with these "`if else`" tests:

```
<HEAD>
<SCRIPT LANGUAGE="JavaScript">
//this function supports the UNIT jump menu
function jump(){
```

43

```
        //find out what is currently selected
        var loc=document.info.jumpMenu.options
➡[document.info.jumpMenu.selectedIndex].text;
        //give the person the page they selected
        if (loc == "Breakfast"){
             location="breakfast.html";
        }else if (loc == "Lunch"){
             location="lunch.html";
        }else if (loc == "Dinner"){
             location="dinner.html";
        }else if (loc == "Feedback"){
             location="feedback.html";
        }else if (loc == "About"){
             location="about.html";
        }
}
</SCRIPT>
<TITLE>main pull-down</TITLE>
</HEAD>
```

5 You can put as many new items in the pull-down menu as you want, as long as you add the following code:

```
if (loc == "whatever you added to the pulldown menu"){
     location="whateverUrlYouWant.html";
```

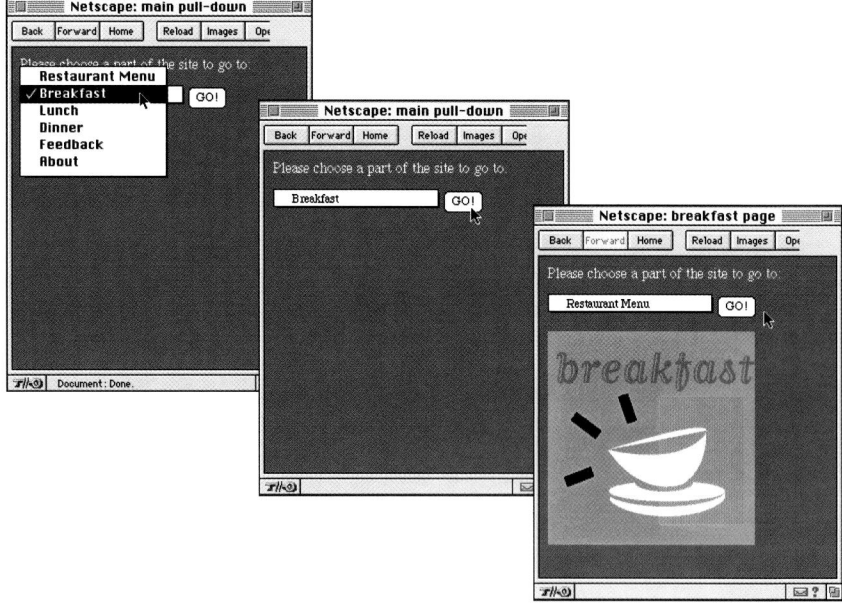

Pull-Down Menu in a Frame

This type of menu works well when it is in a frame and the page that changes is in another frame. The navigation stays with the user at all times. To change the location in another frame you need to replace location= with parent.nameOfFrameThat WillBeChanged.location= Of course, nameOfFrameThatWillBeChanged is whatever you named the frame that is to be changed in the original frameset tags.

Pull-Down Menu without Button

You can omit the "go" button and make your pull-down menus automatic by replacing <select NAME="jumpMenu"> with <select NAME="jumpMenu" onChange="jump()">. The new onChange code, tells the browser to call the jump() function as soon as anything changes in the pull-down menu.

> **NOTE** You should be aware of the cosmetic differences between Macintosh and Windows platforms, as contrasted in The Main Quad pages shown. The Macintosh pull-down menu looks like a flat, white panel with a slight drop shadow, whereas the Windows version has a "down" arrow icon and has a more three-dimensional look. In addition, the Macintosh version requires that the user hold down the mouse to make a selection, whereas the Windows pull-down menu stays open after one click and closes after the selection is made. ■

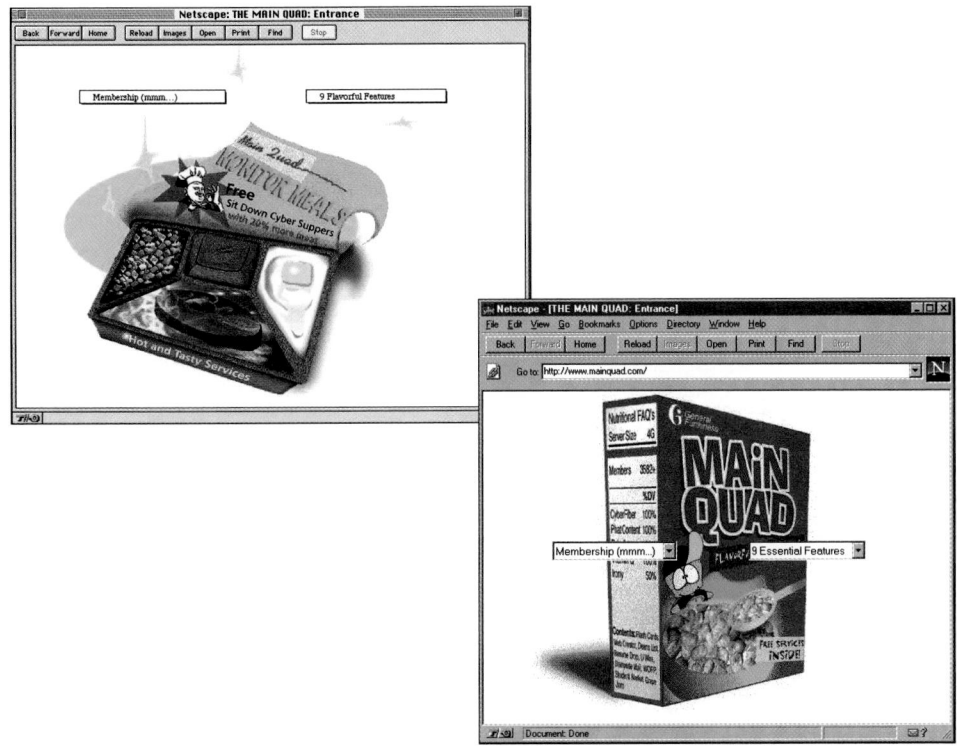

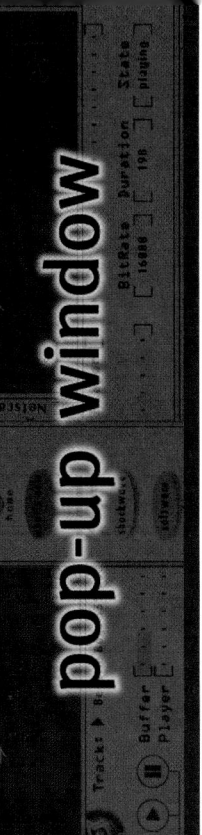

Remote Control Pop-Up Window

Use this technique to:

- **Create a different type of navigation than frames or tables.** Pop-up navigation menus are becoming a common way to navigate through applications. Using these techniques, you can add these same intuitive guideposts to your Web pages.

- **Keep users on your site and grab attention.** Users are attracted to innovation, ease of use, and things that appear by magic. Using a pop-up navigation window gets your site noticed.

- **Enable users to surf off your Web site but still find a way back.** Even if a user strays into a site with no links back to your own pages, this technique makes it easy and painless for users to return.

With so many different ways to control a Web page, the newest phenomenon is controlling your browser window. A remote control window that pops-up when users click on a link is a more creative way to enhance navigation, present animation, or just add fun to your Web site!

By adding a simple JavaScript to your HTML page, you can create a custom-made remote pop-up window in no time!

Writing the HTML

In this technique, you'll build a basic client-side image map. Rather than putting it on the page, however, you'll put it in a separate window created with JavaScript. As the user navigates through the site, the image map window stays put. (You might think of it as a floating navigation palette.)

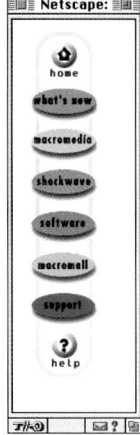

46

1 Create the content for the remote window. Here you use the remote window as a navigation piece, with the navigation bar graphic located inside the window. Mark up your HTML page for the remote window. Make all link references target="mywin" so the links change dynamically in the main window.

```
<HTML>
<HEAD>
<TITLE>navbar.html</TITLE>
</HEAD>

<BODY BGCOLOR="#ffffff" TEXT="#595959" LINK="#337299"
ALINK="#000000" VLINK="#b24c00">

<MAP NAME="headermap">
<AREA SHAPE="RECT" COORDS="9,14,54,47" HREF="main.html"
➥target="mywin">
<AREA SHAPE="RECT" COORDS="0,51,55,84" HREF="whatsnew.html"
➥target="mywin">
<AREA SHAPE="RECT" COORDS="1,92,55,121" HREF="macromedia.html"
➥target="mywin">
<AREA SHAPE="RECT" COORDS="1,132,57,161" HREF="shockwave.html"
➥target="mywin">
<AREA SHAPE="RECT" COORDS="0,173,55,199" HREF="software.html"
➥target="mywin">
<AREA SHAPE="RECT" COORDS="0,209,56,240" HREF="http://
➥www.macromall.com/" target="mywin">
<AREA SHAPE="RECT" COORDS="0,250,55,276" HREF="support.html"
➥target="mywin">
<AREA SHAPE="RECT" COORDS="8,280,48,316" HREF="info.html"
➥target="mywin">

</MAP>
<CENTER>
<img src="images/navigation.gif" width=64 height=329 border=0
➥USEMAP="#headermap" ALT="[ navigation icons turn on graphics or
➥reload please ]">
</CENTER>
</BODY>
</HTML>
```

2 On the page where you want the remote window to "pop-up," type the following JavaScript code between the <HEAD></HEAD> of the document. You want the browser window to hug the graphic so make the default width and height a bit larger than the graphic.

47

```
<HTML>
<HEAD>
<SCRIPT>
var vers = navigator.appVersion.charAt (0)
if (vers >=3) {
     window.name="mywin"
newwin=open("remote.html","win",
➥"width=100 height=360,scrollbars=no,menubar=no");
}
</SCRIPT>
```

3 Load and test the file in your browser. It creates a pop-up window when the page is opened. You can try different uses for the window. Be creative.

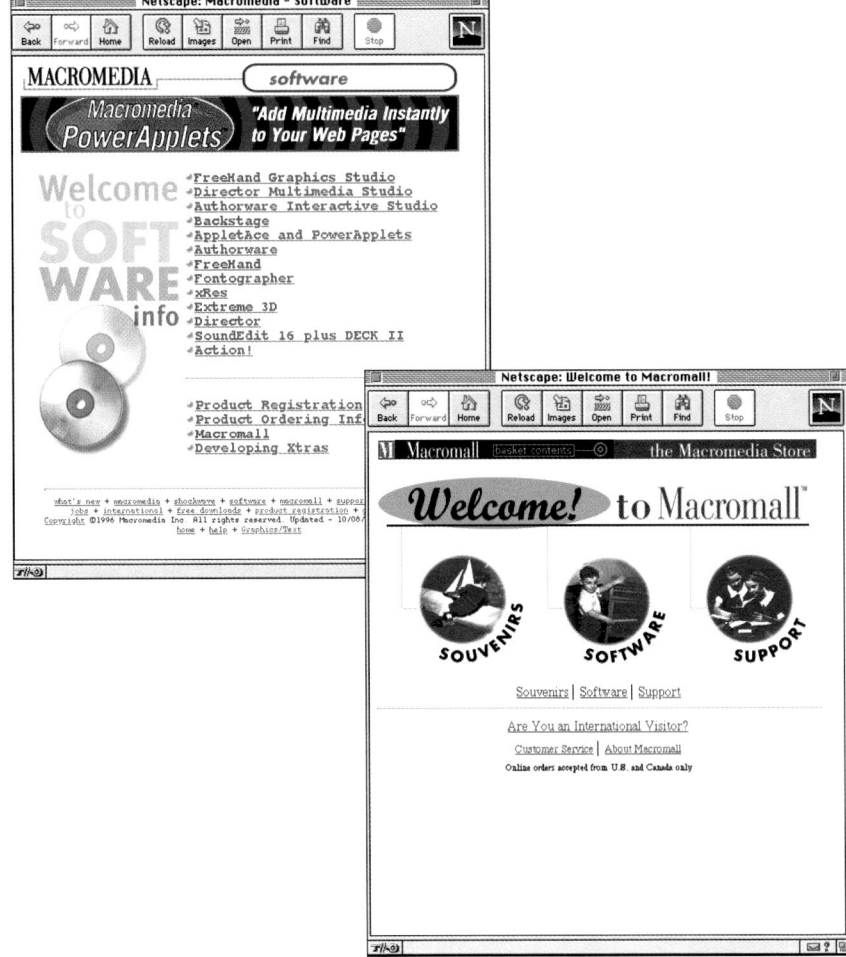

VARIATIONS

Turntable Media uses a pop-up window for a Shockwave audio control interface.

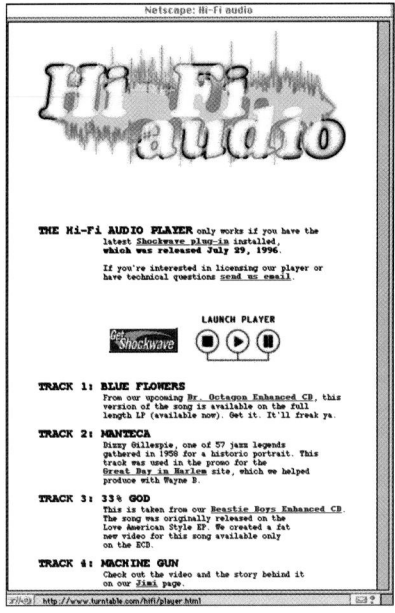

HotWired also uses a pop-up window that links its different Web sites. ■

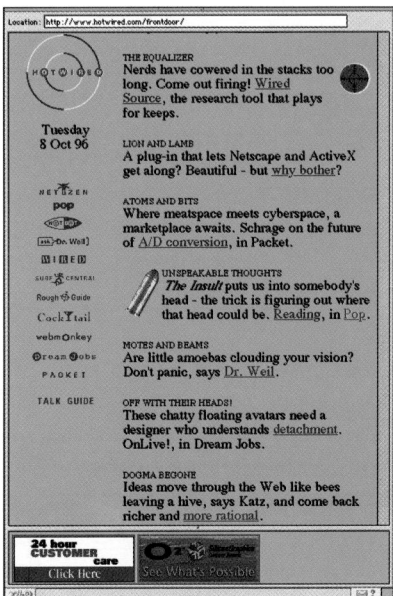

Using Roll-Overs

Use this technique to:

■ **Create an interactive effect for navigation.** You can jazz up a navigation window by adding animation to the buttons. When the mouse moves over one of the button images, the image changes to something new. This signals the reader that the image is also a button and makes the navigation window more interesting.

Roll-overs can create a magical effect bringing your Web pages to life. With simple JavaScript added to your HTML, you can provide an interactive experience for users as they surf around your Web site.

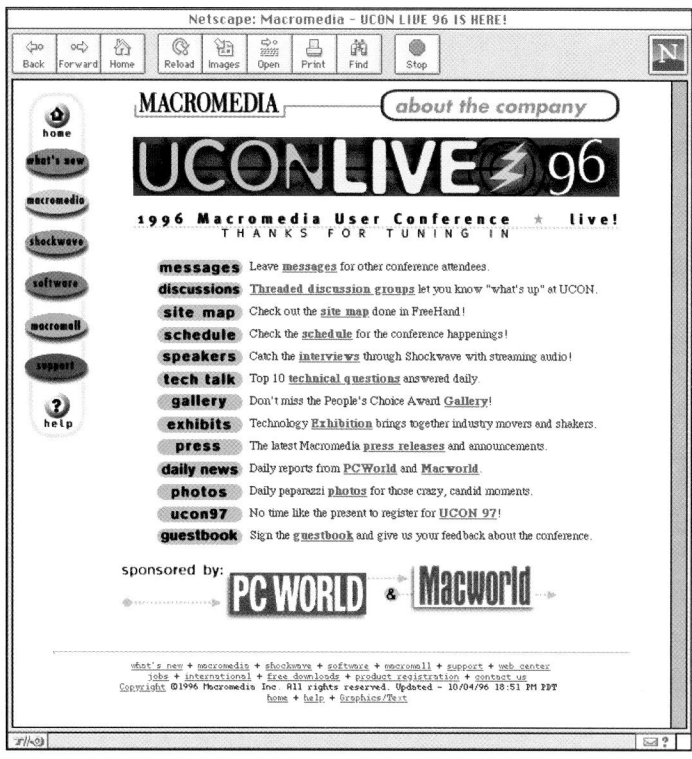

The "Remote Control Pop-Up Window" technique (p.46) introduced remote control windows and showed how useful they are for navigation. Combine remote control windows with the roll-over effect in this example taken from the internal Web site at the 1996 Macromedia User Conference. Before you begin, you need to create your navigation graphics and their corresponding roll-over graphics.

Using Roll-Overs

Writing the HTML

This is a fairly complicated technique. The basic strategy is to create a new window and populate it with image files. Each image tag contains an event handler that reacts to roll-overs. When any of the handlers detects mouse movement, it calls a JavaScript function and swaps in a new image for the current image.

1 Organize your navigation graphics and your corresponding roll-over graphics with a good naming structure and place them into an images directory. In this example you work with 24 small graphics because there are 12 main yellow graphics with their corresponding black roll-overs. Each roll-over is named the same as the regular graphic except a "2" is added (main.gif is the original file and main2.gif is the roll-over).

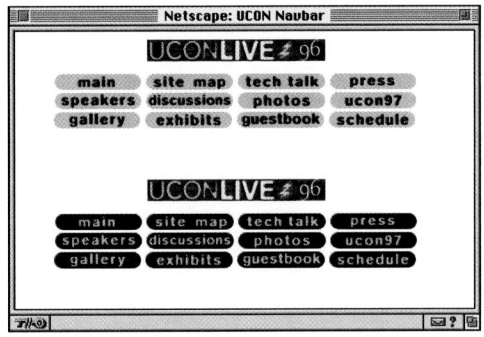

2 The script lives between the <HEAD></HEAD> of the HTML document. Begin by naming each image. In this example, each one is named logo1, logo2, logo3, and so on.

```
<HTML>
<HEAD>
<SCRIPT>
    logo1=new Image();
    logo2=new Image();
    logo3=new Image();
```

3 After this code snippet, add the specific location of each logo graphic named.

```
logo1.src="../uconlive/images/main.gif";
logo2.src="../uconlive/images/main2.gif";
logo3.src="../uconlive/images/map.gif";
logo4.src="../uconlive/images/map2.gif";
```

And so on.

4 Now add the scenarios for each roll-over. The script shows that if the mouse rolls over the main.gif, it is to replace the main.gif image with the main2.gif

51

image and so on for each of the pairs of images specified in Step 3. Begin by adding this line:

```
function display(num) {
```

Next, follow this pattern for images 1-12:

```
if (num=="1") {
        document.images[1].src=logo2.src;
        document.images[2].src=logo3.src;
        document.images[3].src=logo5.src;
        document.images[4].src=logo7.src;
        document.images[5].src=logo9.src;
        document.images[6].src=logo11.src;
        document.images[7].src=logo13.src;
        document.images[8].src=logo15.src;
        document.images[9].src=logo17.src;
        document.images[10].src=logo19.src;
        document.images[11].src=logo21.src;
        document.images[12].src=logo23.src;
    } else if (num=="2") {
        document.images[1].src=logo1.src;
        document.images[2].src=logo4.src;
        document.images[3].src=logo5.src;
        document.images[4].src=logo7.src;
        document.images[5].src=logo9.src;
        document.images[6].src=logo11.src;
        document.images[7].src=logo13.src;
        document.images[8].src=logo15.src;
        document.images[9].src=logo17.src;
        document.images[10].src=logo19.src;
        document.images[11].src=logo21.src;
        document.images[12].src=logo23.src;
                }
    }
</SCRIPT>
```

5 After you have programmed the script, lay out the HTML page that will contain the images and add their links. Add the corresponding <A HREF> links and the <IMG SRC> tags for the main graphics only.

```
<TITLE>UCON Navbar</TITLE>
</HEAD>
<BODY BGCOLOR=ffffff text=000000>
<CENTER>
<IMG SRC="../uconlive/images/navbanner.gif" WIDTH=170 HEIGHT=20
➥BORDER=0 ALT="alt="UCON!"><P>
<A HREF="index.html"><IMG SRC="../uconlive/images/main.gif"
➥WIDTH=85 HEIGHT=15 BORDER=0 ALT="alt="Click here for main UCON
➥LIVE page"></A>
```

```
<A HREF="map.html"><IMG SRC="../uconlive/images/map.gif" WIDTH=85
➥HEIGHT=15 BORDER=0 ALT="alt="Click here for UCON LIVE map page"></A>

<A HREF="techtalk.html"><IMG SRC="../uconlive/images/techtalk.gif"
➥WIDTH=85 HEIGHT=15 BORDER=0 ALT="alt="Click here for UCON LIVE techtalk
➥page"></A>

<A HREF="press.html"><IMG SRC="../uconlive/images/press.gif" WIDTH=85
➥HEIGHT=15 BORDER=0 ALT="alt="Click here for UCON LIVE press page"></A>

<BR>

<A HREF="speakers/index.html"><IMG SRC="../uconlive/images/speakers.gif"
➥WIDTH=85 HEIGHT=15 BORDER=0 ALT="alt="Click here for UCON LIVE speakers
➥page"></A>

<A HREF="http://ucon-messages.macromedia.com/bin/threads/
➥index_internal.html"><IMG SRC="../uconlive/images/discussions.gif"
➥WIDTH=85 HEIGHT=15 BORDER=0 ALT="alt="Click here for UCON LIVE
➥discussions page"></A>

<A HREF="photos/" onMouseOver="display(7)"><IMG
➥SRC="../uconlive/images/photos.gif" WIDTH=85 HEIGHT=15 BORDER=0
➥ALT="alt="Click here for UCON LIVE photos page"></A>

<A HREF="ucon97form.html"><IMG SRC="../uconlive/images/ucon97.gif"
➥WIDTH=85 HEIGHT=15 BORDER=0 ALT="alt="Click here for UCON LIVE 97 form
➥page"></A>

<BR>

<A HREF="gallery/"><IMG SRC="../uconlive/images/gallery.gif" WIDTH=85
➥HEIGHT=15 BORDER=0 ALT="alt="Click here for UCON LIVE gallery
➥page"></A>

<A HREF="exhibitors.html"><IMG SRC="../uconlive/images/exhibit.gif"
➥WIDTH=85 HEIGHT=15 BORDER=0 ALT="alt="Click here for UCON LIVE
➥exhibitors page"></A>

<A HREF="guestbookform.html"><IMG SRC="../uconlive/images/guestbook.gif"
➥WIDTH=85 HEIGHT=15 BORDER=0 ALT="alt="Click here for UCON LIVE
➥guestbook page"></A>

<A HREF="schedule.html"><IMG SRC="../uconlive/images/schedule.gif"
➥WIDTH=85 HEIGHT=15 BORDER=0 ALT="alt="Click here for UCON LIVE schedule
➥page"></A>

</CENTER>
</BODY>
</HTML>
```

53

6 Add the scenarios for each roll-over for each graphic in the <A HREF> tag. Use
   the pattern onMouseOver="display(n) where *n* is the number of the scenario.
   Also add TARGET = "mywin" (the name of our main browser frame) so that each
   link changes the URL in the main browser. Now rollover.html is complete.

```
<A HREF="index.html" TARGET="mywin" onMouseOver="display(1)"><IMG
➥SRC="../uconlive/images/main.gif" WIDTH=85 HEIGHT=15 BORDER=0
➥ALT="alt="Click here for main UCON LIVE page"></A>

<A HREF="map.html" TARGET="mywin" onMouseOver="display(2)"><IMG
➥SRC="../uconlive/images/map.gif" WIDTH=85 HEIGHT=15 BORDER=0
➥ALT="alt="Click here for UCON LIVE map page"></A>

<A HREF="techtalk.html" TARGET="mywin" onMouseOver="display(3)"><IMG
➥SRC="../uconlive/images/techtalk.gif" WIDTH=85 HEIGHT=15 BORDER=0
➥ALT="alt="Click here for UCON LIVE techtalk page"></A>

<A HREF="press.html" TARGET="mywin" onMouseOver="display(4)"><IMG
➥SRC="../uconlive/images/press.gif" WIDTH=85 HEIGHT=15 BORDER=0
➥ALT="alt="Click here for UCON LIVE press page"></A>
```

```
<BR>

<A HREF="speakers/index.html" TARGET="mywin" onMouseOver="display
(5)"><IMG SRC="../uconlive/images/speakers.gif" WIDTH=85
HEIGHT=15 BORDER=0 ALT="alt="Click here for UCON LIVE speakers
page"></A>

<A HREF="http://ucon-messages.macromedia.com/bin/threads/
index_internal.html" TARGET="mywin" onMouseOver="display(6)"><IMG
SRC="../uconlive/images/discussions.gif" WIDTH=85 HEIGHT=15
BORDER=0 ALT="alt="Click here for UCON LIVE discussions
page"></A>

<A HREF="photos/" TARGET="mywin" onMouseOver="display(7)"><IMG
SRC="../uconlive/images/photos.gif" WIDTH=85 HEIGHT=15 BORDER=0
ALT="alt="Click here for UCON LIVE photos page"></A>

<A HREF="ucon97form.html" TARGET="mywin" onMouseOver="display
(8)"><IMG SRC="../uconlive/images/ucon97.gif" WIDTH=85 HEIGHT=15
BORDER=0 ALT="alt="Click here for UCON LIVE 97 form page"></A>

<BR>

<A HREF="gallery/" TARGET="mywin" onMouseOver="display(9)"><IMG
SRC="../uconlive/images/gallery.gif" WIDTH=85 HEIGHT=15 BORDER=0
ALT="alt="Click here for UCON LIVE gallery page"></A>

<A HREF="exhibitors.html" TARGET="mywin" onMouseOver="display
(10)"><IMG SRC="../uconlive/images/exhibit.gif" WIDTH=85
HEIGHT=15 BORDER=0 ALT="alt="Click here for UCON LIVE exhibitors
page"></A>

<A HREF="guestbookform.html" TARGET="mywin" onMouseOver="display
(11)"><IMG SRC="../uconlive/images/guestbook.gif" WIDTH=85
HEIGHT=15 BORDER=0 ALT="alt="Click here for UCON LIVE guestbook
page"></A>

<A HREF="schedule.html" TARGET="mywin" onMouseOver="display(12)"
><IMG SRC="../uconlive/images/schedule.gif" WIDTH=85 HEIGHT=15
BORDER=0 ALT="alt="Click here for UCON LIVE schedule page"></A>

</CENTER>

</BODY>

</HTML>
```

7 Reference .html in your main browser page so that it opens a new browser window.

```
<HTML>
<HEAD>
<SCRIPT>
var vers = navigator.appVersion.charAt(0);
if (vers >= 3) {
  window.name = "mywin";
  newwin=open("rollover.html","win","width=400,height=120,scroll-
bars=no,menubar=no");
}
</SCRIPT>
<TITLE>Macromedia - UCON LIVE 96 IS HERE!</TITLE>
```

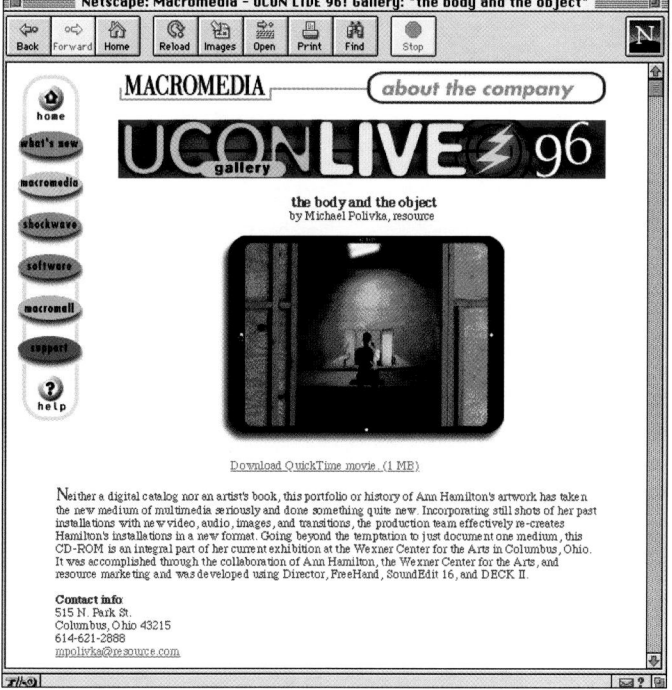

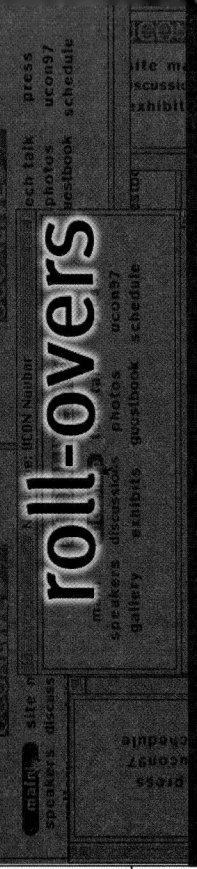

VARIATIONS

More advanced multimedia designers might want to create a Shockwave movie with roll-overs adding streaming audio or sound clips as an enhancement.

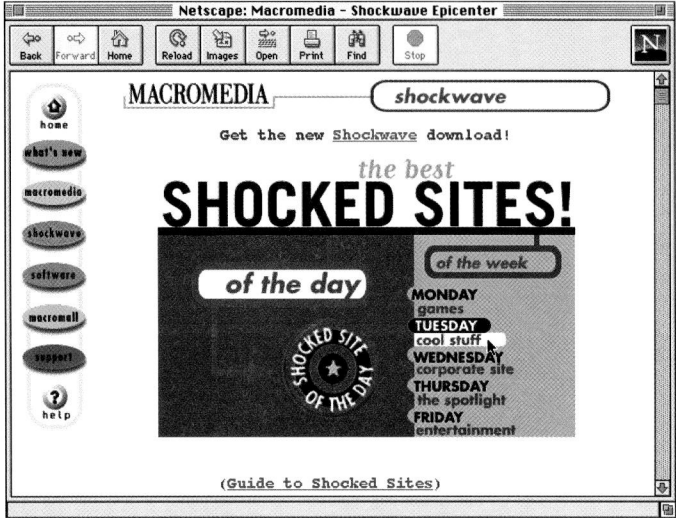

See also "Creating Java Applet Image Maps" (p.214).

Browser Watch

Netscape 3.0 ■

56

Creating Customized Window Status Messages

Use this technique to:

- **Provide specific information about a link destination.** Have you ever noticed the URLs that pop up at the bottom of the browser window when your cursor passes over a "hot" item—a text link or linked graphic? You can personalize these messages with creative or functional comments.

- **Provide more interactivity with your audience.** Creating your own window status messages is just one way to show your visitors that you want to clarify their options and to make your site more navigable for their convenience and happiness.

Window status messages appear at the bottom bar of the Web browser window. The messages indicate the progress of a file loading as well as the URL of a link when the mouse passes over the text link or linked image.

I pay attention to the loading status of a page but usually overlook the standard rollover message when I am about to click a link. I don't particularly care about the exact location of this upcoming page, described by the URL in the status bar. I just care about the content of this next page. The URL makes sense of that site's particular system of directory organization, but may have little significance to the visitor. Notice that by ignoring the rollover status bar message, I am taking chances that the link will take me to where I expect to go. I rely on the text link description or graphical icon to indicate the next destination.

| http://www.mygroovysite.com/portfolio/inspiration/travels/photos/usa/sanfrancisco/ |

Writing the HTML

Creating your own window status messages breaks down the ambiguity of your links, especially for images and image maps. Compare these two different messages that can show up on the status bar.

```
"http://www.mygroovysite.com/portfolio/inspiration/travels/photos/usa
➥/sanfrancisco/embarcadero.html"
```

```
"Click here to see my favorite black-and-white photograph, taken at the
➥Embarcadero Center, San Francisco."
```

59

Revise the `<a href>` Tag by Adding Parameters

JavaScript provides a way to customize window status messages.

Incorporating customized window status messages into your code involves adding a few extra parameters to your `<a href>` tag. The `onMouseOver` tag indicates the rollover event. The `window.status` tag indicates the type of reaction the rollover creates, and `return true` tag erases the message after the mouse passes over the "hot" area.

```
<A HREF="destination.html" onMouseOver="window.status='Your message
→here.'; return true">
```

Plug in the appropriate text within the tags from the preceding code example to create your customized message. This is how I created my personalized window status message:

```
<A HREF=" http://www.mygroovysite.com/portfolio/inspiration/travels/pho-
tos/usa/sanfrancisco/embarcadero.html " onMouseOver="window.status=
'Click here to see my favorite black-and-white photograph, taken at the
Embarcadero Center, San Francisco.'; return true">.
```
Although this small image provides a basic feel for what the full-scale image contains, the text in the status message furnishes additional details and information that such a small, cryptic graphic might fail to relay. The link destination is then a welcomed experience rather than an unpleasant surprise.

Trilogy's Web site provides even more specific information about the event after the click.

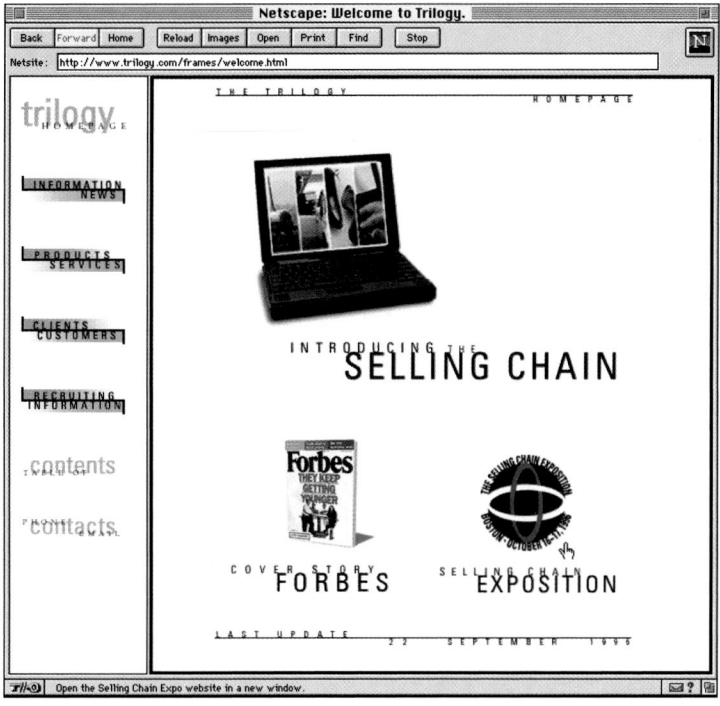

Here is the code used to create the status bar message signaling to the user that the new link will open in a new window:

```
<A HREF="http://www.sellingchain.com/" TARGET="more" onMouseOver="window.
➥status='Open the Selling Chain Expo Web site in a new window.'; return true">
```

By adding customized window status messages to your Web pages, you can chart visitors' possible paths in such a way that they won't have to guess where they are going.

By creating your own window status messages, you make every appearance of text count. You recognize that everything showing up in that browser window is subject to the questioning eyes of your audience. Eliminate any opportunities for second-guessing. And most of all, have fun with this! Talk to your audience! ∎

Using Virtual Headers and Footers

Use this technique to:

- **Provide consistent navigation as well as a consistent look and feel throughout your site.** Using the compact code of a `virtual` tag, you can include consistent headers and footers on each of your pages.

- **Update single header and footer files easily.** Finally, an HTML feature on your side (with the help of JavaScript). Manage changes to your site navigation or header bars with easy adjustments to no more than two documents.

The immediacy of the Web puts demands on Web developers and designers to keep their content fresh and updated.

What if your site has dozens of pages? Hundreds? Thousands? How are you going to update your headers and footers each time you need to make a slight change? Imagine changing the code on each and every one of your pages. By the time you finish this tedious process, it's time to make the next change!

Macromedia's Web site uses server-side "includes" to display headers and footers. Each of the pages contains a vertical navigation graphic, a header graphic to indicate the section, and a text link footer.

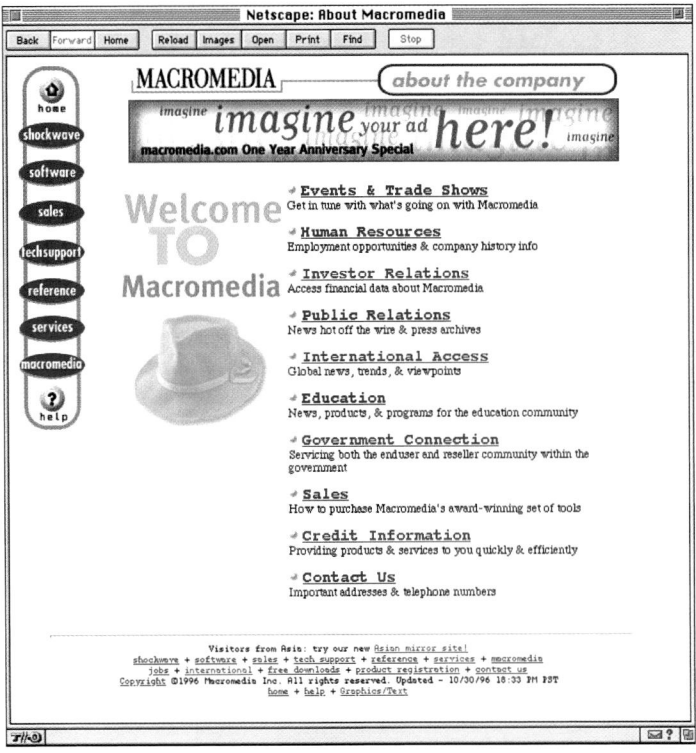

MACROMEDIA —————— (*about the company*)

Visitors from Asia: try our new Asian mirror site!
shockwave + software + sales + tech support + reference + services + macromedia
jobs + international + free downloads + product registration + contact us
Copyright ©1996 Macromedia Inc. All rights reserved. Updated – 10/30/96 18:33 PM PST
home + help + Graphics/Text

63

Writing the HTML

Common applications of server-side "includes" involve writing CGI scripts. The include virtual tag references a separate HTML file that contains the entire code for the header or footer—whatever needs to be substituted. Therefore, several lines of code can be compressed into one line, making it easier to read your code and isolate specific sections.

Here is an example of the code:

```
<html>
<head>
<title>Any given Macromedia page</title>
<body>
```

```
<!--include virtual="/header.html"-->
<!--include virtual="/SECTION/header.html"-->
BODY OF PAGE.
<!--include virtual="/footer.html"-->
</body>
</html>
```

If you cringe at the sound of server or CGI, this technique offers an alternative. All you need is one external JavaScript file and a few additions to your HTML code. The following example describes how to create a virtual footer with JavaScript.

Write the External JavaScript File

Between the <HEAD> tags you must locate the external footer file containing the function that plugs in the footer code for you:

```
<SCRIPT SRC="http://www.yourserver.com/virtualFooter.js">
```

Instead of a standard HTML file, as in the server-side include example, your code accesses an external JavaScript file with the .js extension.

```
//this is the function that writes out the footer
//it will be called remotely from many different html pages
//to change the footer on each and every page, you only need to
//change it here
        function printVirtualFooter(){
                document.write('<IMG SRC="footerImage.jpg"><BR>');
                document.write('All material on this page is
➥ copyrighted by Fred Harkins');
                document.write('of harkins fame and fortune... 1996,
➥1995, and 1994<BR>');
                document.write('You can write whatever else you want
➥down here...');
        }
```

Replace Server-Side "Include" with JavaScript

Instead of using this code...

```
<!--include virtual="/footer.html"-->
```

...in this case, you use:

```
<SCRIPT Language="JavaScript">
        printVirtualFooter();
</SCRIPT>
```

64

Incorporate Virtual Footer in Your Page

Here is what the entire code looks like for a Web page that utilizes a virtual footer created with JavaScript:

```
<HTML>
<HEAD>
<SCRIPT SRC="http://www.yourserver.com/virtualFooter.js">
</HEAD>
<TITLE> Virtual Footer Demo</TITLE>
<BODY BGCOLOR="white" BACKGROUND="" text="black">
This is some regular text...whatever I want.. can be different on every page.
and now for the virtual footer which will be the same in every document in
which it appears...but only in 3.0 or higher.
<SCRIPT Language="JavaScript">
      printVirtualFooter();
</SCRIPT>
</BODY>
</HTML>
```

Like the CGI scenario, all you have to do is update one file whenever you make a change to your navigation.

 TIP You can combine multiple functions in one .js document to manage both your header and footer. By doing so, the function location remains constant.

Browser Watch

Netscape 3.0. ■

65

Using Target Windows

Use this technique to:

- **Find links off your site.** Open a new browser window for links off your site so that users can easily find their way back.

- **Linking between different frame layouts.** You can have single browser windows or different frame layouts open.

- **Keeping users based on your site.** No matter where they link to, users always remain on your site.

Target windows provide a great way for users to find their way back to your Web site. Whether they are just opening a regular browser window, or creating a frame style link, these effective and easy HTML additions keep your Web surfers happy!

Writing the HTML

The target attributes go into the `<A HREF>` tag.

- `TARGET="window"` opens a new browser window

- `TARGET="self"` is used for frame documents. The link always loads in the frame where the link was selected.

- `TARGET="parent"` is used for frame documents. The link loads in the immediate FRAMESET parent of the document.

- `TARGET="top"` for frame documents. The link loads in the full body of the window.

- `TARGET="blank"` link loads in a new blank window.

1 Adding target windows to the Shockwave Gallery is easy. Open the HTML document, and for each URL link add `target="window"` like this:

```
<A HREF="http://www.urlhere.com" target="window">
```

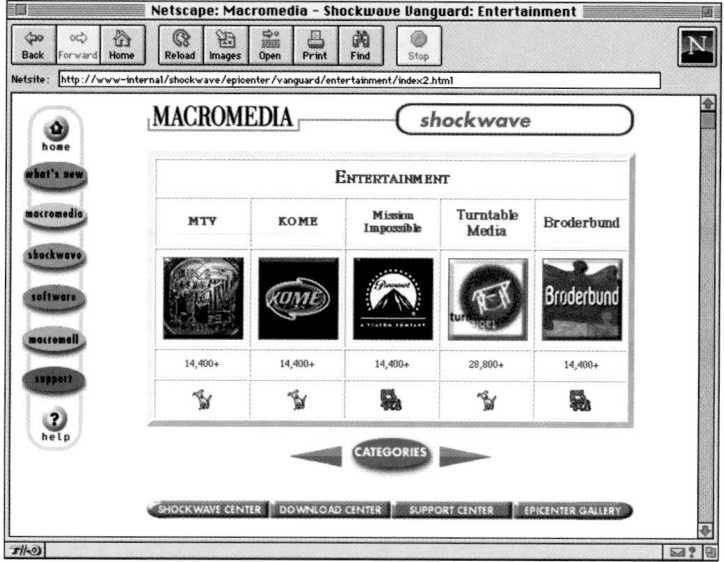

2 Save and upload. Click each icon and it should bring up another browser window.

67

target windows

CHECK OUT THESE

VARIATIONS

For more technical control of your page, you can create a frame link where users who click on a link jump to a frames version of the link containing both the original page and the new page.

1 To create a two-frame Web page, decide on a layout based on what works best with the content you are presenting. The two frames, for example, might look best side-by-side or stacked on top of each other.

2 To stack your frames, as in the second example, create a new HTML document. This is the main frames page linking both frame windows. Define your area as follows:

```
<frameset rows="*, 100">
```

This code states that there are 2 rows, indicated by the values "*," and "100." The top frame is given the "*" property so that it can be as large as the user wants; the second frame is set to 100 and cannot be adjusted.

3 Link the two frames to specific pages by adding this code:

```
<FRAME SRC="gallery.html" NAME="main frame" NORESIZE>
<FRAME SRC="links.html" NAME="bottom link frame" SCROLLING=auto>
```

The page is presented with gallery.html as the main window. After the URLs in links.html are clicked, the main frame dynamically changes to that Web page while the bottom link frame stays intact for easy Web surfing.

4 Create something eye-catching for the opening page gallery.html. Insert a graphic and add directions on use for the page.

5 Create the HTML document "links.html." List your links and use the center tag to align them on the page. Instead of adding a target="main frame" to every link, you can add a base target to the top of the links.html page that affects all the links:

```
<base target="main frame">
```

6 Upload and test the file in your browser. Adjust any row span if necessary.

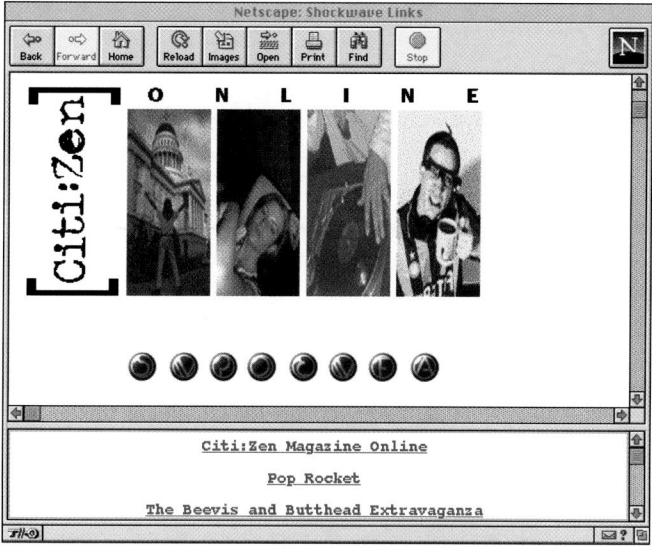

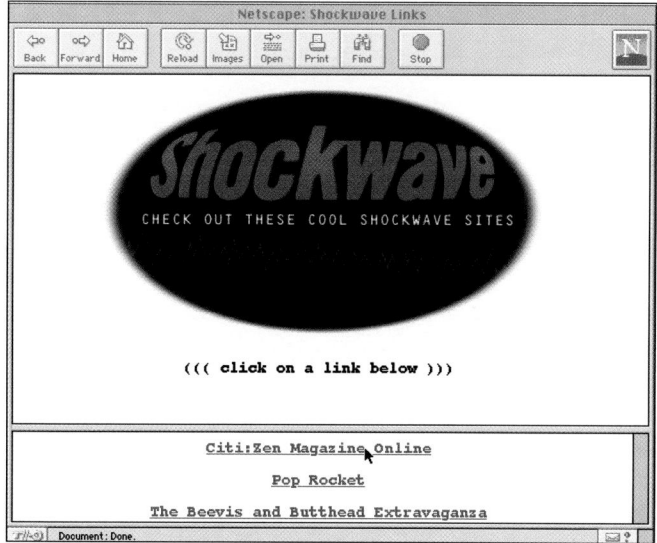

For more on target windows, see the "Remote Control Pop-Up Window" (p.46) or "Linking from One Frame Layout to Another" (p.114) techniques.

Browser Watch

Netscape 2.0 and higher

Internet Explorer 3.0 ∎

Column Layout

Use this technique to:

■ **Create a newspaper or multicolumn page layout.** Laying out your type in columns can make your page look more organized and make the type more legible.

Columns are a great way to provide content especially because many people are already used to reading a newspaper layout. With the introduction of the COLUMN tag, you can create great columns without messy tables!

Writing the HTML

This technique makes use of the new <MULTICOL> tag. In this example, you use <MULTICOL> in conjunction with a table to organize a block of type so that it looks like a traditionally designed page.

1 Decide how many columns you want on your page. In this example, a two-column layout was used for the "Web Designer's Rant" page. You can specify a gutter number in pixels between columns (the default is 10).

```
<MULTICOL COLS=2 WIDTH=90% GUTTER=50>
</MULTICOL>
```

2 Add your content between the <MULTICOL> tags and that's it! No need to worry about placement; the column tags automatically wrap your text to the next column if necessary.

```
<MULTICOL COLS=2 WIDTH=90% GUTTER=50>
<FONT FACE="Arial,Helvetica" SIZE=6 COLOR="red">Tables</FONT><BR>
<HR>
I love tables! There's something about the control and layout you can
get with a table. True, it's useful for adding informational data like a
financial report, but I'm no number cruncher!...
<SPACER TYPE=VERTICAL SIZE=25>
<FONT FACE="Arial,Helvetica" SIZE=6 COLOR="red">Frames</FONT><BR>
<HR>
Ok, well I can't say I love frames because I love tables so much but
really frames have come a long way. I actually like the way you can
create a borderless frame for a seamless page look...
Besides a navigation tool, frames create great multiple page layouts onto
one screen. There is definitely more control here...
</FONT>
<SPACER TYPE=VERTICAL SIZE=25>
<FONT FACE="Arial,Helvetica" SIZE=6 COLOR="red">Fonts</FONT><BR>
<HR>
Fonts are slowing taking their place on the Web! Although I love CODE
and TT, I've probably used them to death in trying to create Web pages
with panache and style...
<P></FONT>
</MULTICOL>
```

3 Save your page and test it in your browser.

Browser Watch

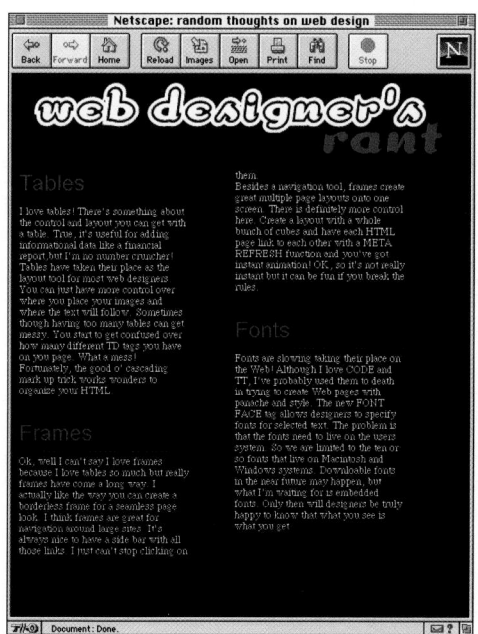

Netscape 2.0 and higher for Windows

Netscape 3.0 for Macintosh

Internet Explorer 3.0 ■

71

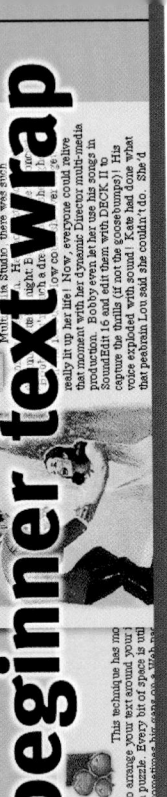

Wrapping Text Around Images–Beginner Example

Use this technique to:

- **Improve the appearance of your page.** Wrapping text around images integrates the content of your Web pages. Use this technique when the content calls for a close relationship between words and pictures, such as a storybook style.

- **Create interesting typographic effects.** Create a drop cap look to dramatize the beginning of your paragraphs.

Polish your Web page layout by arranging text around images. In order for graphics and text to complement each other, they must share space like pieces of a puzzle. Every bit of space is used to create the final layout. Although empty space is just as important as the content itself, sometimes big gaps on a Web page look accidental and awkward. Compare the two different layouts in these figures. The first example illustrates a straightforward alternation between graphics and text, and the second shows how wrapping text around images provides a more effective layout.

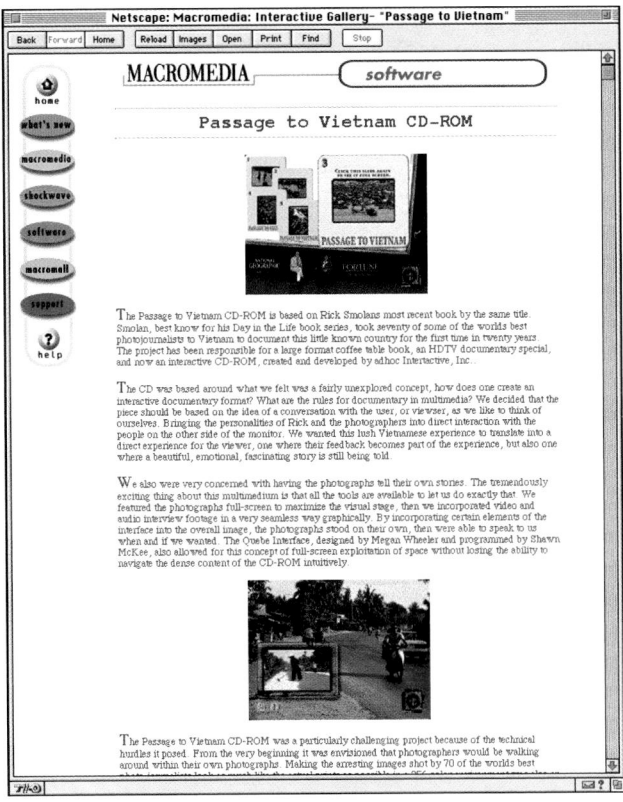

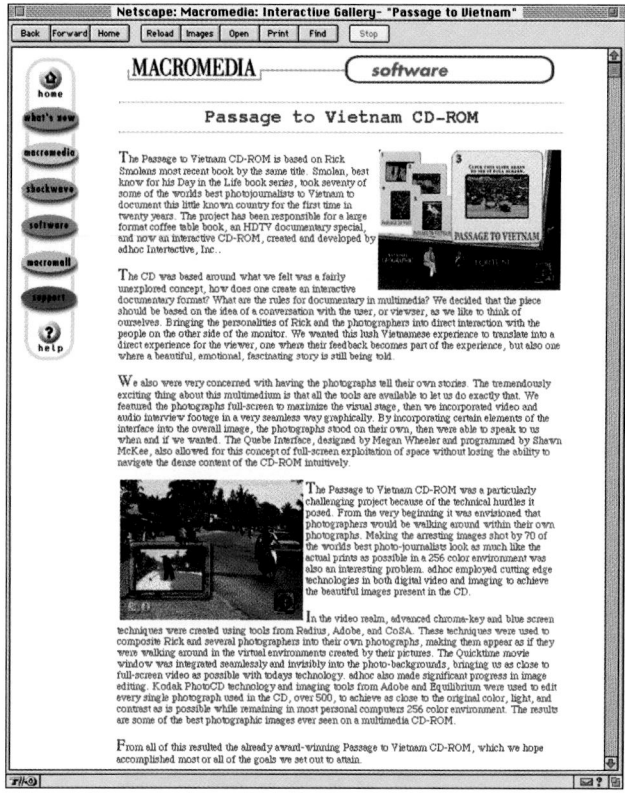

Isolating a graphic works best when you want to showcase the graphic in a gallery or portfolio. When you integrate a graphic within text, the synergy between the two elements communicates information in a cohesive and compelling manner.

Writing the HTML

You can align your text horizontally and vertically in relation to your graphics. Wrapping text around a graphic is as easy as placing the `align` `attribute` within the `img src` tag. Although you need only the simple horizontal alignment tags to arrange paragraphs around images, this technique briefly explains vertical alignment to give you more alignment options.

Horizontal Alignment

This section discusses ways to align graphics horizontally with text. Whether or not you choose left or right alignment, the HTML text automatically starts at the top of your image.

If you put the `image` tag in the middle of a sentence, the first part of that paragraph appears above the image and then wraps around it.

Left Alignment

To align a graphic to the left of the text, use the following code:

```
<img src="yourgraphichere" align=left width="widthgoeshere"
➥height="heightgoeshere" alt="Your graphic aligned to the left">
```

This is where your text would go. Lots and lots of text. Text that's so interesting to read. People will be amazed by your genius.

TIP The drop cap, or an oversized letterform that occupies two or more lines at the start of a paragraph, serves as a useful application of this technique. You can create ornamental letterforms to draw the eye into the copy, especially if other elements such as pictures are prominent. In the "Shocking True Story" of Macromedia's 1996 Annual Report, drop caps enhance the storybook flavor of the narration.

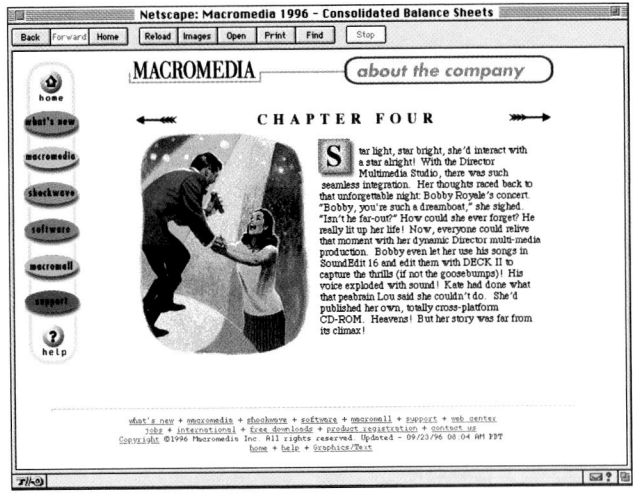

Right Alignment

Use this code to align a graphic to the right of the text. (Notice how this code shows a striking resemblance to the left alignment example except for the `align` position.)

```
<img src="yourgraphichere" align=right width="widthgoeshere" height="height
➡goeshere" alt="Your graphic aligned to the left">
```

```
This is where your text would go. Lots and lots of text. Text that's so
➡interesting to read. People will be amazed by your genius.
```

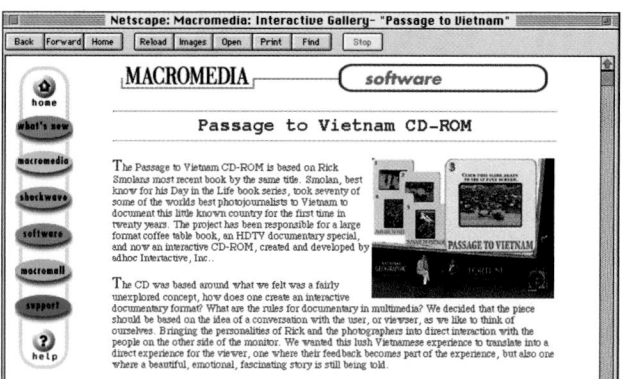

 You might want to use a little variety to spice up your layout. Refer to the first figure in this technique and note that the images alternate between right and left alignment; thus the viewer's eye travels over the entire page.

Center Alignment

Unfortunately, you can't place an image at the center of your body of text with any HTML align tags. `align=center` within the `img src` tag for example, results in aligning the first line of your paragraph to the center of your graphic, (the same result as `align=middle`.) You can place an image at the center of a line of text by adding the `img src` tag between specific words in a sentence. The HTML code looks like this:

```
words words words <img src="image.gif" width="widthgoeshere"
➡height="heightgoeshere" border="0" alt="Here's a graphic that fits right
➡into my sentence."> words words words words
```

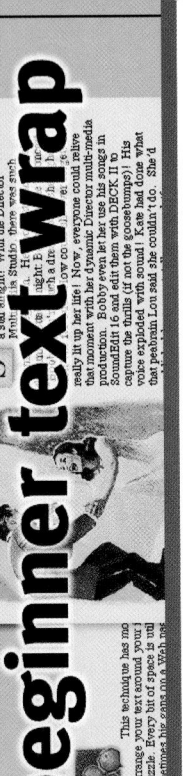

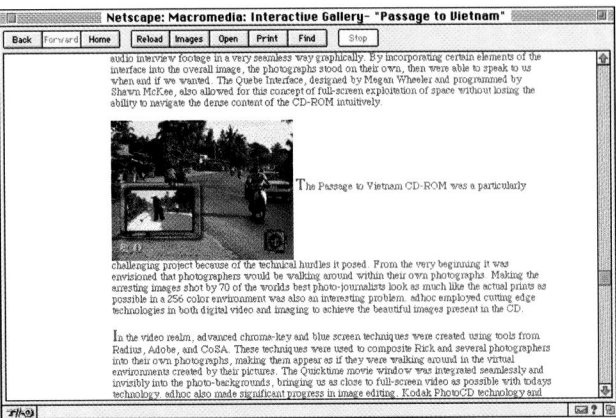

Vertical Alignment

Vertical alignment works best with one-line captions next to a graphic, because any text that wraps automatically drops below the graphic. Aligning paragraphs vertically in relation to a graphic produces some pretty strange results.

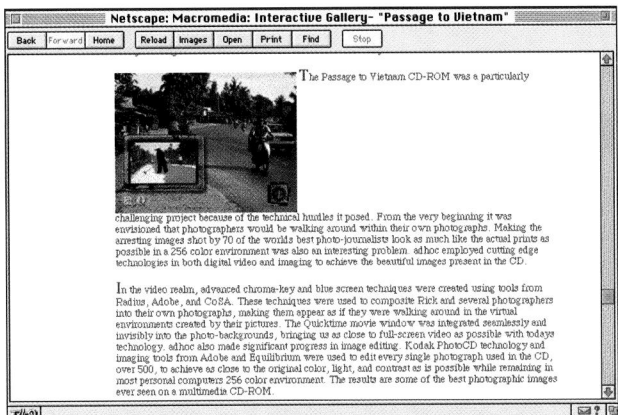

To align text to the top of a graphic, use the following code:

```
<img src="yourgraphichere" align=top width="widthgoeshere"
➡height="heightgoeshere" alt="Your graphic aligned to the left">
Here's a simple line of text aligned to the top of a graphic.
```

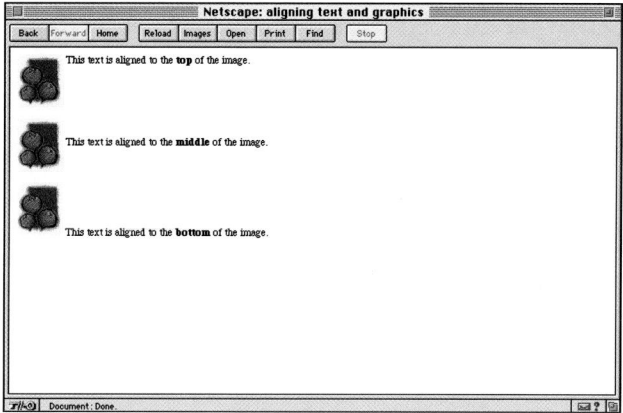

Use this code to align a graphic to the middle of the text:

```
<img src="yourgraphichere" align=middle width=whatever height=whatever alt="Your
➥graphic aligned to the left">
Here's a simple line of text aligned to the middle of a graphic.
```

Unlike the other two vertical alignment attributes, bottom alignment works with paragraphs because the lines flow consistently one after another without any strange breaks. To align a graphic to the bottom of the text, use the following code:

```
<img src="yourgraphichere" align=bottom width="widthgoeshere"
➥height="heightgoeshere" alt="Your graphic aligned to the left">
Here's a simple line of text aligned to the bottom of a graphic.
```

Space Around Your Images

You can also control the space between your graphics and text. By adding the hspace and vspace attributes to the img src tag, you can specify the number of pixels in both horizontal and vertical directions. Here is the code with these added features:

```
<img src="yourgraphichere" align=left hspace="10" vspace="3" width="width-
➥goeshere" height="heightgoeshere" alt="Your graphic aligned to the left">
```

77

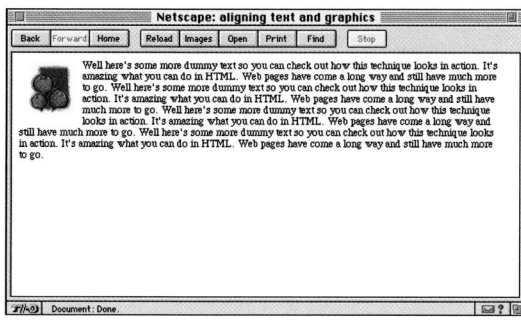

NOTE The space indicated by these tags defines the space all the way around the image, even on sides with no related elements; therefore, if you need your graphic to flush with the text you should avoid using hspace. Instead, create the space within your graphic on the side where you need it. This way, you can still use vspace so that your graphic is spaced from the wrapping text on three sides instead of all four. ■

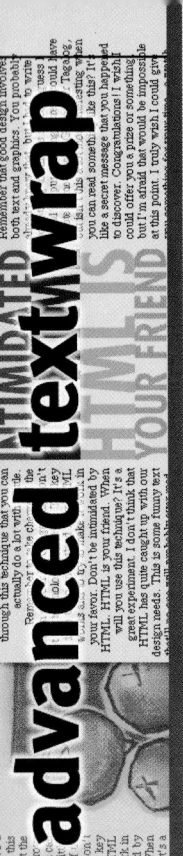

Wrapping Text Around Images–Advanced Example

Use this technique to:

- **Place graphics within the center of your text.** You can find examples of this particular technique in magazine and newspaper articles where an important image or enlarged quote breaks up the space between two columns.

- **Highlight an idea from your text in graphical form.** If you have a Web page with text-intensive content, it is a good idea to highlight important quotes or ideas from the text for readers as they scan your page.

Have you ever wanted to fit a graphic in the middle of two columns with text flowing around it? This technique shows you more options for placing images in unusual places within text.

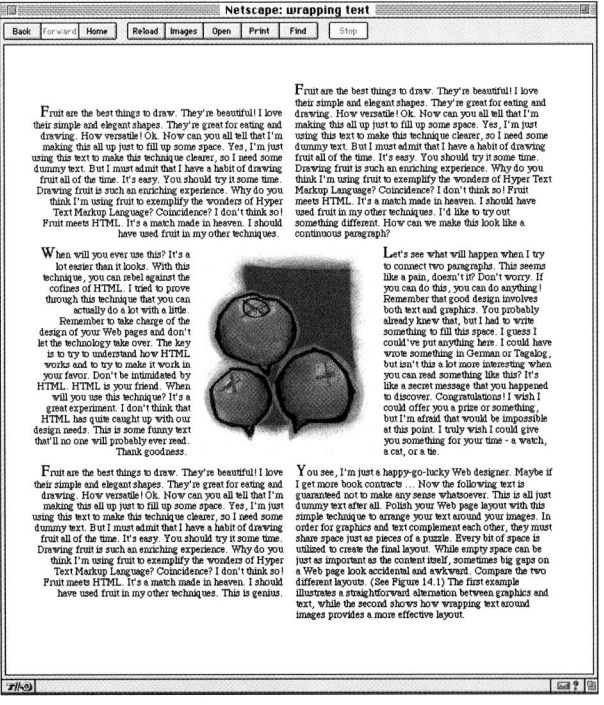

Unlike previous examples, this technique calls for a fixed layout within a set table. Because there isn't a way to place a graphic in the middle of text that automatically resets itself around the image, this example of the wrapping text technique offers a basic solution for this problem.

NOTE Fitting text exactly around a specific image requires a certain amount of experimentation depending on your graphic's dimensions, the font sizes and styles used, as well as the cellpadding and cellspacing you add to your table. Also remember other people might not use the same default font or size as you.

Writing the HTML

Using this technique is as easy as creating basic tables in HTML. If you want to place a graphic snugly between two columns, you have to accommodate for text hanging over and passing under the graphic. You need these five columns to lay out your content:

- A column for the left-hand column of text.

- A column for the right-hand column of text.

- A column for the gutter between the two columns of text.

- A column for the left-hand portion of the graphic.

- A column for the right-hand portion of the graphic.

Your table must have a fixed width to control how the text fits in the individual table data cells. Furthermore, some of your table data entries span across multiple columns to create the wrapping text effect. The graphic spans across three columns to sit within the center table and the top and bottom portions of the text columns span across two columns.

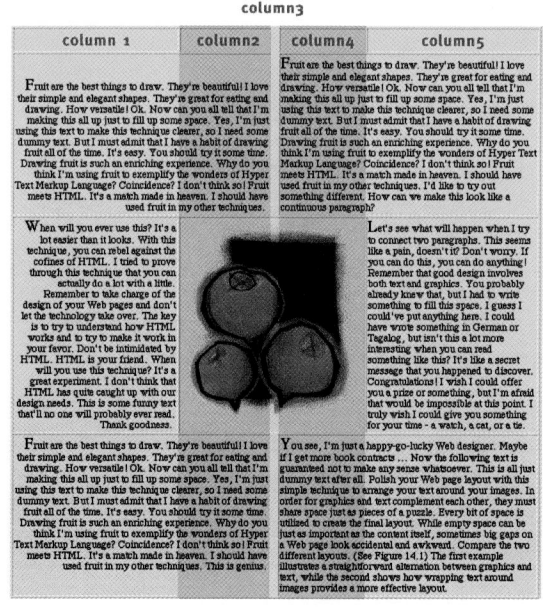

Highlight a Picture

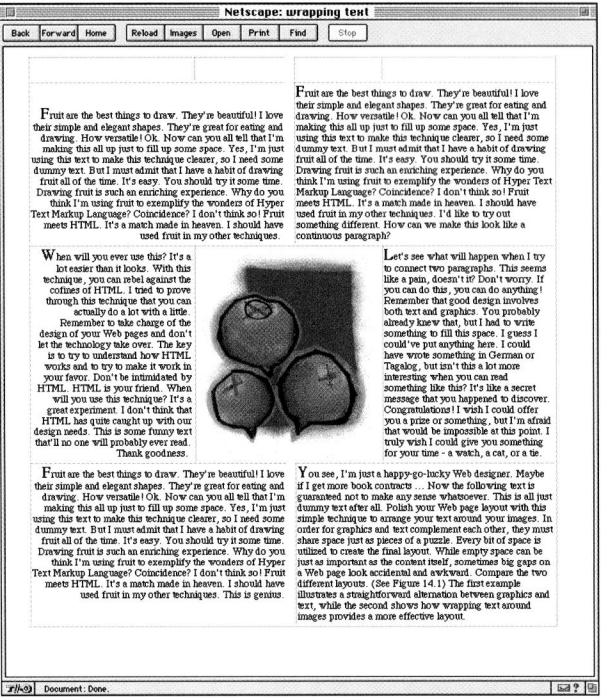

Use the following code for this example by substituting your own text where indicated:

```
<center>
<table width="600" cellpadding="0" cellspacing="0" border="1">
<tr>
        <td width="100"><pre>    </pre></td>
        <td width="100"><pre>    </pre></td>
        <td width="10"></td>
        <td width="100"><pre>    </pre></td>
        <td width="100"><pre>    </pre></td>
</tr>
<tr>
        <td colspan="2" align=right valign=bottom>all the text for the top
➥left column goes here! </td>
        <td width="10"></td>
        <td colspan="2" valign=bottom>all the text for the top right
➥column goes here! </td>
</tr>
<tr>
        <td valign=top align=right> all the text for the middle left
➥column goes here! </td>
```

```
        <td colspan="3" align=center><img src="images/frutas.jpeg" width="200"
➥height="230" border="0" alt="Here's a funky graphic!"></td>
        <td valign=top> all the text for the middle right column goes
➥here!</td>
</tr>
<tr>
        <td colspan="2" align=right valign=top>all the text for the bottom left
➥column goes here!</td>
        <td width="10"></td>
        <td colspan="2"> all the text for the bottom right column goes here</td>
</tr>
</table>
</center>
```

You might have to do some copy editing to make this technique work for you. Notice the center paragraphs in this example fit within the table data cells at the exact height of the graphic. After you are satisfied with your layout, turn the table border off by setting the `border="0"`.

TIP Thanks to a simple `TD align=right` command for the three left-hand table data cells, this effect has a more polished look because of the way the text frames the graphic in a well-defined rectangle.

Highlight a Quote

Remember, a graphic doesn't have to be an illustration or a picture. You can use a graphic to highlight text exactly the way you want by choosing the colors, sizes, and type-faces. This example shows ways you can highlight a quote or a segment of text on your Web page. This code is the same as the code used in the previous example but with a different graphic.

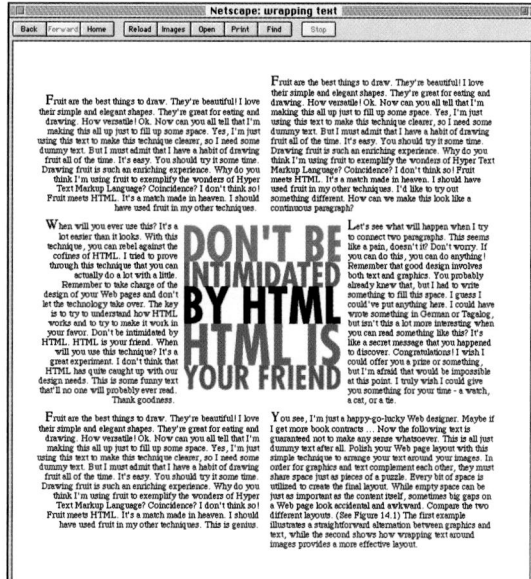

Forcing Alignment

Use this technique to:

- **Align text next to images.** Force text and images to align correctly.

- **Create a layout without tables.** Although you can have better control of alignment with tables, the <BR> tag is a quick and easy way to force alignment

Sometimes it is easier to align graphics and text without complicating your HTML with tables. It is easy to create alignment with images and text by using these three HTML tags:

- <BR CLEAR=RIGHT> to clearing right-aligned images

- <BR CLEAR=LEFT> to clearing left-aligned images

- <BR CLEAR=ALL> to clear all right- and left-aligned images

Writing the HTML

In this section, you look at some pages where the text-picture alignment isn't quite right, and see how variations on the basic <BR> tag are used to solve common alignment problems.

Clearing All Alignment

When redesigning Macromedia's Web site in June of 1996, we were posed with several choices for implementing the side navigation bar. We could have used frames or tables but because there were problems with browser compatibility and unpredictable behavior in early implementations of frames, we chose to have the navigation graphic align to the left. We soon found that small pages with little text caused the navigational footer to align adjacent to the graphic rather than sit below it. We used the <BR CLEAR=ALL> tag to make the page align correctly. Here's what the page looks like without the use of the <BR CLEAR= ALL> tag:

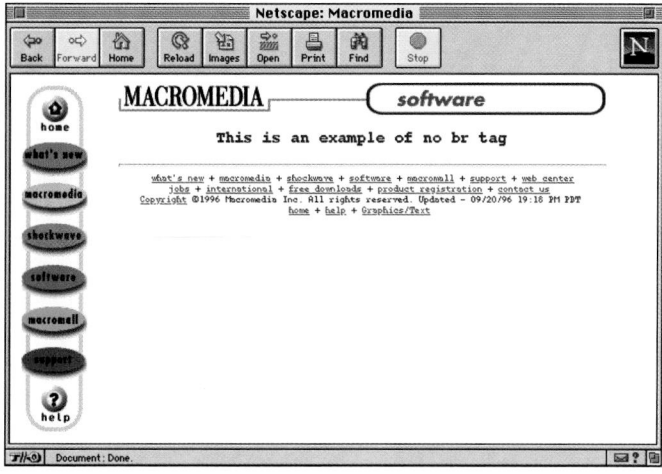

Here's the corrected page, with the caption in the correct position:

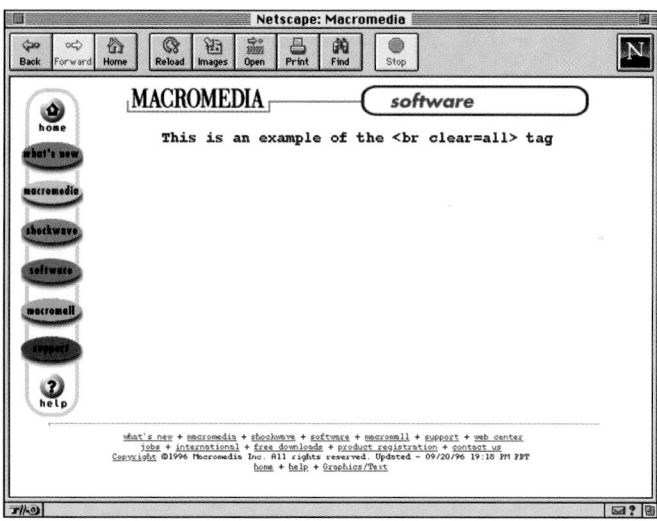

Clearing Right or Left Alignment

Say you have a graphic that you want some but not all of the adjacent text to wrap around and align. (Refer to the "Wrapping Text Around Images–Beginner Example," (p.72), and the "Wrapping Text Around Images–Advanced Example," (p.78), techniques) This can be done with the <BR CLEAR> tags. Clearing left- and right-aligned text does not afford as much control of text flow as you have with tables, but it is an easy alternative, and using the <BR CLEAR> tags definitely make your HTML cleaner in terms of maintenance.

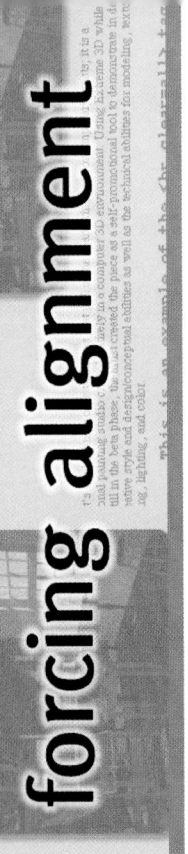

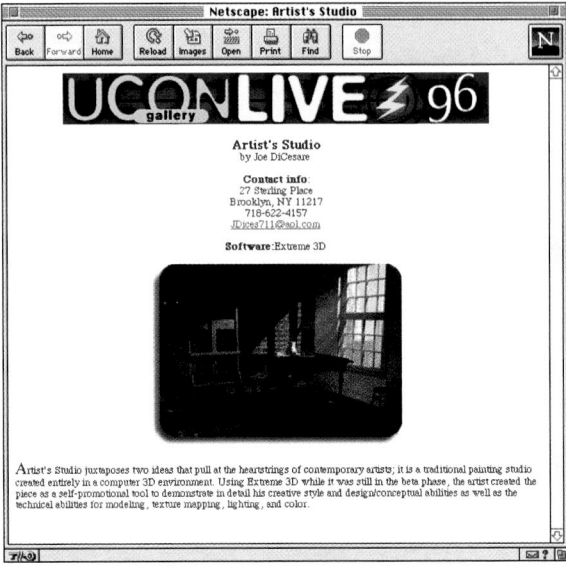

You will work on a winning entry from Macromedia's 1996 User Conference. This piece, which won Best Fine Art, needs to be showcased better on the Web page. You can eliminate a lot of the white space around the graphic by fine-tuning the alignment.

Clearing Right Alignment

1 Open the HTML document. Remove the center tags and move the IMG SRC tag above the title "Artist's Studio."

```
<IMG SRC="7artist.gif" WIDTH=275 HEIGHT=195 ALT="Artist's Studio">
<P>
<B><FONT SIZE=4>Artist's Studio</FONT></B><BR>
by Joe DiCesare
```

2 Add <ALIGN=RIGHT> to the <IMG SRC> tag.

```
<IMG SRC="7artist.gif" ALIGN=RIGHT WIDTH=275 HEIGHT=195
➥ALT="Artist's Studio">
```

3 You want the paragraph that contains the description to stay at the bottom and not wrap to the left of the graphic. (The title, however, stays with the graphic.) Add `<BR CLEAR=RIGHT>` before the beginning of the paragraph like this:

```
<B>Software:</B>Extreme 3D

<P>

<BR CLEAR=RIGHT>


<font size=+2>A</font>rtist's Studio juxtaposes two ideas that pull at
the heartstrings of contemporary artists; it is a traditional painting
studio created entirely in a computer 3D environment. Using Extreme 3D
while it was still in the beta phase, the artist created the piece as a
self-promotional tool to demonstrate in detail his creative style and
design/conceptual abilities as well as the technical abilities for
modeling, texture mapping, lighting, and color.

<P>
```

4 Save your HTML document and upload it.

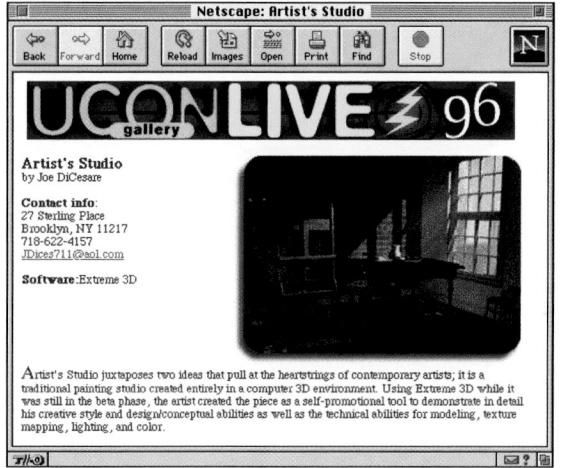

Clearing Left Alignment

1 Open the HTML document. Remove the center tags and move the `IMG SRC` tag above the title "Artist's Studio."

```
<IMG SRC="7artist.gif" WIDTH=275 HEIGHT=195 ALT="Artist's Studio">
<P>
<B><FONT SIZE=4>Artist's Studio</FONT></B><BR>
by Joe DiCesare
```

2 Add `<ALIGN=left>` to the `<IMG SRC>` tag.

```
<IMG SRC="7artist.gif" WIDTH=275 HEIGHT=195 ALT="Artist's Studio">
```

3 You want to have the title and information on the right this time, so add `<BR CLEAR=LEFT>` before the beginning of the paragraph.

```
<B>Software:</B>Extreme 3D
<P>
<BR CLEAR=LEFT>
<font size=+2>A</font>rtist's Studio juxtaposes two ideas that pull
at the heartstrings of contemporary artists; it is a traditional
painting studio created entirely in a computer 3D environment.
Using Extreme 3D while it was still in the beta phase, the artist
created the piece as a self-promotional tool to demonstrate in
detail his creative style and design/conceptual abilities as well
as the technical abilities for modeling, texture mapping, lighting,
and color.
<P>
```

4 As you can see there is too little space between the graphic and the text. You can solve this by adding a few spacer tags ` ` like this:

```
 <A HREF="mailto:JDices711@aol.com">JDices711@aol.com</A>
<p>
 <BSoftware:</B>Extreme 3D
 <B><FONT SIZE=4>Artist's Studio</FONT></B><BR>
 by Joe DiCesare
<P>
```

 <B>Contact info</B>:
 27 Sterling Place
 Brooklyn, NY 11217
 718-622-4157
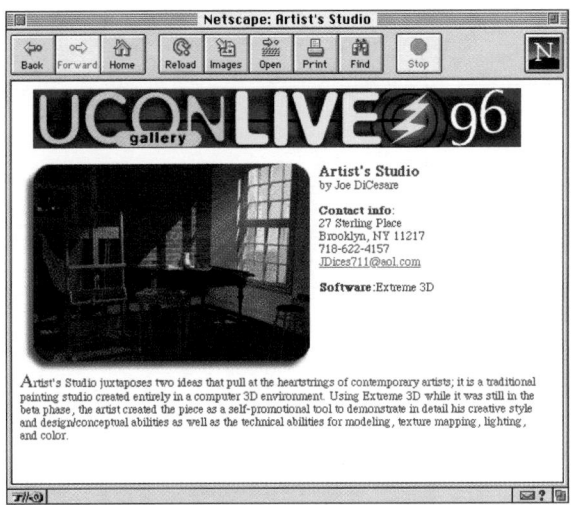

Using Different Styles of Lists

Use this technique to:

■ **Emphasize your main ideas with HTML bullets or characters.** Both ordered and unordered lists enable you to indent and highlight important points with standard numbers, letters, and bullets.

■ **Maintain indented alignments easily.** Although definition lists provide standard indenting, HTML lists enable you to indent your points effortlessly because the bullet or character is separate from the list item text.

■ **Manage enumerated lists efficiently.** If your list items need to be in a certain order, the ordered list tag, `<ol>`, keeps your list in numerical order no matter how many times the list is modified.

Perhaps the best-kept secrets of HTML, lists offer easy ways to align text clearly and effectively. Key points on a page lose their impact when they follow the same alignment as the rest of the body of text.

Writing the HTML

This section focusses on the most popular and most useful types of lists. Regardless of type, a list has opening and closing tags around the entire list and each individual list items. Browsers tend to forgive certain omitted closing tags, `</dt>`, `</dd>`, and `</li>`, but remember that proper HTML form is to close all of your tags.

Bulleted Lists

Within the `<ul>` or unordered list tag, you can create bullets shaped as circles, `type=circle`; discs, `type=disc`; or squares, `type=square`.

1 The default `ul` type automatically displays disc bullets; therefore, if you don't specify the `ul` type, you get a list with solid, circular bullets. For this example, use the following code:

Solid Circle Bullets

- First list item
- Second list item
- Third list item
- Fourth list item

```
<ul type=disc>
<li>    First list item</li>
<li>    Second list item</li>
<li>    Third list item</li>
<li>    Fourth list item</li>
</ul>
```

2 To create a list with open, circular bullets or discs, use this code:

Open Circle Bullets

○ First list item
○ Second list item
○ Third list item
○ Fourth list item

```
<ul type=circle>
<li>    First list item</li>
<li>    Second list item</li>
<li>    Third list item</li>
<li>    Fourth list item</li>
</ul>
```

3 Create a list with open, square bullets by using the following code:

```
<ul type=square>
<li>    First list item</li>
<li>    Second list item</li>
<li>    Third list item</li>
<li>    Fourth list item</li>
</ul>
```

Square Bullets

- First list item
- Second list item
- Third list item
- Fourth list item

TIP Try alternating bullet styles between circles and squares for an added effect. You can assign the bullet type within the <li> tag. To do this, use the following code:

```
<ul>
<li type=square>      First list item</li>
<li type=disc>        Second list item</li>
<li type=square>      Third list item</li>
<li type=disc>        Fourth list item</li>
</ul>
```

Alternating Bullets

- First list item
- Second list item
- Third list item
- Fourth list item

TIP You might want to experiment with different text colors. Remember the color of the bullets follows the color set for the body text of your page; therefore, you must change the font color of the list items. Here is what the code looks like:

```
<font color="red"><b>Solid Circle Bullets with Color</b>
<ul type=disc>
<li>    First list item</li>
<li>    Second list item</li>
<li>    Third list item</li>
<li>    Fourth list item</li>
</ul>
</font>
```

Barbell Design's Web site effectively shows off their colors with bulleted lists.

Solid Circle Bullets with Color

- First list item
- Second list item
- Third list item
- Fourth list item

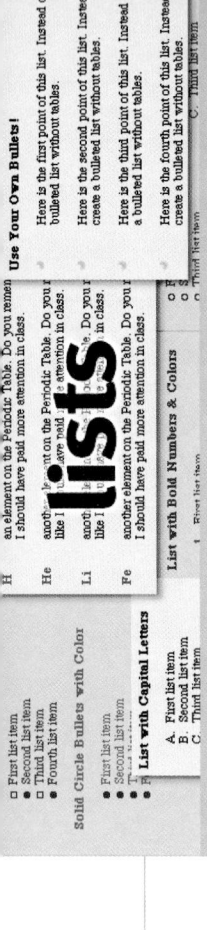

TIP If you have a blockquoted text layout where additional indented lists might look extreme, you can add the `compact` attribute to align your list text with the blockquote margin and let the bullets hang out beyond it. Macromedia's Web site uses extensive blockquoting because of its vertical navigational graphic. For areas such as the job listings, the blockquoting technique was used to maximize the use of space. Here is an abbreviated version of the code:

```
<blockquote>
<hr>
<p>
<b><font size=+2>T</font>ECHNICAL <font size=+2>S</font>
➥UPPORT</b>
<p>
<ul=compact>
<li> <b>Position Available</B>
<BR>
<B>Responsibilites</b>: Responsibilities go here.
<BR>
<B>Requirements</B>: Requirements go here.
<BR>
```

```
<B>Ideal Requirements</B>: Ideal requirements go here.
</li>
</ul>
</blockquote>
```

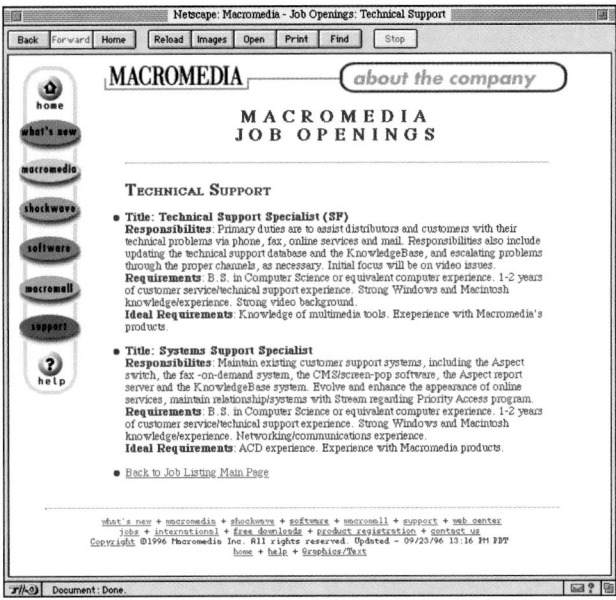

Ordered Lists

If you need to list items in a specific sequence, ordered lists can get the job done. Each type of ordered list enables you to display items in a specific order according to the style you've chosen regardless of how often you rearrange the items. Within the `<ol>` or ordered list tag, you can itemize your list with:

- **numbers**, 1, 2, 3, (`type=1`)
- **capital Roman numerals**, I, II, III, (`type=I`)
- **lowercase Roman numerals**, i, ii, iii, (`type=i`)
- **capital letters**, A, B, C, (`type=A`)
- **lowercase letters**, a, b, c, (`type=a`).

The following code examples illustrate how to create the various types of ordered lists described above.

1 An <ol> tag without `type` specified results in the default 1, 2, 3 type. Here is an example of the code:

Default Ordered List

1. First list item
2. Second list item
3. Third list item
4. Fourth list item

```
<ol>
<li>      First list item</li>
<li>      Second list item</li>
<li>      Third list item</li>
<li>      Fourth list item</li>
</ol>
```

2 To create a list with capital Roman numerals, use the following code:

List with Roman numerals

I. First list item
II. Second list item
III. Third list item
IV. Fourth list item

```
<ol type=I>
<li>      First list item</li>
<li>      Second list item</li>
<li>      Third list item</li>
<li>      Fourth list item</li>
</ol>
```

Replace the type=I tag with one of the values suggested to vary your lists.

3 Unlike bulleted lists, you can specify font colors and boldface style for the numbers and characters of ordered lists. Here is an example of the code:

```
<ol type=1>
<b><font color=purple><li></font></b>      First list item</li>
<b><font color=purple><li></font></b>      Second list item</li>
<b><font color=purple><li></font></b>      Third list item</li>
<b><font color=purple><li></font></b>      Fourth list item</li>
</ol>
```

List with Bold Numbers & Colors

1. First list item
2. Second list item
3. Third list item
4. Fourth list item

TIP You might run into a situation where you have to interrupt your list with regular paragraphs formatted with flushed text. You can still jump back into your list from where you started by assigning the value of the first item in this chunk of the list. All of the ordered list examples, for instance, include four items. If you want to continue the list later on in the page, all you have to do is assign `value="5"` to the first `<li>` of the next list like this:

<table>
<tr><td colspan="2">

Alternative Starting Number

5. First list item
6. Second list item
7. Third list item
8. Fourth list item

</td><td>

```
<ol>
<li value="5">      First list item</li>
<li>                Second list item</li>
<li>                Third list item</li>
<li>                Fourth list item</li>
</ol>
```

</td></tr>
</table>

Definition Lists

Definition lists, indicated by the `<DL>` tag, enable you to set up a glossary-like layout; therefore, instead of bullets or characters, you use your own words to offset blocks of text. Instead of list items, these lists contain definition terms, `<DT>`, and definition definitions, `<DD>`. Here is a basic example:

```
<DL>
<DT>Hydrogen</DT>
<DD>an element on the Periodic Table. Do you remember it from Chemistry class?
I'm pretty sure it's hydrogen. I feel like I should have paid more attention in
class.</DD>
<p>
<DT>Helium</DT>
<DD>another element on the Periodic Table. Do you remember it from Chemistry
class? I'm pretty sure it's helium. I feel like I should have paid more atten-
tion in class.</DD>
<p>
<DT>Lithium</DT>
<DD>another element on the Periodic Table. Do you remember it from Chemistry
class? I'm pretty sure it's lithium. I feel like I should have paid more atten-
tion in class.</DD>
<p>
<DT>Iron</DT>
<DD>another element on the Periodic Table. Do you remember it from Chemistry
class? I'm pretty sure it's iron. I feel like I should have paid more attention
in class.</DD>
</DL>
```

93

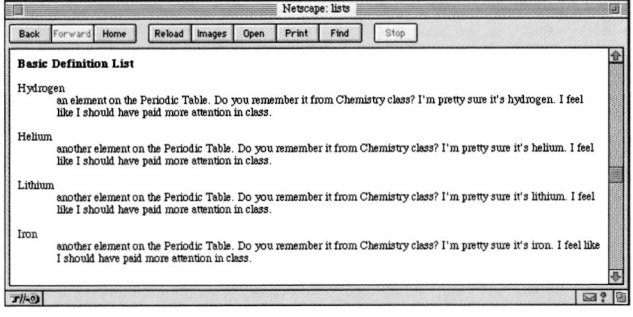

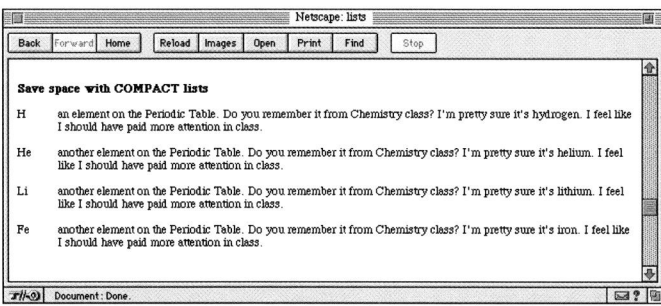

You can use a space-saving version of the definition list by adding the `compact` attribute within the `<DL>` tag. In this example, your `<DT>` becomes the bullet, and your `<DD>` indents as it normally would except this time, it begins on the same line as the `<DT>`. Here is what the code looks like:

```
<DL COMPACT>

<DT>H</DT>

<DD>an element on the Periodic Table. Do you remember it from Chemistry
class? I'm pretty sure it's hydrogen. I feel like I should have paid more
attention in class.</DD>

<p>

<DT>He</DT>

<DD>another element on the Periodic Table. Do you remember it from
Chemistry class? I'm pretty sure it's helium. I feel like I should have
paid more attention in class.</DD>

<p>

<DT>Li</DT>

<DD>another element on the Periodic Table. Do you remember it from
Chemistry class? I'm pretty sure it's lithium. I feel like I should have
paid more attention in class.</DD>

<p>

<DT>Fe</DT>

<DD>another element on the Periodic Table. Do you remember it from
Chemistry class? I'm pretty sure it's iron. I feel like I should have
paid more attention in class.</DD>

</DL>
```

TIP Remember to use font styles and text colors when you use definition lists. Here is an example of a glossary-like list with bold and colored definition terms:

```
<DL COMPACT>

<DT><font color="red"><b>H</b></font></DT>

<DD>an element on the Periodic Table. Do you remember it from
Chemistry class? I'm pretty sure it's hydrogen. I feel like I
should have paid more attention in class.</DD>

<p>
```

```
<DT><font color="red"><b>He</b></font></DT>
<DD>another element on the Periodic Table. Do you remember it from
Chemistry class? I'm pretty sure it's helium. I feel like I should have
paid more attention in class.</DD>
<p>
<DT><font color="red"><b>Li</b></font></DT>
<DD>another element on the Periodic Table. Do you remember it from
Chemistry class? I'm pretty sure it's lithium. I feel like I should have
paid more attention in class.</DD>
<p>
<DT><font color="red"><b>Fe</b></font></DT>
<DD>another element on the Periodic Table. Do you remember it from
Chemistry class? I'm pretty sure it's iron. I feel like I should have
paid more attention in class.</DD>
</DL>
```

Make sure that the colors that you specify are not the same as the ones used for active or visited links. People who turn off the underlining of their links have a hard time distinguishing colored text from clickable text links.

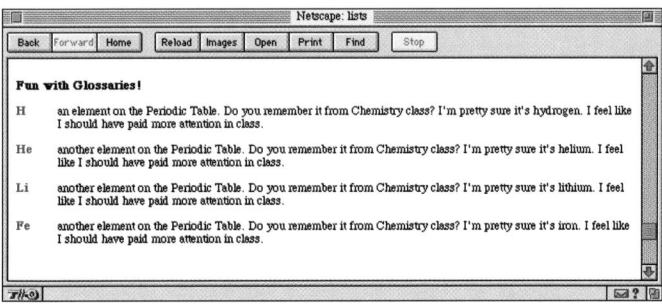

Custom Graphical Bullets

You can use your own graphical bullets with compact definition lists as long as the image height is no larger than the height of the text. All you have to do is substitute the preceding text definition terms with the `image` tags for your bullets. This is an easy way to align your lists properly with your customized bullets without using tables. Here is an example of the code:

```
<DL COMPACT>
<DT><img src="/images/dot.gif" width="10" height="10" alt="*"></DT>
<DD>Here is the first point of this list. Instead of using standard HTML
➥bullets, you can use your own graphics to create a bulleted list without
➥tables.</DD>
<p>
```

95

Dynamic Table Resizing

Use this technique to:

- **Resize your tables to fit any browser window size exactly.** Frustrated with your previous over- and underestimations of your visitors' window settings? With this technique, you can set the corners of your tables to match those of any window size.

- **Economize the space on your Web page.** Use the entire page as your canvas instead of settling for a fixed table size.

- **Create an effective layout for an introduction or welcome page.** Usually sparse and minimal, these pages can benefit by utilizing all available space.

This technique works best with tables containing modular elements that look fine spread apart. Small graphics and brief text also work well. Without this technique, a table looks too short in a long window or too narrow in a wide one.

Writing the HTML

Writing the HTML for this technique is as simple as adding width and height percentages to the table tag. Here is an example of the code (a table border was assigned in order for you to see the dynamic layouts):

```
<center>
<table width="100%" height="100%" border="1">
<tr>
<td align=left valign=top><font size="+2" color="red">This is the upper
➥left-hand corner.</font></td>
<td align=right valign=top><font size="+2" color="brown">This is the upper
➥right-hand corner.</font></td>
</tr>
<tr>
<td align=left valign=bottom><font size="+2" color="purple">This is the
➥lower left-hand corner.</font></td>
<td align=right valign=bottom><font size="+2" color="green">This is the
➥lower right-hand corner.</font></td>
</tr>
</table>
</center>
```

That's it! Seems easy, doesn't it? You're right! Remember to set the vertical alignments for your <td> tags so that your text or graphics meet the corners of any given window size.

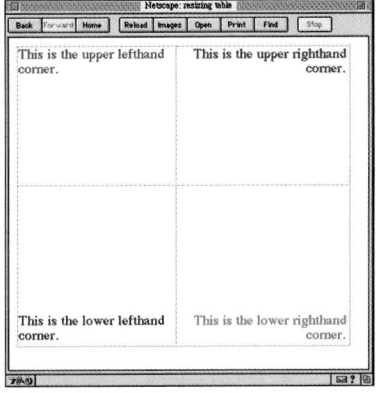

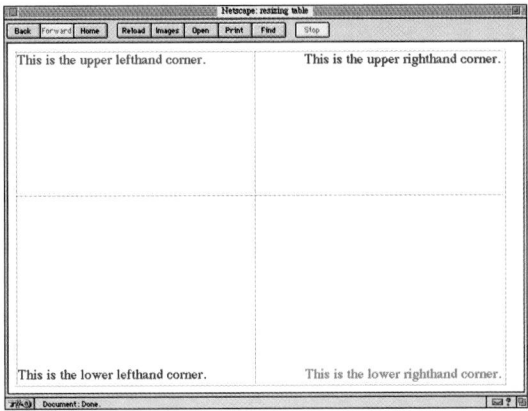

When The Main Quad launched a sophisticated new version of their Web site, they introduced pull-down navigation and special browsing buttons within a sandwich-like frames layout. Geared toward college students, The Main Quad created the new look and feel to make all of its services clear and accessible from every section of the site. They decided, based on strong audience feedback, to add instructions to clearly define the new menus or buttons at the corners of each of their pages. Using an automatically resizing table enabled The Main Quad to make each instruction match its corresponding button or menu, regardless of the size of the browser window. ▪

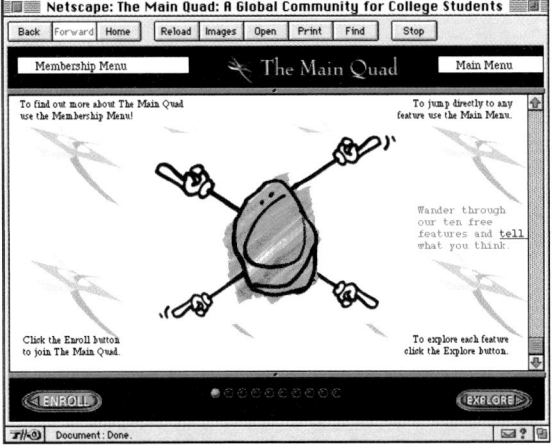

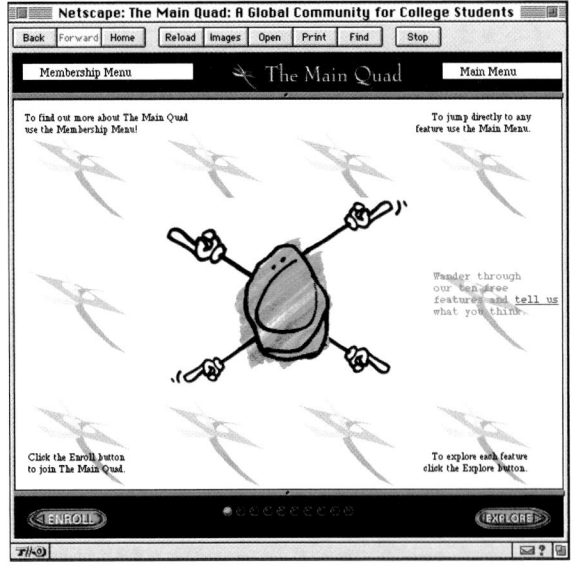

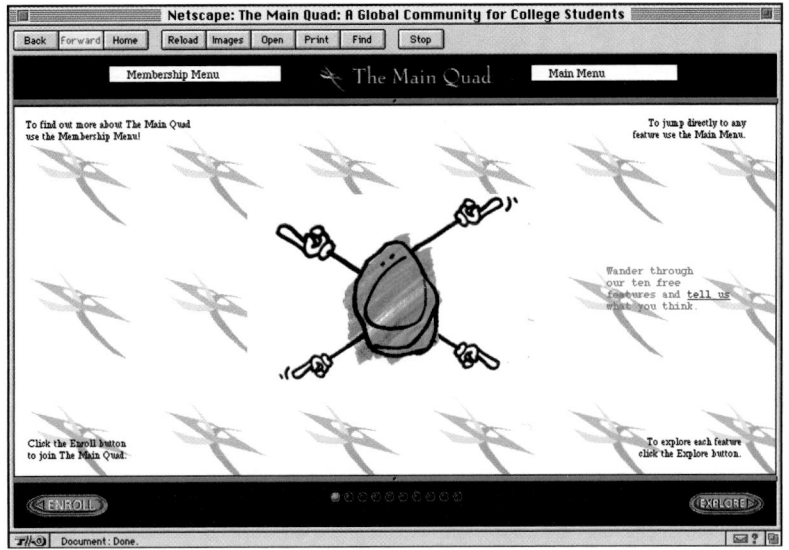

Nesting Tables Within Tables

Use this technique to:

■ **Have more control over your layout.** You can simplify your content management and maintenance by grouping elements within separate tables.

■ **Maintain a cohesive layout with different groups of elements while preserving the independent characteristics of each group.** You can run a long list of text links along the side of your page.

When you need to divide your page in a complicated grid of columns and rows, much like a newspaper or newsletter type format, HTML tables can get the job done. When elements relate to each other in a specific way, grouping them together in units enables you to rearrange your page more easily. You can do this by laying out elements in a table and then placing them within another table to relate to the rest of the elements on the page.

To demonstrate this example, the Macromedia Web team's prototype of a home page redesign is used. The design includes the following elements:

■ List of navigational text links.

■ Macromedia corporate identity as a prominent header.

■ One large main graphic to promote a service or product.

■ "What's New" list of "hot" headlines accompanied by short descriptions.

■ "Perspective" quote or tip from a Macromedian.

■ "Xtra Xtra" featuring a special developer tool.

■ "Shocked Site of the Day" spotlighting the day's cool site that implements Shockwave technology.

■ "Support Central" area to highlight programs and services for Macromedia customers.

Writing the HTML

Nesting tables within tables means placing smaller tables within the `<td>` of one large main table. It is important to set `<table>` and `<td>` widths to prevent resizing windows from ruining the layout within the tables.

> **NOTE** Browsers wait for the closing `</table>` tag before displaying the contents of the table, instead of loading them as it reads the HTML; therefore, a very large table might appear to download slowly.

Main Table

The prototype for the Macromedia home page contains one table that has one table row and two table data cells. The first `<td>` accommodates the navigation—the long list of text links—and the second <td> creates an area for the main content that can grow and shrink independently from the left sidebar. Though the page contains a tremendous amount of information, a simple table holds it all together.

```
<table width="620">
<tr>
<!----side quickmarks-->
        <td valign=top>
        </td>
<!----main content-->
        <td valign=top width="440">
        </td>
</tr>
</table>
```

To build a successful main table for nesting smaller tables, do the following steps:

1 Set the width for the entire table to prevent any strange changes when the browser is resized.

2 Set each table data cell to <td valign=top> to make sure that the page layout remains cohesive even when some columns are longer than others.

3 Set the specific widths of the columns according to the proportions you need.

4 Add comments marked with <!-- and --> to find the sections of your page easily in your HTML code.

uropean UCON
in us in Amsterdam for the
uropean User Conference,
ocking Your World!

reate Audio Co
ur step-by-step Director for
ows you how!

upport Central
New in the Tech Support ar

nesting tables
Perspective
"As we look
forward, Macromedia
is well-positioned
to extend our reach
and take advantage
Check out our mirror site for speedier

FreeHand Shocks the Web
FreeHand Graphics Studio 7 arrives on the scene,
bringing enhanced features and Shocking content.

European UCON

SALES
Business Internet
All Software
Free Downloads
Software Updates
Product Registration
Macromall
International
Education
Government
Local Reseller

Inner Content Table

This new table contains two table rows with three table data cells. The first column holds the "What's New" list, "Support Central," and "Shocked Site of the Day." The second column represents an empty gutter to enable breathing room between the two content columns. The last column holds the "Perspective" and "Xtra Xtra" blurbs. The prominent Macromedia graphic and the large main graphic at the top of the page live in a separate row with a table data cell of <colspan=3>.

```
<table width="440">
<tr>
<!----main graphics-->
        <td colspan=3></td>
</tr>
<tr>
<!----first column-->
        <td width="240" valign=top></td>
<!----gutter-->
        <td width="19"><img src="images/space.gif" alt="empty
➥space"></td>
<!----second column-->
        <td width="181" valign=top></td>
</tr>
</table>
```

Sub-Content Table

Within this inner table lies another table with a specific background color to highlight the "Support Central" section. Macromedia's Web team producer, Lori Hylan, chose to use a separate table for this area in order to create extra columns on each side of the text to keep it from running up against the walls of one <td> tag.

```
<table width="100%" bgcolor="#ffcc00" border="0" cellspacing="0"
➥cellpadding="0">
<tr>
        <td bgcolor="#ffcc00" width="5">   </td>
        <td bgcolor="#ffcc00" width="230"><br>
<!----content-->
        <p>
        </td>
        <td bgcolor="#ffcc00" width="5">   </td>
</tr>
</table>
```

Set the following table parameters:

1 Use width=100% to make this section conform to the width of the column where it is located.

2 Set the background colors to highlight the information in the table.

3 Turn off the border, cellspacing, and cellpadding to create seamless color between the individual <td> tags.

Support Central
New in the Tech Support area: **developer discussion boards**! Ask questions and share solutions with other multimedia and Web developers who are using Macromedia software to power their ideas.

Tables serve as powerful layout tools in HTML. Nesting tables within tables opens the door to more sophisticated and fun Web design. ■

Using Table Borders for Gallery Presentation

Use this technique to:

■ **Add a picture frame effect.** The 3D shading used to create table borders can be used to create the illusion that an image or animation is in a real-world wooden picture frame.

Not only are tables good for cell data, but they are also used as a great visual tool to create frames around graphics or animations.

Writing the HTML

To create the picture frame effect, you can use the <TABLE> tag to wrap up pictures and other content, and then alter the table's border parameters to create different looks.

1 Choose the graphic you want to showcase. In this example an art piece called "Search for Aphrodite" created by Unique Editions was used. You can name it aphrodite.jpeg.

2 In your HTML document lay out the basic HTML tags and insert <IMG SRC="aphrodite.jpeg" ALT="Search for Aphrodite"> between the opening <TD> and closing </TD> tags.

3 Wrap up the image between <TABLE BORDER = 8> and </TABLE> tags. The Border attributes indicate the thickness of the "picture frame." You can add any value for the Border attribute—the larger the value, the thicker the border.

You can tweak the <TABLE> tag's border, cellpadding, and width attributes to create your desired look. You can even change the color of the picture frame with the bordercolor attribute.

```
▤                           aphrodite.html                           ▤
<html><head>

<title>Gallery</title>

</head>
<body bgcolor="#000000" text="#595959" link="337299" alink="#000000" vlink="#b24c00">

<p>

<center>
<font size=4><a href="/gallery/credits/unique.editions.html">
Unique Editions</font></a><br>

<font size=6>S</font><font size=5>EARCH FOR APHRODITE</font><br>

<p>

<center>

<table border=8>
    <tr>
        <td><img src="aphrodite.jpeg" alt="Search for Aphrodite"></td>
    </tr>
</table>

</center>

</body></html>
```

4 Load the page in your browser. If it doesn't look quite right, go back and tweak the attributes of the <TABLE> tag.

VARIATIONS

Expand the border size to 20.

Use the table border to frame Shockwave movies. ■

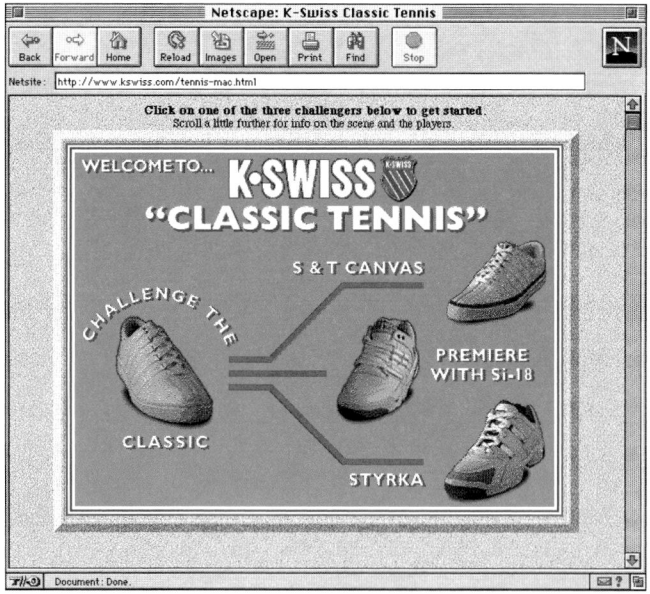

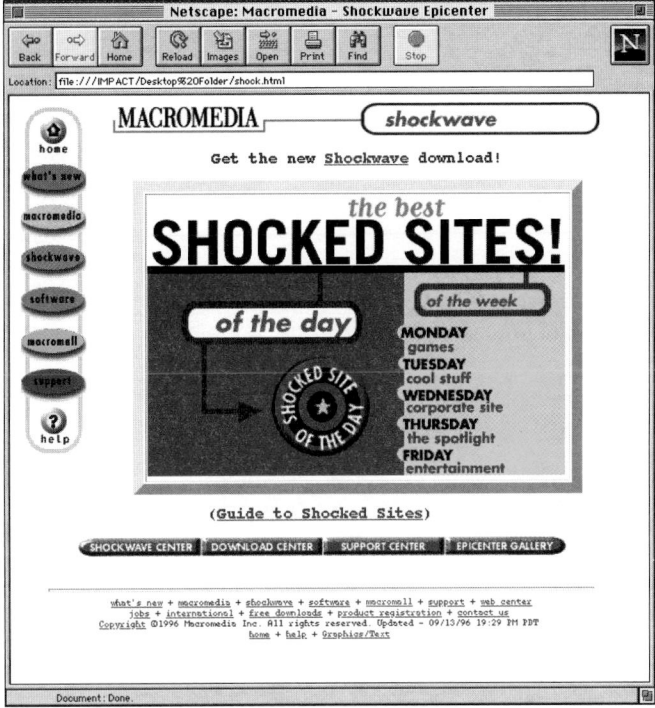

Defining Space

Use this technique to:

- **Make room for lots of space on your HTML page.** Forget about adding in the dozens of
s and the <p>s manually. You have HTML on your side now! Make your adjustments within one HTML tag.

- **Specify space to the exact pixel.** If you are a stickler for detail, this HTML feature enables you to define pixels of space exactly.

- **Clean up your HTML code.** You can cut down on extraneous tags and efficiently organize your HTML.

Space plays as much a part in your layout as do the visible elements. You can control space with several methods:

Traditional HTML Spacing Methods

 	A break is equivalent to one carriage return. This tag breaks up text line by line. Netscape 3.0 now reads each tag literally. While Netscape 2.0 handles successive s as one , 3.0 reads each one as a blank line.
<p>	A paragraph is equivalent to two carriage returns. It creates a blank line between two lines of text.
<pre>	Depending on the server, preformatting creates exactly as many blank lines and horizontal spaces as you leave between the <pre> and </pre> tags.
	HTML tag that creates one character space (indenting examples with blockquotes and lists) The blockquote tag creates a consistent left-hand margin of a Web page, while various HTML lists create automatic enumerated indentations.
<vspace>	Vertical space creates a buffer above and below an image.
<hspace>	Horizontal space specifications create a buffer to the left and the right of an image.

Alternative HTML Spacing Methods

transparent 1-pixel GIF	Enables you to specify the width and height of an empty space by adjusting the dimensions within the `img src` tag.
<spacer>	Creates the same results as the 1-pixel GIF except without the need to access a graphic in the latest versions of Netscape and Internet Explorer.

Spacer tags provide a limited degree of control, as spacing variations might occur across varying browsers or platforms.

Design challenges also affect spacing choices. Although one blank line between two elements might suffice in some instances, other circumstances might call for two to perhaps ten blank lines!

Writing the HTML

Creating space through traditional HTML methods can produce unpredictable results as well as create extremely muddled HTML code. Quick spacing fixes through the use of the small transparent GIF help you work around these issues.

Spacing Needs

When would you need large areas of blank space? Perhaps you have a line of text that needs to be a certain amount of space below the top of the page. Or you need to accommodate a background image that plays an important role in the layout. Using the tried and true `<br>` tag provides the most straightforward way to create a large area of vertical space in both old and new browsers. Representing a carriage return, a `<br>` creates blank space line by line. Say you've determined you need 10 blank lines of space. You need to write 11 successive `<br>` tags, since the first `<br>` represents the carriage return to get to the first blank line.

Be warned, however, that platform, browser, and even default font variations can change the effect of inserting space. You might measure a needed space to be 20 lines, but that might change to 35 lines or 15 lines on someone else's browser. Here is an example of detailed code to describe how each `<br>` creates a new line of space:

109

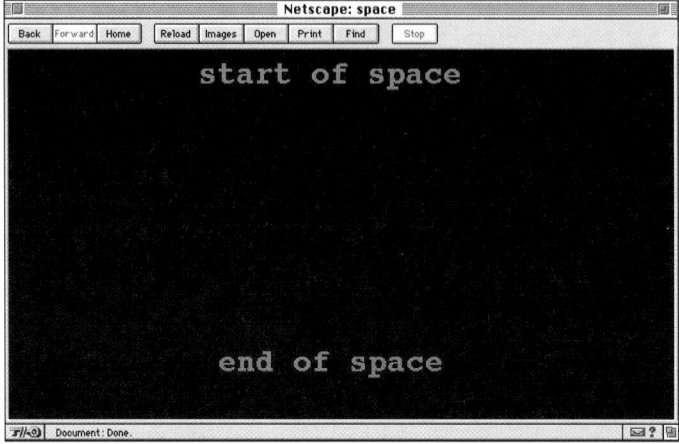

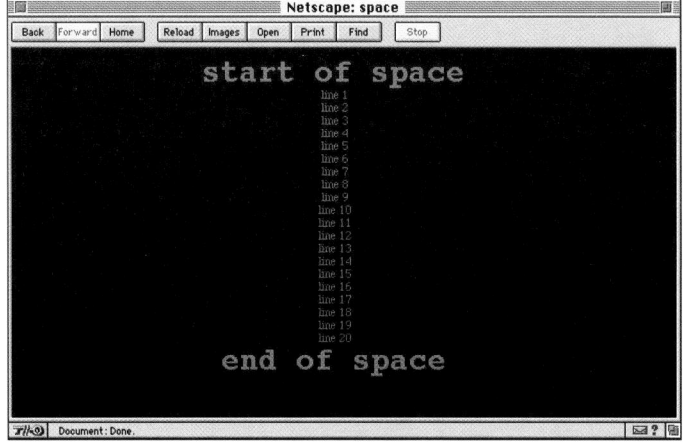

```
<center>
<code><b><font size="7">start of space</font></b></code>
<br><!--this first BR represents the carriage return to get to the first
blank line.  that's why there are 11 BR'S-->
line 1<br>
line 2<br>
line 3<br>
line 4<br>
line 5<br>
line 6<br>
line 7<br>
line 8<br>
```

```
line 9<br>
line 10<br>
<code><b><font size="7">end of space</font></b></code>
</center>
```

The actual code, of course, does not include the text that marks each line.

 It might seem more intuitive to have used 20 <P> tags. Notice, however that browsers interpret 20 successive <P> tags as only one <P>.

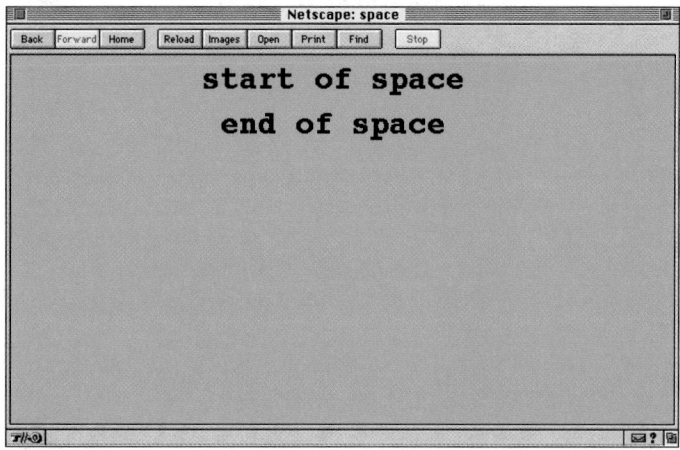

The <pre> tags provide another way to create the desired space described above. Instead of using 21 <br> tags to create 20 blank lines, you could use the <pre> tag and simulate the 20 carriage returns. The difference in this scenario manifests itself only in your code. You would see an enormous gap between the <pre> tags, but what if *one* line of code could take care of all of this space? You can by using a single transparent image!

111

Quick Spacing Fixes

Compare the previous code examples with the following:

```
<center>
<code><b><font size=7>start of space</font></b></code><br>
<img src="" width=10 height=290 alt="Blank Space! Yahoo!"><br>
<code><b><font size=7>end of space</font></b></code>
</center>
```

What a difference! The transparent image in this example literally acts as a place holder for the space. I determined that I needed 290 pixels of space vertically; therefore, I set the height of the image at 290, set the width to any number since I was only concerned with vertical space and voilá! Blank space at my fingertips. (I intentionally produced a broken icon so that you are able to see the image boundaries.)

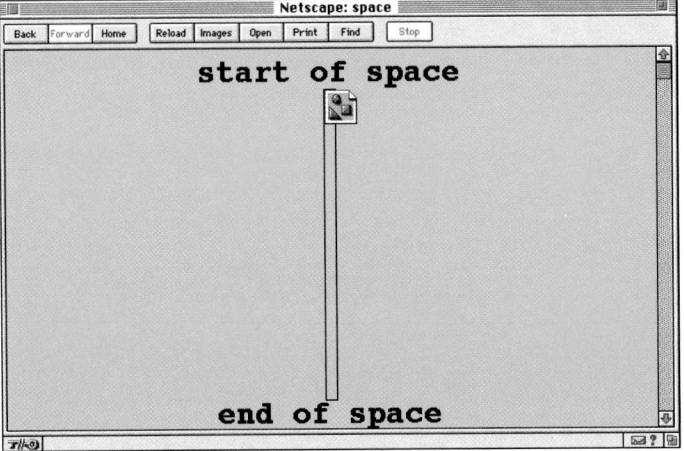

Defining Space with an Image

Where does this image come from? It's easy to make.

1 Create the new, square image 8 pixels wide × 8 pixels high. This is all you need because you can manipulate the dimensions manually in your HTML code.

2 Color the graphic with one flat color.

3 Index the color as you normally would to create a GIF.

4 Save the image as a GIF. Do not interlace the image since it is invisible.

5 Make the image color transparent with your preferred transparency helper application or plug-in.

This one image can open up a host of new possibilities for your layouts. Not only can you control vertical space, but you can control horizontal space as well. In other words, you can define space exactly the way you want down to the last pixel!

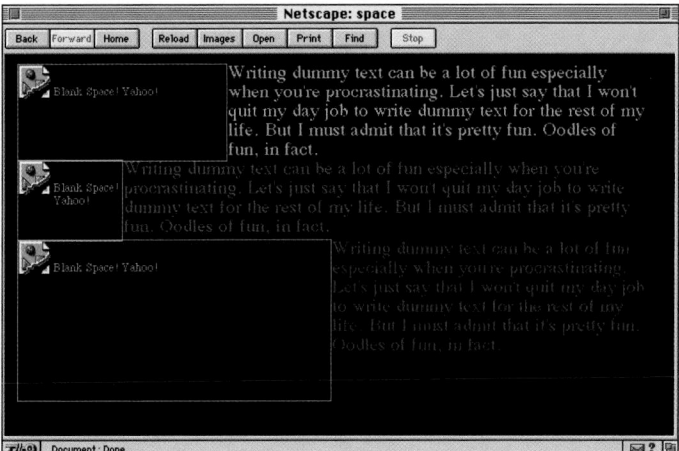

The helpfulness of the transparent GIF is more obvious when defining both vertical and horizontal space. Here is an example of code defining space vertically and horizontally:

```
<img src="" width=200 height=90 align=left alt="Blank Space! Yahoo!">
dummy text goes here.
<br clear=all>
<img src="" width=100 height=75 align=left alt="Blank Space! Yahoo!">
dummy text goes here.
<br clear=all>
<img src="" width=300 height=150 align=left alt="Blank Space! Yahoo!">
dummy text goes here.
```

NOTE Remember that when you align text with images, you must account for text wrapping that occurs according to a user's browser window size. Placing your entire text layout, such as the one described in the previous example, in a fixed size table works around this problem. All you need is one table set to your desired width with one table row and one table data cell. ■

113

Linking from One Frame Layout to Another

Use this technique to:

- **Have better control over frames.** By having different frame layouts you have better control over links on and off your site.

- **Coordinate content with the best frame look.** Fit the best frame layout to match the content of your pages.

Designers can get constrained with their Web site frame layout. Perhaps the main window isn't large enough to display content or maybe it's too large for too little content. A way to solve this problem is through the creative use of the TARGET tags. By linking to another frame layout or even by opening a new browser window, you can have better control over your frames.

Writing the HTML

Frames:

- `<FRAMESET ROWS="rowheight,%,*" COLS="colwidth, %,*">` Start of main container for frames

- `%=` Relative height or width

- `*=` Optional; gives frame all remaining space in accordance with other frames

- `<FRAME>` Start of frames tag

Attributes:

- `NAME="name of frame"` Name of the frame

- `SRC="url"` The location of the HTML page for the frame

- `MARGINWIDTH="number"`

- `MARGINHEIGHT="number"`

- `SCROLLING="yes¦no¦auto"` Controls the scrollbar in the frame

- `NORESIZE` Frame size is not resizable by the user

- `</FRAME>` Closing frame tag

- `</FRAMESET>` Closing frame container

- `TARGET="framename"` Link will load in a frame specified by frame name

- `TARGET="_self"` For frame documents: the link will always load in a frame where the link was clicked

- `TARGET="_parent"` For frame documents: the link will load in the immediate FRAMESET parent of the document

- `TARGET="_top"` For frame documents: the link will load in the full body of the window

Linking from One Frame Layout to Another

In this example, we want the links from the first frame layout to jump to the second layout when the links are clicked.

1 First, create the second frame layout for all the links in the left column of the main frame layout. This frame layout is divided into two sections with the added left side navigation frame included as the target link.

```
<FRAMESET rows="80,*">
        <FRAME SRC="banner.html" NAME="top frame" SCROLLING=No NORESIZE>
        <FRAME SRC="http://www.crushed.com/" NAME="main frame"
➡SCROLLING="auto">
</FRAMESET>
```

2 Save the file as the name of the link. Call the first one "crushed.html." Continue the same pattern for all the links, changing only the target URL for the third `frame src` in each document.

3 In the side frame page for the jumplist of links (shocklinks.html), add `TARGET="mainframe,"` which will load the page in the middle frame.

```
<A HREF="crushed.html" TARGET="main frame">
```

Browser Watch

Netscape 2.0 and higher

Internet Explorer 3.0 ◾

Nesting Frames

Use this technique to:

- **Create more streamlined frames customized for your Web site.** By nesting frames inside other frames, you can create a flexible grid for your Web page.

- **Better organize your content.** Using the nested frames techniques enables you to subdivide frames as needed, so you can organize your page to mirror the editorial organization of your content. You don't need to wedge your content into simple frame setups.

So you want to transform your Web site to frames? Do you feel limited to standard rows and columns? Worry no more because you can create as many frame panels as you want by nesting frames.

Writing the HTML

In this section, you learn some of the subtler applications of the frame tags and how (and why) to put one <FRAMESET></FRAMESET> pair inside another.

1 Because you want the side frame to run up and down the side of the browser, type <FRAMESET> tag for your main frame.

```
<FRAMESET COLS="85,*">
    <FRAME SRC="side.html" NAME="navbar" SCROLLING="no">
    <FRAME SRC="middle.html" NAME="main" SCROLLING="Auto">
</FRAMESET>
```

2 Start another <FRAMESET> tag directly under the first column SRC for the first frame. Specify the width for the rows.

```
<FRAMESET COLS="85,*">
    <FRAME SRC="side.html" NAME="navbar" SCROLLING="no">
        <FRAMESET rows="80,*">
        <FRAME SRC="top.html" NAME="banner" SCROLLING=No>
        <FRAME SRC="middle.html" NAME="main" SCROLLING="Auto">
    </FRAMESET>
</FRAMESET>
```

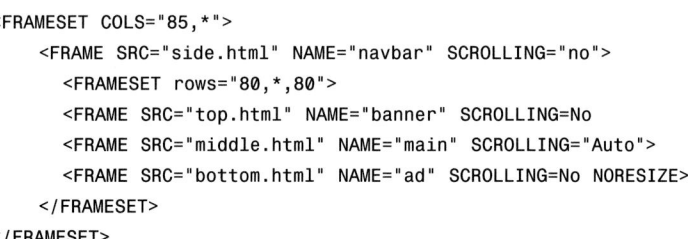

3 Add the final <FRAME SRC> tag for the bottom frame space. Adjust the <FRAMESET rows> tag to accomodate this frame.

```
<FRAMESET COLS="85,*">
    <FRAME SRC="side.html" NAME="navbar" SCROLLING="no">
        <FRAMESET rows="80,*,80">
        <FRAME SRC="top.html" NAME="banner" SCROLLING=No>
        <FRAME SRC="middle.html" NAME="main" SCROLLING="Auto">
        <FRAME SRC="bottom.html" NAME="ad" SCROLLING=No NORESIZE>
    </FRAMESET>
</FRAMESET>
```

Browser Watch

Netscape 2.0 and higher

Internet Explorer 3.0 ■

Using Floating Frames

Use this technique to:

- **Create a "Window" effect for HTML page.** Using floating frames, you can create a free-standing frame that's not bound to the edges of the page and does not necessarily divide the page into separate panels. The floating frame can be positioned like an image, table, or any other HTML object.

- **Keep main page intact while frame contents change dynamically.** The contents of a floating frame can contain anything that an ordinary Web page can contain. You might think of it as a mini-page within your page. And like any page, it can change when links are clicked or a JavaScript is activated.

Floating frames are a great way to create windows into other HTML pages. This is useful when your main page is the navigation tool for the smaller window.

In this technique you are converting the FreeHand Graphics Studio (FGS) software pages into a floating frame format. The main page lists all the links related to the FGS. The box shot starts as the opening main window.

Writing the HTML

In this section, you'll use Microsoft Internet Explorer's new <IFRAME> tag to add a floating frame to your page. The HTML syntax used to add a floating frame is similar to techniques used to add a basic image, but the floating frame can display *anything* a conventional Web page can. (Including another floating frame!)

Creating the Floating Frame

1 You want the frame to left-align so the floating frame and the links will be in a table for better layout. Type in your floating frame elements and name the floating frame "main frame" for easy reference.

```
<TABLE>
<TR>
<TD>
<IFRAME WIDTH=550 HEIGHT=300 ALIGN=LEFT SRC="main.html" NAME="main frame">
        <FRAME WIDTH=550 HEIGHT=300 ALIGN=left SRC="main.html" NAME="main
➥frame">
</IFRAME>
</TD>
```

TIP You must use the **IFRAME** in conjunction with the normal **FRAME** tag in order for this to work. As you can see, the data within these two tags is the same.

TIP By adding values within the **IFRAME** and **FRAME** tags you can better control your frame's look. Attributes are:

- Borderless frames—(**FRAMEBORDER=0**)

- Alignment—**ALIGN** (left, right)

- scrollbar—(**SCROLLING=NO**)

- Horizontal spacing—**HSPACE** (in pixels)

- Vertical spacing—**VSPACE** (in pixels)

2 The links on the right need to have a TARGET reference, so that when clicked on the HTML page, they load within the floating frame window. Add TARGET="main frame" to each <A HREF> link. Add the following after the table data code you entered in Step 1:

```
<TD>
<DL>
<B><FONT SIZE=2>
<DT><IMG SRC="/images/dot.gif" WIDTH=10 HEIGHT=10 ALT="[o]">
<A HREF="main.html" TARGET="main frame">Main</A>
<DT><IMG SRC="/images/dot.gif" WIDTH=10 HEIGHT=10 ALT="[o]">
<A HREF="/shockwave/" TARGET="main frame">Get Shocked Now!</A>
<DT><IMG SRC="/images/dot.gif" WIDTH=10 HEIGHT=10 ALT="[o]">
<A HREF="/software/fgs/features.html" TARGET="main frame">Overview
➥&amp; Key Features</A>
<DT><IMG SRC="/images/dot.gif" WIDTH=10 HEIGHT=10 ALT="[o]">
<A HREF="/software/fgs/requirements.html" TARGET="main
➥frame">System Requirements</A>
<DT><IMG SRC="/images/dot.gif" WIDTH=10 HEIGHT=10 ALT="[o]">
<A HREF="/software/freehand/awards.html" TARGET="main
➥frame">Awards</A> &amp;
<A HREF="/software/fgs/kudos.html" TARGET="main frame">Kudos</A>
<DT><IMG SRC="/images/dot.gif" WIDTH=10 HEIGHT=10 ALT="[o]">
<A HREF="/software/freehand/competitive.html" TARGET="main
➥frame">Competitive Analysis</A>
<DT><IMG SRC="/images/dot.gif" WIDTH=10 HEIGHT=10 ALT="[o]">
<A HREF="/support/" TARGET="main frame">Support</A> &amp;
<A HREF="/support/technotes/index.html" TARGET="main
➥frame">TechNotes</A>
<DT><IMG SRC="/images/dot.gif" WIDTH=10 HEIGHT=10 ALT="[o]">
<A HREF="/shockwave/epicenter/vanguard/fgs/" TARGET="main
➥frame">Shockwave Vanguard</A> &amp;
<A HREF="/gallery/guides/product/freehand.html" TARGET="main
➥frame">Gallery</A>
<DT><IMG SRC="/images/dot.gif" WIDTH=10 HEIGHT=10 ALT="[o]">
<A HREF="/software/freehand/updates.html" TARGET="main
➥frame">Updates</A> &amp;
<A HREF="/software/freehand/resources.html" TARGET="main
➥frame">Resources</A>
<DT><IMG SRC="/images/dot.gif" WIDTH=10 HEIGHT=10 ALT="[o]">
<A HREF="/bin/pubs.cgi" TARGET="main frame">Reference Library</A>
<DT><IMG SRC="/images/dot.gif" WIDTH=10 HEIGHT=10 ALT="[o]">
<A HREF="/software/ordering/index.html" TARGET="main frame">Product
➥Ordering Info</A>
<DT><IMG SRC="/images/dot.gif" WIDTH=10 HEIGHT=10 ALT="[o]">
<A HREF="/software/register/" TARGET="main frame">Product
➥Registration</A>
<DT><IMG SRC="/images/dot.gif" WIDTH=10 HEIGHT=10 ALT="[o]">
<A HREF="http://www.harte-hanks.com/macromedia/showcase_qualification
➥form.cgi" TARGET="main frame">Qualify for a Showcase CD-ROM</A>
```

```
</FONT></B>
</DL>
</TD>
</TR>
</TABLE>
```

3 Test your page in Internet Explorer 3.0. Click each link and you'll see the contents of your floating frame change instantly! (The following figures show how the page changes after the Overview and Vanguard buttons are pressed.)

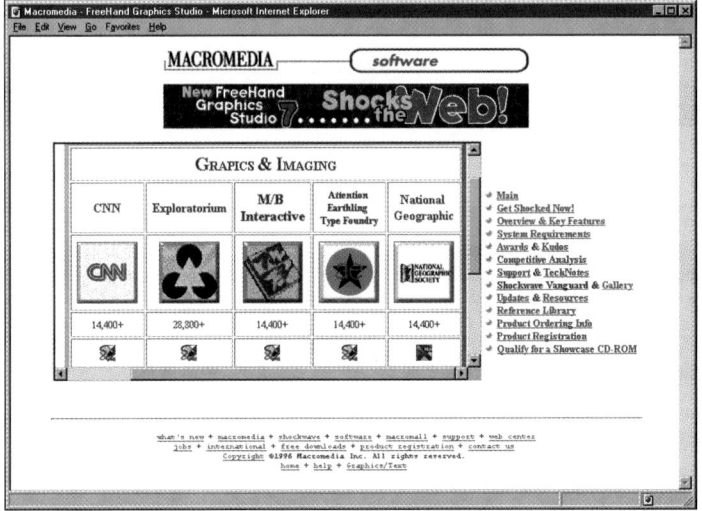

VARIATIONS

Combine floating frames with the META REFRESH function and create a window to a gallery, portfolio, video cam, or anything else you want dynamically updated.

Creating a Floating Gallery

1 Set up your gallery frame with the first frame as your opening gallery entry.

```
<IFRAME WIDTH=300 HEIGHT=300 SRC="travolta.html" NAME="gallery">
        <FRAME WIDTH=300 HEIGHT=300 SRC="travolta.html"
➥NAME="gallery">
</IFRAME>
```

2 For each gallery entry, add the META REFRESH tag between the <HEAD> and the <TITLE> of the document. (META REFRESH causes the page to reload from a new URL after a specified delay once the current page is loaded.) Specify the URL of the next gallery entry you want it to cycle. Continue this step for each entry until you are done.

```
<HTML>
<HEAD>
<META HTTP-EQUIV="REFRESH" CONTENT="20; URL=cover.html">
<TITLE>FGS Gallery</TITLE>
</HEAD>
<BODY BGCOLOR="white">
<CENTER>
<FONT SIZE=6>T</FONT><FONT SIZE=5>RAVOLTA</FONT><BR>
<FONT SIZE=4>Don Assmussen</FONT>
<p>
<IMG SRC="images/travolta.gif" WIDTH=263 HEIGHT=184 alt="John
Travolta">
</CENTER>
</BODY>
</HTML>
```

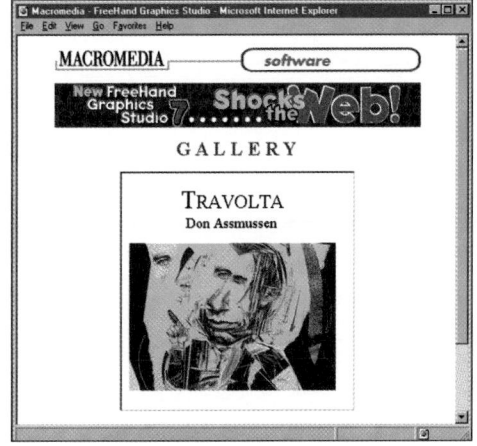

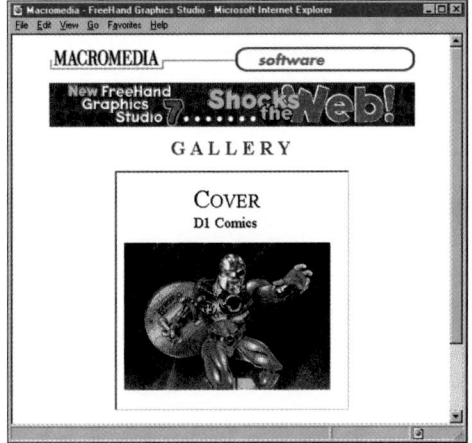

Browser Watch

Internet Explorer 3.0 ■

Hidden Frames

Use this technique to:

■ **Present material in a fun, interactive way.** There hasn't been much fun use of frames. Creating a game-like interface will make your Web site different from all the others.

■ **Grab the user's attention.** Having a "secret" area attracts users to open and move various frames to find "hidden" information.

Want a unique way to interact with frames? Used more for fun rather than functionality, a hidden frame is a unique way to present an interactive game, announce a special event, or anything you want!

Writing the HTML

Frames:

■ `<FRAMESET ROWS="rowheight,%,*"`
`COLS="colwidth, %,*">` Start of main container for frames

■ `%=` Relative height or width

■ `*=` Optional; gives frame all remaining space in accordance with other frames

■ `<FRAME>` Start of frames tag

Attributes:

■ `NAME="name of frame"` Name of the frame

■ `SRC="url"` The location of the HTML page for the frame

■ `MARGINWIDTH="number"`

■ `MARGINHEIGHT="number"`

■ `SCROLLING="yes¦no¦auto"` Controls the scroll bar in the frame

■ `NORESIZE` Frame size is not resizable by the user

■ `</FRAME>` Closing frame tag

■ `</FRAMESET>` Closing frame container

This technique shows you how to use a hidden frame to create a party announcement. Here is the frame layout you need for this technique. When the user pulls down the frame border as directed in the graphic, the party announcement page is revealed.

1 Open the HTML page that contains the <FRAMESET> for the main layout.

```
                    <FRAMESET rows="80,*">
                        <FRAME SRC="groove.html" NAME="top" SCROLLING=No
    ➥ NORESIZE>
                        <FRAME SRC="funkygal.html" NAME="main"
    ➥ SCROLLING="No">
    </FRAMESET>
```

2 Add the <FRAME SRC> for the hidden frame. Modify the <FRAMESET rows> making the hidden frame 1 pixel.

```
                    <FRAMESET rows="80,1,* ">
                        <FRAME SRC="groove.html" NAME="top" SCROLLING="No"
    ➥ NORESIZE>
                        <FRAME SRC="party.html" NAME="hidden">
                        <FRAME SRC="funkygal.html" NAME="main" SCROLLING="No">
    </FRAMESET>
```

3 Save and test in your browsers. Pull down on the frame border and you see the contents appear!

125

Browser Watch

Netscape 2.0 and higher

Internet Explorer 3.0 ■

Transforming Graphics as They Download

Use this technique to:

■ **Keep your Web site visitors from becoming impatient with long download times for large graphics.** The img lowsrc tag displays an image of your choice as a placeholder while the final image is downloading and dropping into the HTML page. Many use a small, 1-bit graphic for their lowsrc image.

■ **Surprise your Web site viewers.** Depending on the effect you want to achieve, you can display any manipulated version of a graphic before the final image drops in—even a different graphic altogether! Use your favorite filters, play with different color schemes, or display a written message on the img lowsrc image to present your final image dramatically.

■ **"Interlace" your JPEG images.** Although Progressive JPEG technology already exists to display JPEGs in stages, using the img lowsrc tag to display an interlaced graphic prior to the regular JPEG image provides a reliable way to shorten the perceived download time.

The Web site for the band Toad the Wet Sprocket (http://www.sony.com/Music/ArtistInfo/Toad) first introduced me to the magic of img lowsrc. Their home page started with a graphic of a closed refrigerator. To my surprise, the blueprint image of the interior of the refrigerator downloaded immediately afterward to reveal the table of contents. The design and sequence of the illustrations effectively exploit the img lowsrc tag. The clever, yet simple graphics surprise the viewer while providing necessary information.

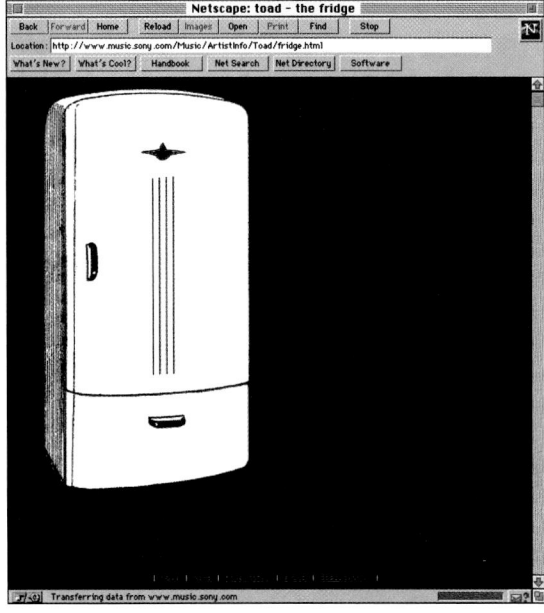

With just one simple addition to the usual `img src` tag to display your Web graphics, you can surprise and entertain visitors to your site by creating the illusion that the graphics transform as they download. The speed of the effect depends upon bandwidth and the viewer's computer capacity. The faster the connection the faster the transition.

> **NOTE** Bear in mind that this `img lowsrc` effect will appear to happen only once in a visit. Subsequent loading of the page will rely on cached images, thus moving past the initial low-resolution graphic so quickly it usually won't be visible at all. The user must remove the disk cache or have it set to zero to see the effect each time.

Eligible Graphics

Your final image may either be a GIF or a JPEG. Make sure your first image has a smaller file size than your final image. Using a "heavy" initial image causes a much slower download time than using a lighter one and consequently defeats the purpose of the transformation effect. Also, make sure your two images share the same dimensions to set the best graphical placements for an effective transition.

This is the final, full-color version of the image we want to load. The following code enables you to use any variation of a lowsrc image to create different transformations for arriving at this image.

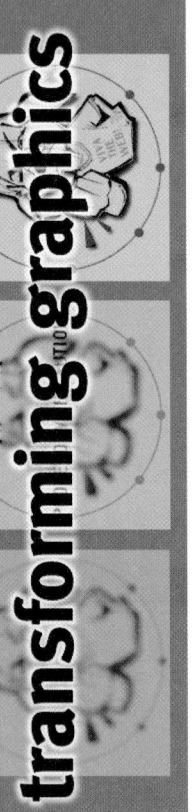
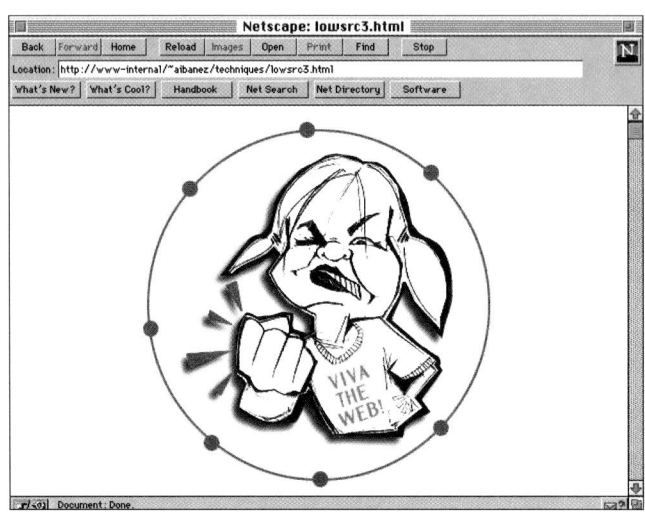

Writing the HTML

Writing the HTML to create an image transformation is as simple as adding a lowsrc reference within the regular img src tag:

```
<img lowsrc="images/tuffgirl_first.gif" src="images/tuffgirl_last.jpeg"
➥width="" height="" alt="Here is my transforming Tough Girl image.">>
```

Use the preceding code for any of the "low-resolution" image variations described below. Take the filename of the version of your choice and plug it into the img lowsrc= reference.

VARIATIONS

Transforming from Black-and-White to Color

A two-color graphic is a one-bit image, which provides the smallest file size for a low-resolution version of your graphic and therefore the fastest download time. A one-bit image is also the easiest variation of the final image to create. All you have to do is set the number of colors in your image to "2" when you index the colors before saving it as a GIF. The result is a black-and-white version of your final image.

130

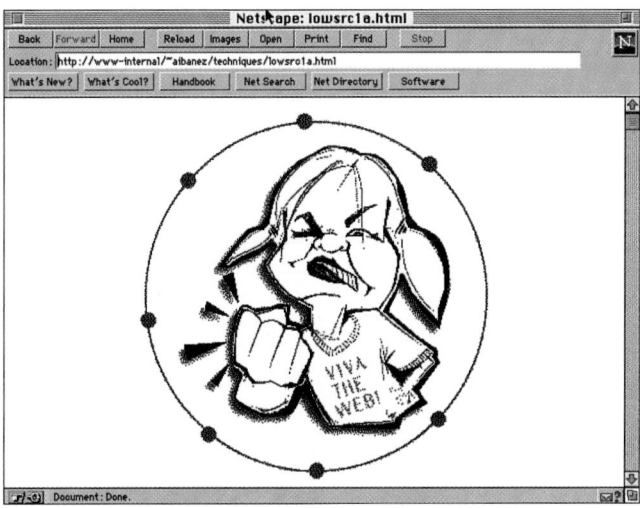

Transforming from Inverted to Normal Color

Try creating a cool negative film strip effect by inverting the colors while the image is still in RGB mode before indexing it to two colors. To do this in Photoshop, select the entire image and go the Images menu. Under Map, choose Invert.

In the "tough girl" example, as shown, I inverted the colors only in the layer that contained the drawing of the girl and then filled the circle with black for fun. Keep in mind that I had access to the original Photoshop file with layers. Working in layers simplifies the manipulation process for individual objects in your graphics.

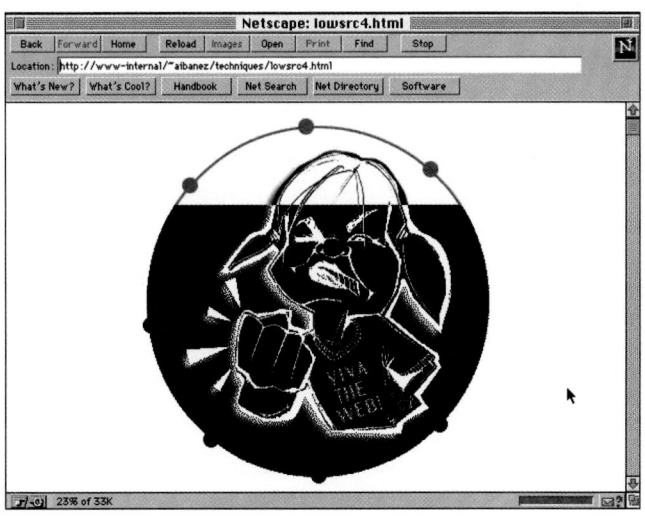

131

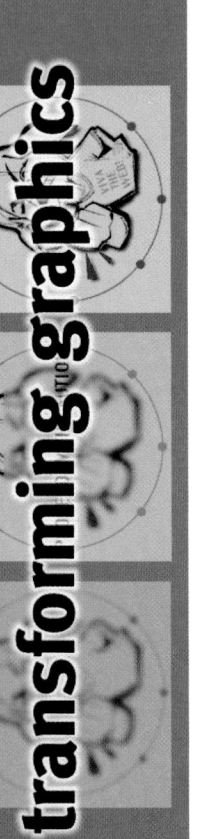
Transforming Colors and Shapes

A "light" graphic does not have to be black-and-white. Spice up the `img lowsrc` effect with two colors that correspond with your Web site look and feel. This effect involves using the black-and-white version with the background shape colored in. Therefore, the end result creates a transformation between colors and filled, open shapes.

Applying a Filter to an Image

You may not always have an illustrator on hand to create unique graphics for such effects as demonstrated by the Toad the Wet Sprocket site. Never fear! Your options are only limited by your imagination. Creating special effects with `img lowsrc` can be as easy as the flick of a filter. Experiment with the standard filters and image controls included in Photoshop.

Keep in mind that not all manipulations work for all images. In general, Gaussian Blur and Fractalize create excellent results for a wide range of images, Solarize works best with full-color images, and Flip transforms images against symmetrical color panels well.

Blurring an existing image is an easy and simple way to show off the `img lowsrc` in action. This section utilizes the Gaussian Blur for its simplicity and expert results. In your own experimentation, you may prefer other blurs to select specific blur angles and directions.

NOTE **If the image you are working with is a "floating" image on a transparent background, you might have to adjust the Canvas Size to leave allowance for the blurred effect. An image too close to the canvas boundaries results in blurred edges, which conform to these straight edges. If you adjust the canvas size, be sure to do the same with the final image for a smooth transition.**

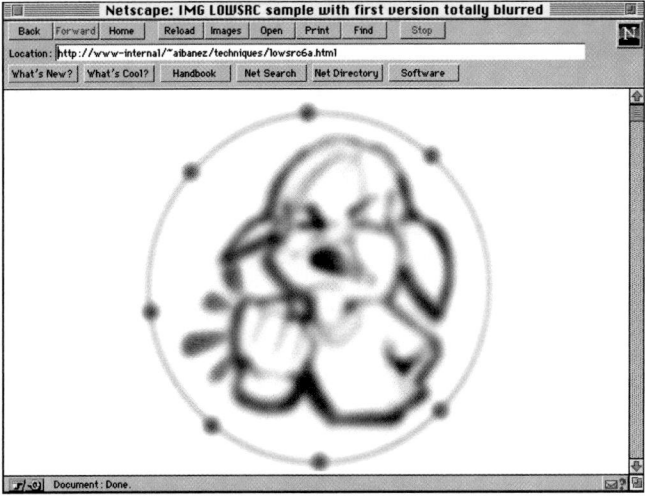

TIP Add a written message, such as Welcome!, or a Loading Image over the blurred graphic for added effect.

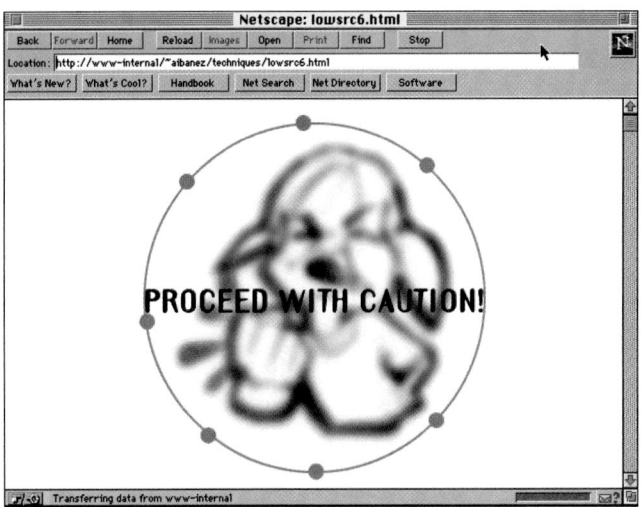

133

Do not get carried away by these special effects. The blurred image from the previous example is actually heavier than the final image, although the blurred image shown here is almost the same size as the final image. By adjusting the number of colors in your blurred graphic, you can still achieve a cool filtered effect, but without the cost of too many extra bytes. ■

text on graphics

Placing Text on Graphics

Use this technique to:

- **Create modular artwork for constantly changing items.** Ideal for sections headers, this technique offers a dynamic method for updating the text within graphics.

- **Save file space.** Repurposing one graphic allows you to minimize the bytes your visitors need to download in order to view your pages.

- **Save time in creating images.** Create one graphic for the foundation and leave the rest to HTML!

- **Highlight sections of your text.** Not all viewers may use browsers that support background colors for individual table data cells. You can adapt or trick your tables to create overlaying effects.

Though we will use section headers to demonstrate this technique, you can apply this trick to any instance where you would like to overlay text over graphics—forms, lists, and so on.

Writing the HTML

Although the most common way to overlay pictures and text over graphics involves using a background image within your `<body>` tag, you can also trick your HTML tables into overlaying graphics from different table data cells.

1 Use the `background` option within the `<body>` tag to add a specific background image to your HTML page:

```
<BODY background="images/fadedgraphic.gif" BGCOLOR="#FFFFFF"
➥link="#595959" link="#000000" vlink="#B24C00">
```

When adding a background image to your page, remember that the image tiles or repeats itself within the entire browser window. Faded or subdued images without a lot of distracting texture work best as backgrounds especially when text must be read. The overview Web page for the "Global Collage" art project uses a background image in an invisible frame so that the graphic does not overlap and interfere with the top header.

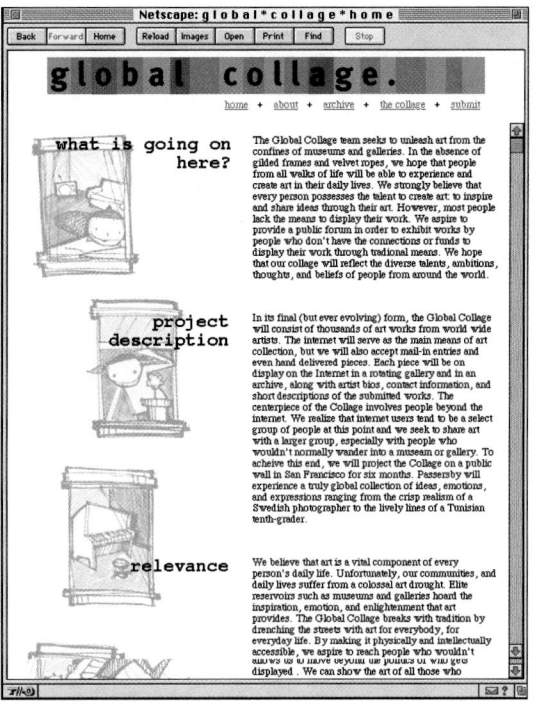

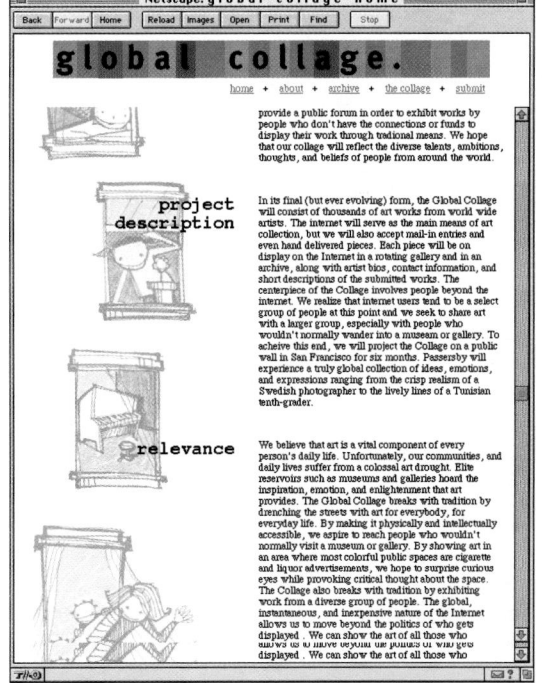

text for section header

text for section

project description

relevance

what is going on here?

text for section header

text on graphics

2 Create a regular table. Understanding the HTML code for this technique involves understanding the dynamics of a regular table. Each table consists of at least one table row that contains at least one table data cell. You can manipulate the width and alignment of the <td> tag as well as adjust the cellpadding, cellspacing, and border width of the entire table. Here is the code for an ordinary table where table data items exist exclusive of each other:

```
<center>
<table cellpadding="1" border="1">
  <tr>
    <td><img src="graphic.gif" width="290" height="50" border="0"
↪alt="This is the background for our header."></td>
    <td align=center><code><b><font size="5">text for section
↪header</font></b></code></td>
  </tr>
</table>
</center>
```

text for section header

3 Compress the table. Although tables tend to serve as layout tools, we use the table in this technique to update a graphic instantly. By tweaking the table data dimensions, you can force your table data contents to overlap each other.

```
<center>
<table cellpadding="1" border="1">
  <tr>
    <td width="5"><img src="graphic.gif" width="290" height="50"
↪border="0" alt="This is the background for our header."></td>
    <td align=center width="200"><code><b><font size="5">text for
↪section header</font></b></code></td>
  </tr>
</table>
</center>
```

text for section header

Setting the <td> tag for the graphic to a much smaller width than its actual one forces the graphic to overhang the <td> boundaries, thus creating the overlap effect. You must always set your image and <td> widths for controlled results. Keep your table border visible as you test for your desired overlap. Once you are satisfied with the results, turn the border off by setting border="0."

text for section header

 TIP This HTML trick works only when the compressed table is located offscreen. If the table is located at the top of the Web page or onscreen, then the bottom graphic actually covers the text until you scroll below it and then back up again. You want to place your compressed tables below where you think your viewer's window ends. ■

Placing Graphics on Graphics

Use this technique to:

- **Create interesting visual effects.** Enrich your Web pages by floating images on top of interesting graphical backgrounds.

- **Create modular artwork for constantly changing needs or styles.** Similar to working with layers in a graphics program, this technique offers unique ways to integrate graphics using HTML. Add, subtract, and change alignments in graphic elements instantly.

- **Save file space.** Recycling graphics enables you to minimize the bytes your visitors must download to view your pages.

- **Signal a new section or category with specific combinations of colors, shapes, and your own graphics.** A viewer might need visual cues to understand the boundaries between different sections or ideas.

This technique follows the same principles as the "Placing Text on Graphics" technique (p.134). In addition, it emphasizes your signature graphics and enhances the strength of your Web site's visual identity.

Be warned, though—your viewer might need to scroll above the graphic and down again to get the image to appear correctly. The final effect might also be affected by browser type and screen resolution.

Writing the HTML

Although the most common way to place graphics on graphics involves using a background image within your <body> tag, you can also trick your HTML tables into placing graphics from different table data cells.

Using the Background Option Within the <body> Tag

To add a specific background image to your HTML page, insert the background option in your <body> tag:

```
<body bgcolor="black" background="images/stripes.gif" text="white"
link="red" alink="black" vlink="cyan">
```

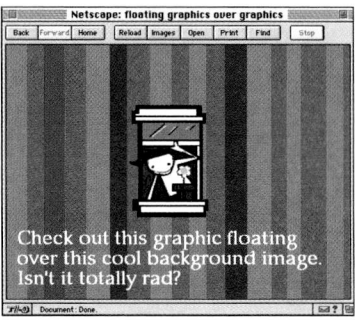

When adding a background image to your page, remember that the image tiles or repeats itself. Images without a lot of distracting texture work best as backgrounds, especially when used with small body text.

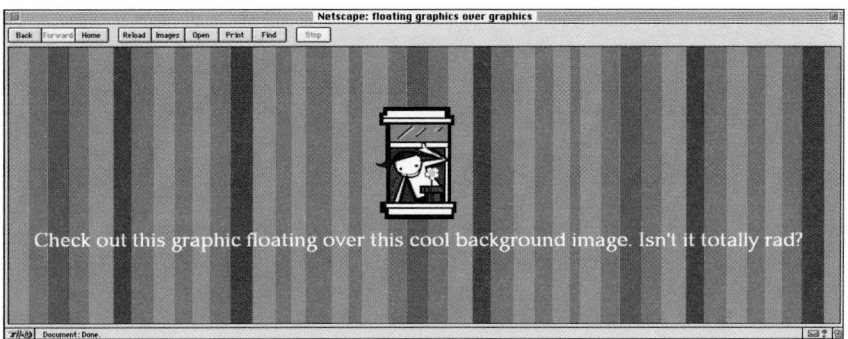

TIP Make specific parts of your background image transparent to reflect changing background colors. The background stripe for Macromedia's home page is an image 1,200 pixels wide created with panels of red, purple, and white. White was designated as the transparency just in case they decide to change the background color.

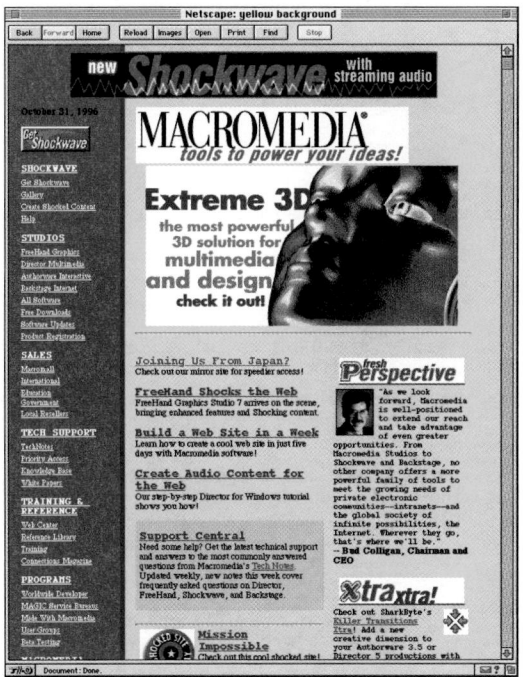

Using Compressed Tables with a Graphic Header

Say your home page includes thumbnails of different sections of your site. For each of these sections, you want to incorporate its corresponding graphic into a graphical header. You can do this with HTML tables. You can tweak the table data dimensions just as you would in the "Placing Text on Graphics" technique.

139

Regular Table

Before trying to overlay images in a table, consider how two graphics would look in a regular table without compression. You need a table with one table row and two table data cells:

```
<center>
<table cellpadding="1" border="1">
        <tr>
                <td><img src="images/dot.gif" width="300" height="55"
➥border="0" alt="This is the background for our header."></td>
                <td align=center><img src="images/thumbnail.gif" width="40"
➥height="55" border="0" alt="This is the section graphic."></td>
        </tr>
</table>
</center>
```

Compress the Table

Now you're ready to overlay your graphics. Adjust the <td> widths according to how much you want each graphic to hang over its table data boundaries. Keep the table border on to monitor the overlap easily. When you are satisfied with the results, turn the border off by setting border="0."

```
<table cellpadding="1" border="1">
        <tr>
                <td width="5"><img src="images/dot.gif" width="300"
➥height="55" border="0" alt="This is the background for our header."></td>
                <td align=center width="5"><img src="images/thumbnail.gif"
➥width="40" height="55" border="0" alt="This is the section
➥graphic."></td>
                <td width="265" align=right><code><b><font size="6">section
➥header text</font></b></code></td>
        </tr>
</table>
```

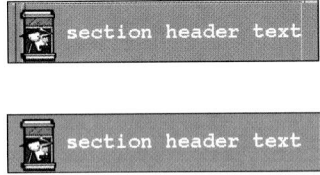

Notice this technique utilizes HTML text as well as the given graphics. This combination maximizes the versatility of the graphical elements. Now all you have to do for a different section is change the thumbnail and header text.

Create Drop Shadows

Can't decide whether to use drop shadows or not? Use them or lose them with quick HTML editing.

Combined with the "Manipulating Image Dimensions" technique (p.152), you can create quick and simple drop shadows with one small graphic. The bottom graphic or drop shadow is a small 8×8 GIF stretched out to specific dimensions. Depending on how you want to offset the drop shadow, adjust the `valign` of your table data and add space above or below the images. Here's what the code looks like:

```
<center>
<table cellpadding="1" border="1">
      <tr>
              <td width="5" valign=bottom><p><br><img src="images/dot.gif"
➥width="300" height="300" border="0" alt="This is the drop shadow for the
➥graphic."></td>
              <td width="5" valign=top><img src="images/talisman.gif"
➥width="300" height="300" border="0" alt="This is the main graphic."><p></td>
      </tr>
</table>
</center>
```

NOTE When using compressed tables to overlay graphics, be sure that the topmost image has a larger file size than the bottom image. Otherwise, the bottom graphic obliterates the top until you scroll above or below it. The only other instance that allows you to overlay a "light" graphic over a heavier one is when the compressed table is downloaded offscreen or below the browser window boundaries. ■

141

Creative Horizontal Dividers

Use this technique to:

■ **Clearly define the sections of your Web pages with creative dashed lines.** Bored with the regular HR tag? Take this HTML tag a few steps further with a few variations combined with the basic TABLE tag. HR tags will never be the same again!

■ **Create simple, but interesting graphical elements using only HTML.** You won't have to open a sophisticated graphics application to draw these lines. It all happens in HTML!

Why use the hr tag in the first place? Unless your Web pages fit on a standard 640×480 pixel screen, you probably have enough information that requires visual cues to break up the space for your viewers. The hr or "hard rule" acts like punctuation in a sentence or between sentences. Incorporating punctuation in vocabulary makes it easier to understand the relationships between different groups of words and to isolate these very groups. The presence of an hr usually signals either the beginning or the end of a section. Many often use an hr to delineate a header or footer from the body of a page.

Writing the HTML

The default <hr> creates a horizontal, shaded three-dimensional line stretching across the entire browser window. This simple tag comes with a myriad of other possibilities. You may also set the dimensions and a solid, unshaded look for your hr.

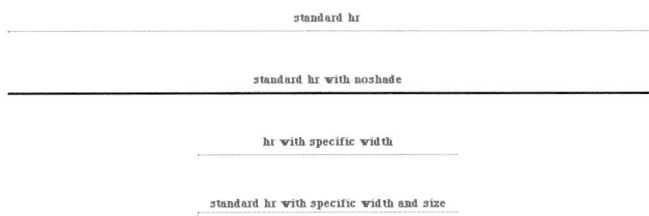

Standard HRs

1 Using an hr is as simple as adding brackets around the initials:

```
<hr>
```

2 You can also set the width:

```
<hr width="250">
```

3 You can also set the size or height:

```
<hr width="250" size="10">
```

4 In addition, you can specify whether or not your hr will appear as a solid line with no shading. To do this, you simply add a noshade attribute within the hr tag.

```
<hr noshade>
```

TIP Combine your favorite hr shade, width, and size settings to customize your horizontal dashed lines. I specified **noshade** and a particular size to create a distinctive horizontal divider that matched the look and feel of my page.

Incorporating the HR with Tables

In order to create dashed lines, you must place separate hr tags within individual table data cells. Without a table, a series of hr tags will result in a stack of lines—one on top of the other.

VARIATIONS

Small "Stitch"

Start with a row of three squares, each 10 pixels wide × 10 pixels high. The code looks like this:

```
<center>
<table>
  <tr>
    <td><hr width="10" size="10" ></td>
    <td><hr width="10" size="10" ></td>
    <td><hr width="10" size="10" ></td>
  </tr>
</table>
</center>
```

Alternating "Stitch"

Next, try playing with various dimensions to create a new symmetrical pattern. Scale down the two outer squares to 5 pixels wide × 5 pixels high. The code looks like this:

```
<center>
<table>
  <tr>
    <td><hr width="5" size="5" ></td>
    <td><hr width="10" size="10" ></td>
    <td><hr width="5" size="5" ></td>
  </tr>
</table>
</center>
```

Gradual Alternating "Stitch"

You might also want to try a more gradual change in scale by increments of 2 pixels. The code looks like this:

```
<center>
<table>
  <tr>
    <td><hr width="4" size="4" ></td>
    <td><hr width="6" size="6" ></td>
    <td><hr width="8" size="8" ></td>
    <td><hr width="10" size="10" ></td>
    <td><hr width="8" size="8" ></td>
```

```
      <td><hr width="6" size="6" ></td>
      <td><hr width="4" size="4" ></td>
    </tr>
  </table>
</center>
```

Alternating Lines and Boxes

You can alternate lines and boxes in new horizontal patterns. The code looks like this:

```
<center>
<table>
  <tr>
    <td><hr width="25" ></td>
    <td><hr width="5" size="5" ></td>
    <td><hr width="25" ></td>
    <td><hr width="5" size="5" ></td>
    <td><hr width="25" ></td>
    <td><hr width="5" size="5" ></td>
    <td><hr width="25" ></td>
    <td><hr width="5" size="5" ></td>
    <td><hr width="25" ></td>
    <td><hr width="5" size="5" ></td>
    <td><hr width="25" ></td>
    <td><hr width="5" size="5" ></td>
  </tr>
</table>
</center>
```

```
width="25" width="25" width="5" size="5" width="25" width="25" width="5"
➥size="5" width="25" width="25" width="5" size="5" width="25" width="25"
➥width="5" size="5" width="25" width="25" width="5" size="5" width="25"
➥width="25" width="5" size="5"
```

> **TIP** Make sure the table width containing your horizontal divider adds up to about 1,200 pixels if you want the dashed line to stretch across the widest window size. You can never be sure how wide someone decides to stretch out their browser window. ■

145

Creative Vertical Dividers

Use this technique to:

- **Create boundaries between columns.** Adding vertical lines between text and graphics enhances yours columns and keeps the viewer's attention focused section-by-section.

- **Lead the viewer's eye down your page.** When you add something such as a vertical line down the length of your page, you emphasize the verticality of the layout. The line subtly guides the eye from the top to the bottom of the page.

- **Separate paragraphs and keywords in a résumé style format.** Use vertical lines to enhance the impact of your layouts.

Didn't think you could create vertical lines in HTML? Think again. Exercise boundless variations by manipulating HR dimensions or using various characters for creative dashed lines! Although the horizontal dividers discussed in the previous technique exist in their own tables, exclusive from the graphics and text on the rest of the page, vertical dividers must be incorporated in the same table with the rest of the corresponding graphics and text to work properly.

Writing the HTML

Although the standard HR or "Hard Rule" commonly used in HTML appears horizontally, creating vertical HRs involves simple size manipulations within the HR tag. You can adjust the width and size or height as well as the three-dimensional appearance of your vertical HR just as you can with a horizontal one.

Standard HRs

Creating a vertical line with an HR requires set dimensions for both width and size:

```
<center><hr width=5 size=100%></center>
```

 TIP The maximimum dimension for a vertical HR is 100 pixels; therefore size=100% yields 100 pixels. To create the illusion of a longer line, you need to stack numerous HRs on top of each other. In this case, there is a slight space between each segment creating a dashed-line effect.

Start with a 3-column layout that calls for two vertical dividers.

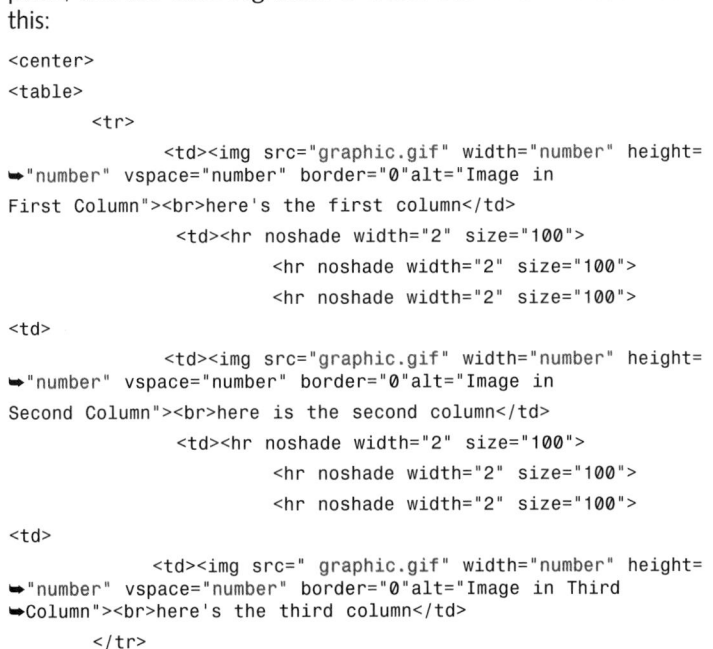

1 Use a table to create the three columns for your layout. Inserting the vertical lines involves inserting two additional table data cells into the table row. Give each vertical segment a width of 2 pixels, a height of 100 pixels, and use three segments to create each line. The code looks like this:

```
<center>
<table>
        <tr>
                <td><img src="graphic.gif" width="number" height=
➥"number" vspace="number" border="0"alt="Image in
First Column"><br>here's the first column</td>
                <td><hr noshade width="2" size="100">
                        <hr noshade width="2" size="100">
                        <hr noshade width="2" size="100">
        <td>
                <td><img src="graphic.gif" width="number" height=
➥"number" vspace="number" border="0"alt="Image in
Second Column"><br>here is the second column</td>
                <td><hr noshade width="2" size="100">
                        <hr noshade width="2" size="100">
                        <hr noshade width="2" size="100">
        <td>
                <td><img src=" graphic.gif" width="number" height=
➥"number" vspace="number" border="0"alt="Image in Third
➥Column"><br>here's the third column</td>
        </tr>
</table>
</center>
```

2 Add more or fewer sets of HRs to accommodate the size of your graphics and text on the page.

here's column 1   here's column 2   here's column 3

> **TIP** Remember to adjust the cell spacing and cell padding in your table to adjust the spacing between the line and other page elements.

VARIATIONS

Shorter "Stitch"

You can create other versions of the dashed line to suit your style. Here is an example with a shorter stitch than the previous example:

```
<hr width=2 size=25>
<hr width=2 size=25>
<hr width=2 size=25>
<hr width=2 size=25>
<hr width=2 size=25>
<hr width=2 size=25>
<hr width=2 size=25>
<hr width=2 size=25>
<hr width=2 size=25>
<hr width=2 size=25>
```

Alternating "Stitches"

You can also alternate the sizes of the HR:

```
<hr width=2 size=25>
<hr width=2 size=5>
<hr width=2 size=25>
<hr width=2 size=5>
<hr width=2 size=25>
<hr width=2 size=5>
<hr width=2 size=25>
<hr width=2 size=5>
<hr width=2 size=25>
<hr width=2 size=5>
<hr width=2 size=25>
<hr width=2 size=5>
<hr width=2 size=25>
<hr width=2 size=5>
<hr width=2 size=25>
<hr width=2 size=5>
<hr width=2 size=25>
```

Alternating Lines and Spaces

Another interesting example groups HRs and adds spacing between them:

```
<hr width=2 size=15>
<hr width=2 size=15>
<p>
<hr width=2 size=15>
<hr width=2 size=15>
<p>
<hr width=2 size=15>
<hr width=2 size=15>
<p>
<hr width=2 size=15>
<hr width=2 size=15>
<p>
<hr width=2 size=15>
<hr width=2 size=15>
<p>
<hr width=2 size=15>
<hr width=2 size=15>
<p>
<hr width=2 size=15>
<hr width=2 size=15>
<p>
<hr width=2 size=15>
<hr width=2 size=15>
<p>
<hr width=2 size=15>
<hr width=2 size=15>
```

Dotted Lines

Don't be limited by dashed lines! You can also use the "period" punctuation mark to create a dotted vertical line. The <br> tag at the front of each text column enables the text to align with the top dot. By using a character instead of an HR, you also have the opportunity to add color to your vertical divider:

```
<center>
<table height="100" cellspacing="20" bor-
der="0">
<tr>
  <td width="50" valign="top"><br>Some text
➥here, with lots more text and even more
➥text.</td>
  <td width="1" valign="top"><font size="+2"
➥color="red">.<br>.<br>.<br>.<br>.<br>.<br
➥>.<br>.</font></td>
```

Some text here, with lots more text and even more text. · Some text here, with lots more text and even more text. · Some text here, with lots more text and even more text.

```
    <td width="50" valign="top"><br>Some text here, with lots more text and
➥even more text.</td>
    <td width="1" valign="top"><font size="+2"
➥color="red">.<br>.<br>.<br>.<br>.<br>.<br>.<br>.<br>.</font></td>
    <td width="50" valign="top"><br>Some text here, with lots more text and
➥even more text.</td>
</tr>
</table>
</center>
```

Résumé Style

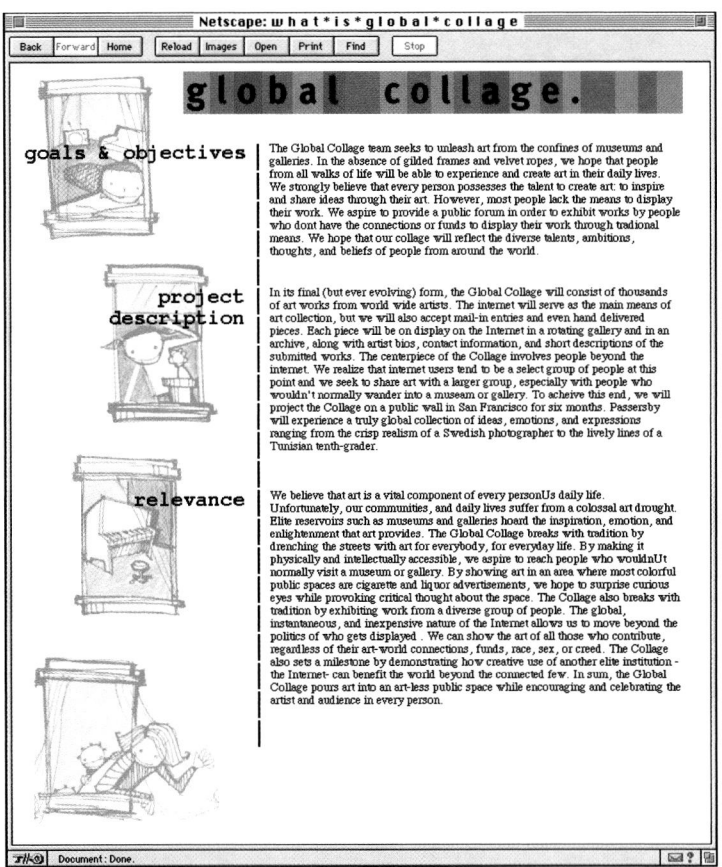

You can make a résumé or glossary look more interesting by adding a vertical line as shown in the adjacent figure. I chose a vertical dashed line of the "short stitch" variety without the three-dimensional look by setting my `height`, `size`, and `no shade` tags for my HRs. Use the following code.

```
<center>
<table>
    <tr>
                <td valign="top" align="right"><code><b><font size="6">
➥section title goes here</b></code></font></td>
                <td rowspan="3" width="10" valign="top">
<hr noshade width=2 size=25>
<hr noshade width=2 size=25>
<hr noshade width=2 size=25>
<hr noshade width=2 size=25>
<hr noshade width=2 size=25>
<hr noshade width=2 size=25>
<hr noshade width=2 size=25>
<hr noshade width=2 size=25>
<hr noshade width=2 size=25>
<hr noshade width=2 size=25>
<hr noshade width=2 size=25>
<hr noshade width=2 size=25>
<hr noshade width=2 size=25>
<hr noshade width=2 size=25>
<hr noshade width=2 size=25>
<hr noshade width=2 size=25>
<hr noshade width=2 size=25>
<hr noshade width=2 size=25>
<hr noshade width=2 size=25>
</td>
                <td width="500" valign="top">lots and lots of text goes
➥here</td>
        </tr>
        <tr>
                <td width="500" valign="top">lots and lots of text goes
➥here</td>
        </tr>
        <tr>
            <td valign="top" align="right"><code><b><font size="6">section
➥title goes here</b></code></font></td>
            <td width="500" valign="top">lots and lots of text goes ➥here</td>
        </tr>
</table>
</center>
```

TIP When using columns with large bodies of text, remember to keep your columns relatively short. Although people expect to scan up and down long pages of newspapers or magazines, scrolling back to the top of the next column of an article on a Web page is rather annoying. ■

Manipulating Image Dimensions

Use this technique to:

- **Create colored lines.** This technique offers the versatility of HTML hard rules with colors of your choice!

- **Create continuous vertical lines.** Because the maximum size for a vertical hr or "hard rule" is 100 pixels, this technique offers an excellent solution for creating continuous vertical lines within your layout.

- **Save file space.** Repurposing one graphic enables you to minimize your site's download time to view your pages.

Writing the HTML

Manipulating image dimensions involves adjusting the figures set by the width and height attributes of the img src tag.

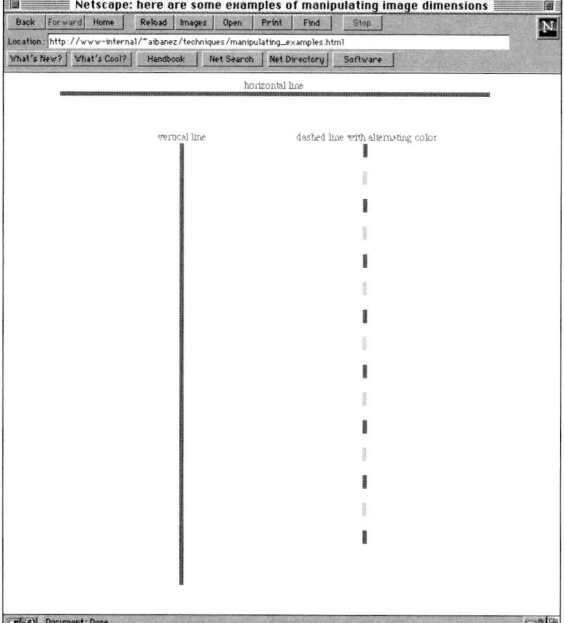

Basic Image Manipulation

1 If you've used images in an HTML page before, you already know how to place these lines on your pages! Here's how to create a 480 pixels wide × 5 pixels high horizontal line with an image, called dot.gif, measuring 16 pixels wide × 16 pixels high.

```
<img src="dot.gif" width="480" height="5" alt="Here's a Bonafide
➥Horizontal Line!">
```

Adjust the dimensions to create the thickness and length you need.

2 Here's how to create a vertical line with the same image:

```
<img src="dot.gif" width="5" height="480" alt="Here's a Bonafide
➥Vertical Line!">
```

Adjust the dimensions to create the thickness and length you need.

Incorporating the Image with Tables

You can use the same examples from the "Creative Horizontal Dividers" (p.142) and "Creative Vertical Dividers" (p.146) techniques to apply these image manipulations.

1 Vertical lines separate columns effectively. The code looks like this:

```
<center>
<table>
        <tr>
                <td><img src="graphic.gif" width="150" height="500"
➥vspace="3"alt="Image in First Column"><br>here's the first
➥column</td>
                <td><img src="dot.gif" width=2 height=500></td>
                <td><img src="graphic.gif" width="150" height="500"
➥vspace="3"alt="Image in
Second Column"><br>here's the second column</td>
                <td><img src="dot.gif" width=2 height=500></td>
                <td><img src="graphic.gif" width="150" height="500"
➥vspace="3"alt="Image in Third Column"><br>here's the third
➥column</td>
        </tr>
</table>
</center>
```

153

Many companies are adopting the clean columns layout with lines. Prototypes of the Macromall Web site design utilize a subtle vertical line, whereas c|net uses both vertical and horizontal lines generated from one graphic.

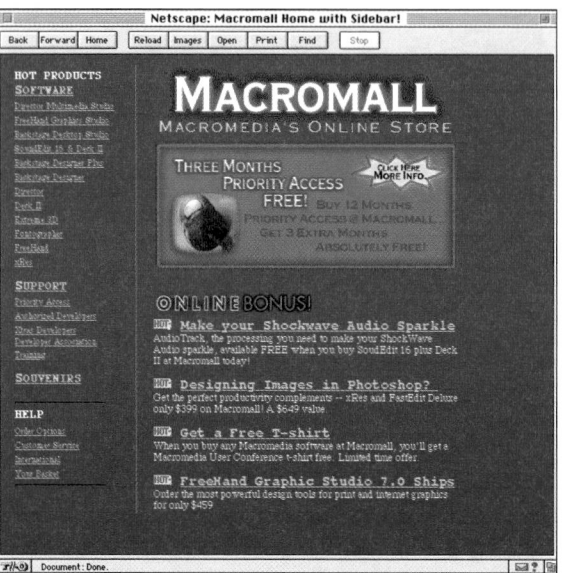

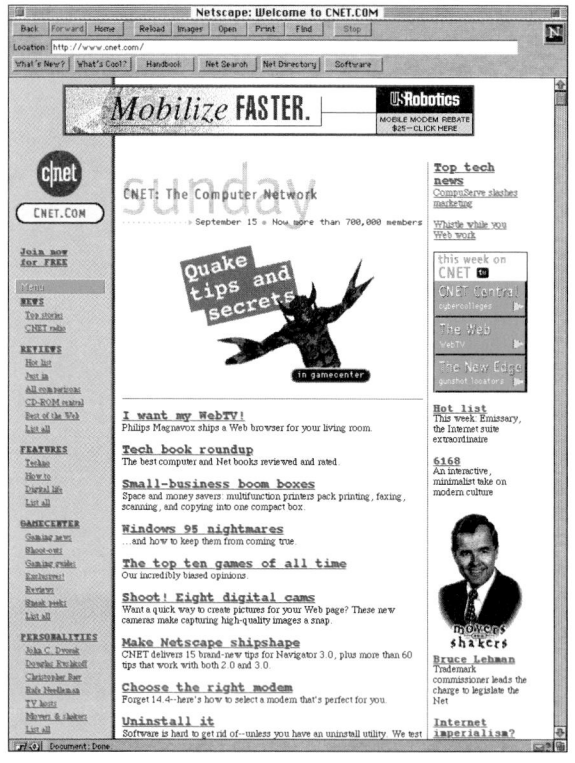

TIP Remember to adjust the `cellspacing` and `cellpadding` in your table to adjust the spacing between the line and other page elements.

TIP Create dashed lines with alternating colors. Substitute the following `img src` tags with the one above. Repeat the pattern as often as necessary:

```
<img src="dot.gif" width="2" height="15" alt="Here's a Vertical Line in the
➥Color I Want"><p>
<img src="dot2.gif" width="2" height="15" alt="Here's a Different Colored
➥Line"><p>
<img src="dot.gif" width="2" height="15" alt="Here's a Vertical Line in the
➥Color I Want"><p>
<img src="dot2.gif" width="2" height="15" alt="Here's a Different Colored
➥Line"><p> ■
```

System Typefaces

Use this technique to:

■ **Specify fonts in HTML.** Choose specific Macintosh or Windows fonts for any text in your Web page.

■ **Change the typographic look.** Add style to your Web pages by moving away from the standard default look of Times New Roman and Courier.

■ **Create stylized headers.** Customize your headers by specifying fonts that differentiate them from the rest of the text.

Typography on the Web has thus far been limited to the browser default settings of Times New Roman and Courier. Now with the new `font face` tag you can set any text within an HTML document to a specific font. The font is visible to the user, provided the user has it installed on his or her machine.

Macintosh	Windows 95
Chicago	Arial
Courier	Courier
Geneva	Courier New
Helvetica	Comic Sans
Monaco	Impact
New York	Times New Roman
Times New Roman	Verdana

Here are the standard system fonts for Macintosh and Windows machines.

1 Here is what the normal Web page looks like with the default browser fonts.

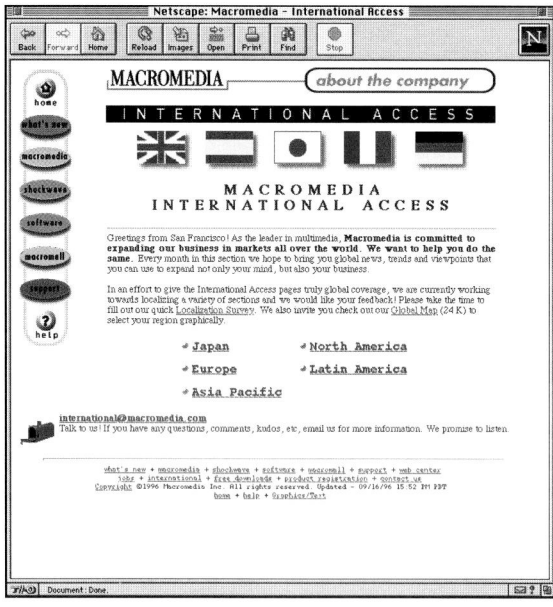

2 Select the text area or heading. Make the header, "Macromedia International Access," an Arial font. Insert `<font face="Arial">` before the heading and close the heading with a `</font>` tag. Add some extra default fonts to your header. Because Arial is a Windows font, Helvetica was added as the second font after Arial so that Macintosh viewers could have a special font face.

TIP It is a good idea to have a few font face selections. You should choose one Macintosh-specific font and one Windows-specific font. You can have as many defaults as you want, just make sure you place the fonts in order of appearance and that they are all separated by commas. If any of your selections are unavailable on the client machine, the browser reverts back to its default settings.

3 Do the same for the body of the text. Before the start of the text specify:

```
<font face="Arial, Helvetica">
```

At the end of the text, insert the closing `</font>` tag.

157

4 Now upload your HTML document and test it in your browser.

TIP It's a good idea if you have multiple font face selections to test each font face (on a Macintosh and Windows machine if you can) so that you know what the user sees if they can't view your first selection.

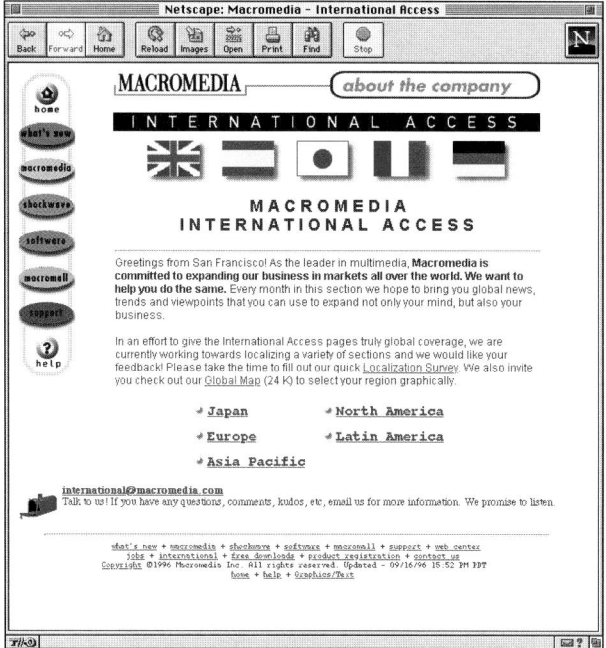

VARIATIONS

By varying font size and adding color you can create unique HTML headers. See the "Fine Tuning Header Typogaphy" technique (p.192) for more information on how to create your own custom HTML headers.

Create a typographical effect by changing font names and sizes. ■

Using Standard HTML Typeface Styles

Use this technique to:

- **Change text.** Use different font styles within the realm of HTML without having to define Font Face.

- **Create links.** Differentiate links from the body of text

Typography on the Web is gaining momentum. Designers are getting frustrated by simple browser default text styles. Although there is much talk of embedded fonts for the future, there is a quick and easy way to create different looks for your Web pages.

Writing the HTML

There are a few HTML tags you can use to create different typographic looks without having specific fonts loaded on the user's system.

```
<CODE></CODE>    code: small fixed-width font
<TT></TT>        teletype: creates keyboard typeface
<PRE></PRE>          preformatted text
```

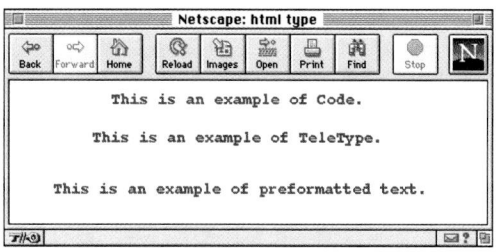

As you can see all three fonts have about the same look (shown here bold font size 5). The difference is their width. Most sites use code and teletype to specify the font and use preformatted text for layout purposes. Code is a great "font" to use for links because it differentiates the link from the normal text on a Web page. Fonts can make the links more eye-catching and create a unique look for your Web site. You can play around with the font size or attributes such as bold to create headers, quotes, or anything else that you might want to emphasize.

Keep in mind that users have the option to set the font and font size in their browser preferences.

You start by creating stylish links for this Macromedia index page.

1 Open the HTML document and insert the HTML tag <CODE> by each link.

```
<IMG SRC="/images/dot.gif" WIDTH=10 HEIGHT=10 ALT="[o]">
<CODE><B><A HREF="ucon/european.html">1996 European User Conference</A>
➥</B></CODE><BR>
December 4 - 6, 1996, Rai Center, Amsterdam, the Netherlands
<P>
<IMG SRC="/images/dot.gif" WIDTH=10 HEIGHT=10 ALT="[o]">
<CODE><B><A HREF="ucon/index.html">1996 User Conference</A> </B></CODE>
➥<BR>
Find out what happened this year and register for 1997!
<P>
<IMG SRC="/images/dot.gif" WIDTH=10 HEIGHT=10 ALT="[o]">
<CODE><B><A HREF="investors/annual96/index.html">1996 Annual Report</A>
➥</B></CODE><BR>
This year's Annual Report plus a "Shocking True Story!"
<P>
```

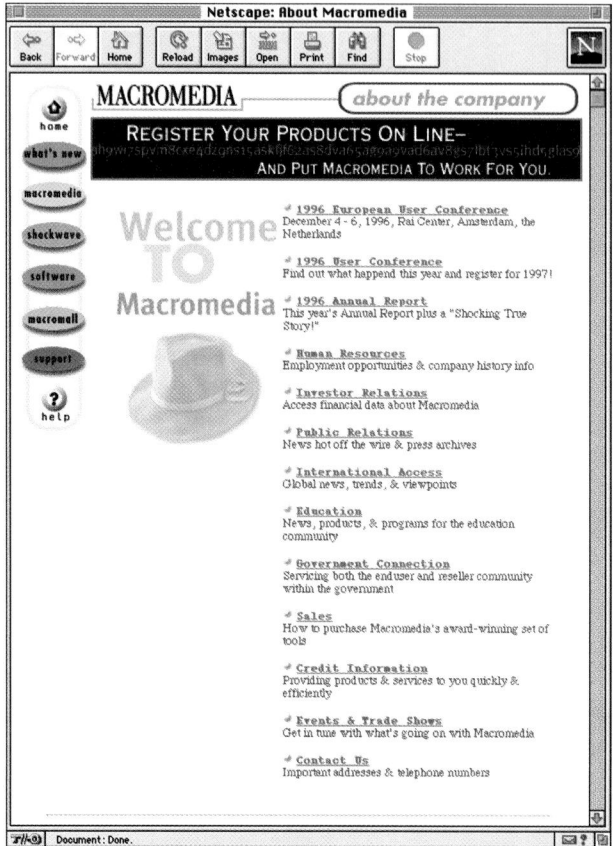

2 The code looks great but to make the links even more powerful visually, add FONT SIZE=5 to each of the links.

```
<IMG SRC="/images/dot.gif" WIDTH=10 HEIGHT=10 ALT="[o]">
<CODE><FONT SIZE=5><b><A HREF="ucon/european.html">1996 European
➡User Conference</A></B></FONT></CODE><BR>
December 4 - 6, 1996, Rai Center, Amsterdam, the Netherlands
<P>
<IMG SRC="/images/dot.gif" WIDTH=10 HEIGHT=10 ALT="[o]">
<CODE><FONT SIZE=5><b><A HREF="ucon/index.html">1996 User
Conference</A></B></FONT></CODE><BR>
Find out what happened this year and register for 1997!
<P>
<IMG SRC="/images/dot.gif" WIDTH=10 HEIGHT=10 ALT="[o]">
<CODE><FONT SIZE=5><b><A HREF="investors/annual96/index.html">1996
➡Annual Report</A></B></FONT></CODE><BR>
This year's Annual Report plus a "Shocking True Story!"
<P>
```

Browser Watch

Netscape 1.1 and higher

Internet Explorer 2.0 and higher ■

Unusual Text Alignment

Use this technique to:

- **Create unusual shapes with blocks of text.** Just as combinations of illustrations and text work together to communicate the content so can the actual form of the text.

- **Align your text along unusual curves and shapes**. Using little text and a simple background, you can create a dramatic effect with unusual alignment.

The most legible and obvious way to layout text is to left-align it. Left alignment is a tried and true formula, but you can add interest by making the text part of your message.

Writing the HTML

The HTML code involves a straightforward application of the `<pre>` tag that uses the font set in the browser preferences as a fixed-font width. Here are some things to keep in mind when you preformat your text.

- Make sure that you use a fixed-width code when entering the HTML in order to make it easy to set up the example.

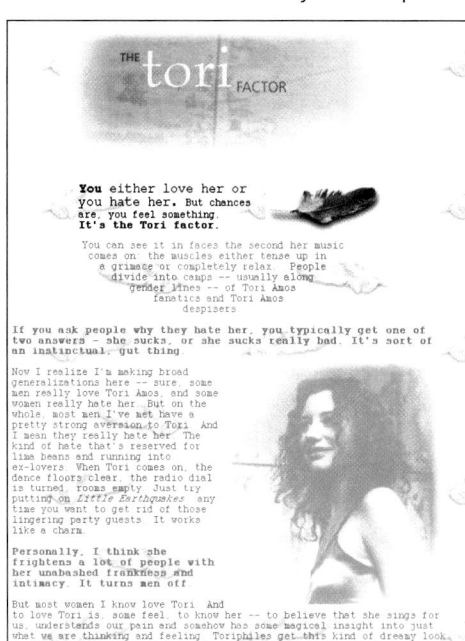

- Enter the text first to see the desired text formations more easily onscreen.

- Set the horizontal or character spacing manually by pressing the spacebar on your keyboard where appropriate. Within the preformatting tags, your browser reads each character space as it would if you had put an   HTML tag to represent the spaces outside of the preformating tags.

- Add the appropriate HTML tags for font color and size last, after you have achieved the desired effects.

Aligning Text in Abstract Patterns and Shapes

On a Web page with a commentary on singer Tori Amos, designer Michael Merrill accentuated his curving text alignment by using two different font colors.

```
<FONT COLOR="slateblue">
<FONT SIZE="+1">
<PRE>
        You can <FONT COLOR="gray">see it in faces the second her</FONT> music
          comes on: <FONT COLOR="gray">the muscles either tense</FONT> up in
            a grimace <FONT COLOR="gray">or completely relax.</FONT> People
              divide into <FONT COLOR="gray">camps</FONT> — <FONT
➥COLOR="gray">usually</FONT> along
                gender <FONT COLOR="gray">lines</FONT> — <FONT
➥COLOR="gray">of Tori </FONT>Amos
                  fanatics <FONT COLOR="gray">and </FONT>Tori Amos
                    despisers.
</PRE>
```

As a result, the text content of the page takes on a distinctive shape. The curved forms relate to a certain flow and energy indicated by the article.

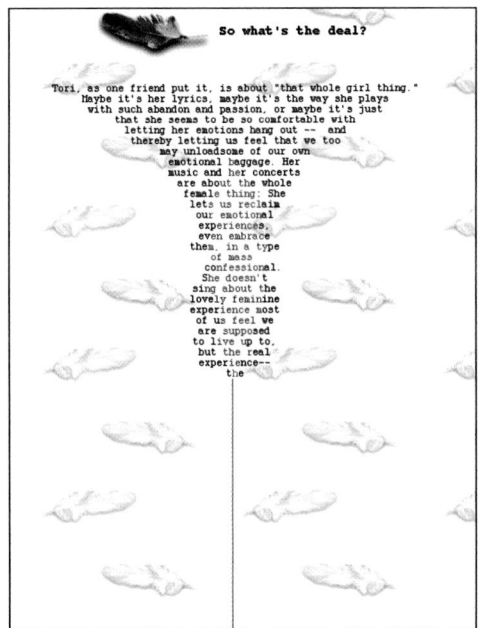

Creating an Interesting List

The Netscape `<spacer>` tag or transparent GIF trick serves as an alternative to using preformatted text to specify special horizontal spacing. The following example combines two lists of text

aligned along different curves set by the size of the `<spacer>` or width of the GIF.

One set of words displays a large font size and different hues of green, whereas the other set lists the same phrase at a smaller font size. Placing the entire layout within a table orients the specified spaces along a consistent boundary.

Set Up First Group Words

1 Standardize the font size, style, and color of the group. The green words use the `code` style with a bold, large font size like this:

```
<code><b><font size="7" color="#006600">funky!</font></b></code>
```

As the list of words goes down, the green color becomes lighter. Set `color=` according the desired green color of that row.

2 Set up the table. Start with a `<table border="0" width="600">`.

3 Put each word in its own table row with one table data cell.

4 Align each `<td>` tag. Set horizontal alignment to `<td align=left>`.

5 Set the horizontal space for the curving alignment. Use the Netscape `<spacer>` tag, that produces the same results as the transparent GIF discussed in "Defining Space." Place this defined space before the word. Set the space for the first word at `<spacer type=horizontal size="235">`.

6 With each new row, increase the space by some standard increment, such as 15 pixels. When you reach the center point of the curve, decrease the size by 15 pixels again in order to create a mirror image of the first part of the curve.

Set Up Second Group of Words

1 Standardize the font size, style, and color of the group. The phrase "html * i love it!" is repeated throughout this list, using a small font size and spaced out lettering:

```
<font size="-1">h t m l   *   i   l o v e  
➥i t !</font>
```

2 Set up the same table as the first with a `<table border="0" width="600">`.

3 Put each word in its own table row with one table data cell.

4 Align each `<td>`. This time, set horizontal alignment to `<td align=right>`.

5 Set the horizontal space for the curving alignment. Instead of placing the extra space before the words in the table data, place it after. Set the space for the first word at `<spacer type=horizontal size="250">`.

6 With each new row, increase the space by some standard increment, such as 15 pixels. When you reach the center point of the curve, decrease the size by 15 pixels again in order to create a mirror image of the first part of the curve.

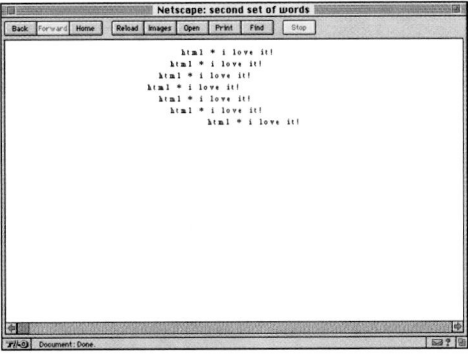

Combine the Groups

Put the table information together by alternating the table rows from the two different tables.

1 Start with the first green word:

```
<tr>
    <td align=left><spacer type=horizontal size="235"><code><b>
➥<font size="7" color="#006600">funky!</font></b></code></td>
</tr>
```

2 The second `<td>` should be the first row from the second set of words.

```
<tr>
    <td align=right><font size="-1">h t m l   *   i
➥  l o v e   i t !</font><spacer type=horizontal
➥size="250"></td>
</tr>
```

3 The third `<td>` comes from the second row of the first group:

```
<tr>
    <td align=left><spacer type=horizontal size="250"><code>
➥<b><font size="7" color="#009900">crazy!</font></b></code></td>
</tr>
```

4 Repeat the pattern for the rest of the table. ■

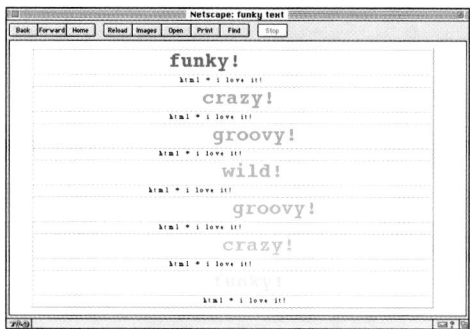

Varying Font Sizes

Use this technique to:

- **Create inner cap look.** Inner caps, such as large letters in the middle of a line of all-caps type, are a great way to give your pages a sophisticated, stylized look. This look is used most by banks or for businesses related to finance, and they are great for main headers or tag lines.

- **Create drop cap look.** First letters of paragraphs can be increased in size to create a different look. This can also be done with a graphic.

- **Emphasize words or letters.** Sometimes it is appropriate to emphasize type by changing its size, rather than bolding, italicizing, or underlining the type. Used effectively, you can put just the right spin on your message.

- **Stylize headlines.** The default headlines built into HTML (<H1></H1> through <H6></H6>) lack typographic flair. To create interesting effects, you can tweak the sizes of individual letters in your headlines.

- **Brand your Web site.** By mimicking your company or organization's official name mark with HTML, you can add your corporate identity to your Web pages.

By modifying your font size you can create specialized looks for your Web pages. From inner caps to simple or elegant headers, you can choose how and which text gets emphasized.

Font sizes run from 1-7 with the default base size of 3. You can vary your font size from the default size by "+1", "-1", "+2", "-2", and so on; therefore, <font size=6> and <font size="+3"> produce the same sized type.

Writing the HTML

In this section, you take a block of basic text and apply the <FONT> tag's size attribute in several different ways. You get a feel for the different kinds of special typographic effects that are possible with some tweaking of simple HTML.

The International Access page in the figure contains the basic HTML tags, an <H1> header and default-sized links. You want to enhance this Web page using various font sizes and spacing techniques.

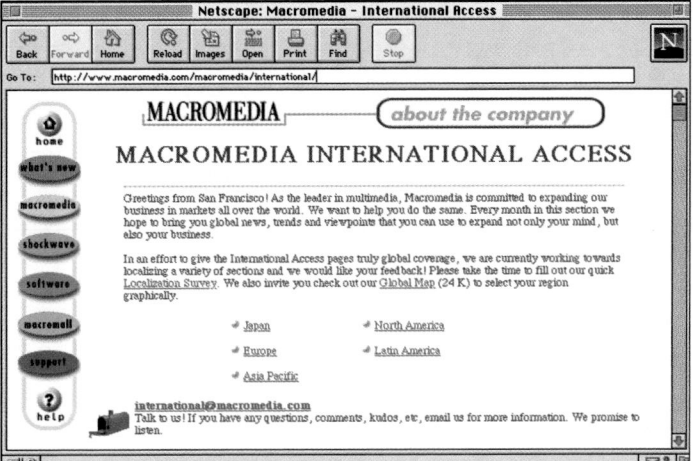

1 Open the existing HTML document. As you can see, the existing header is quite large as an <H1>. Change the header to a smaller size at <H3>.

```
<H3>MACROMEDIA INTERNATIONAL ACCESS</H3>
```

2 Make the font size for the "M," "I," and the "A" 3 sizes bigger than the rest of the text to create the effect.

```
<H3><FONT SIZE="+3">M</FONT>ACROMEDIA
<FONT SIZE="+3">I</FONT>NTERNATIONAL
<FONTSIZE="+3">A</FONT>CCESS</H3>
```

TIP The inner cap look should not be used for links. The URL underline creates an uneven jagged line under the larger letters.

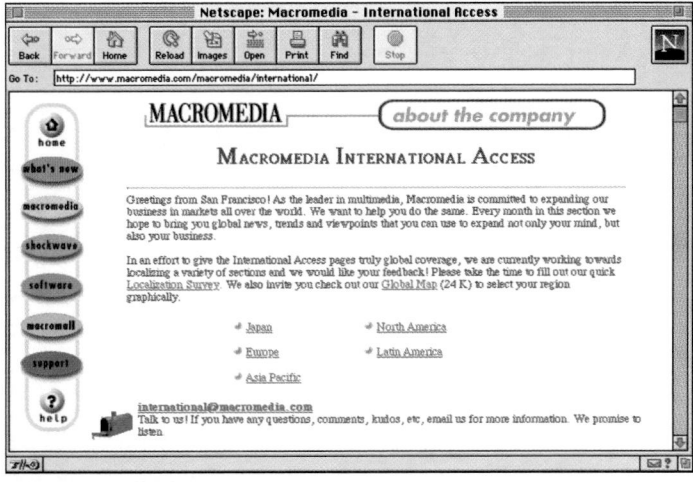

3 As you can see, the inner cap effect works but the rest of the page lacks weight, especially relative to the powerful header. You can create a drop cap look for the two main paragraphs by increasing the first letter to `font size=5`.

```
<font size=5>G</font>reetings from San Francisco! As the leader in
multimedia, Macromedia is committed to expanding our business in
markets all over the world.  We want to help you do the same.
Every month in this section we hope to bring you global news,
trends and viewpoints that you can use to expand not only your
mind, but also your business.
<p>
<font size=5>I</font>n an effort to give the International Access
pages truly global coverage, we are currently working towards
localizing a variety of sections and we would like your feedback!
Please take the time to fill out our quick <a
href="survey.html">Localization Survey</a>.
We also invite you check out our <A HREF="map.html">Global Map</A>
(24K) to select your region graphically.
<P>
```

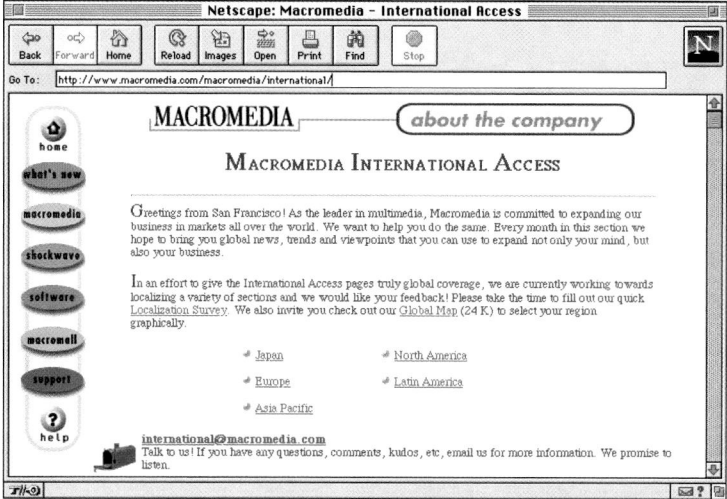

4 You can also give the links below the second paragraph some pizzazz by making them `font size=5`. It may get a bit complicated because all the links are formatted within the table; therefore you must tag all the text links.

```
<TABLE WIDTH=300>
    <TR>
        <TD VALIGN=TOP>
        <IMG SRC="/images/dot.gif" alt="[o]">
        <A HREF="japan.html"><font size=5>Japan</font></A>
        <P>
        <IMG SRC="/images/dot.gif" alt="[o]">
    <a href="europe.html"><font size=5>Europe</font></a>
```

```
        <P>
       <IMG SRC="/images/dot.gif" alt="[o]">
       <A HREF="asiapacific.html"><font size=5>Asia
Pacific</font></A>
           </TD>
         <TD VALIGN=TOP>
         <IMG SRC="/images/dot.gif" alt="[o]">
       <A HREF="northamerica.html"><font size=5>North
America</font></A>
           <P>
       <IMG SRC="/images/dot.gif" alt="[o]">
             <A HREF="latinamerica.html"><font size=5>Latin
America</font></A>
         </TD>
       </TR>
    </TABLE>
```

5 Finish the look by making the text links bold and adding the font type code.

```
  <TABLE WIDTH=300>
         <TR>
            <TD VALIGN=TOP>
          <IMG SRC="/images/dot.gif" alt="[o]">
         <A HREF="japan.html"><B><CODE>
          <font size=5>Japan</font></CODE></B></A>
          <P>
        <IMG SRC="/images/dot.gif" alt="[o]">
        <a href="europe.html"><B><CODE>
         <font size=5>Europe</font></CODE></B></a>
         <P>
       <IMG SRC="/images/dot.gif" alt="[o]">
          <A HREF="asiapacific.html"><B><CODE>
            <font size=5>Asia Pacific</font></CODE></B></A>
        </TD>
          <TD VALIGN=TOP>
        <IMG SRC="/images/dot.gif" alt="[o]">
           <A HREF="northamerica.html"><B><CODE>
         <font size=5>North America</font></A>
       <P>
       <IMG SRC="/images/dot.gif" alt="[o]">
        <A HREF="latinamerica.html"><font size=5>Latin
America</font></CODE></B></A>
          </TD>
          </TR>
    </TABLE>
```

Add a graphic to the top and the page is complete.

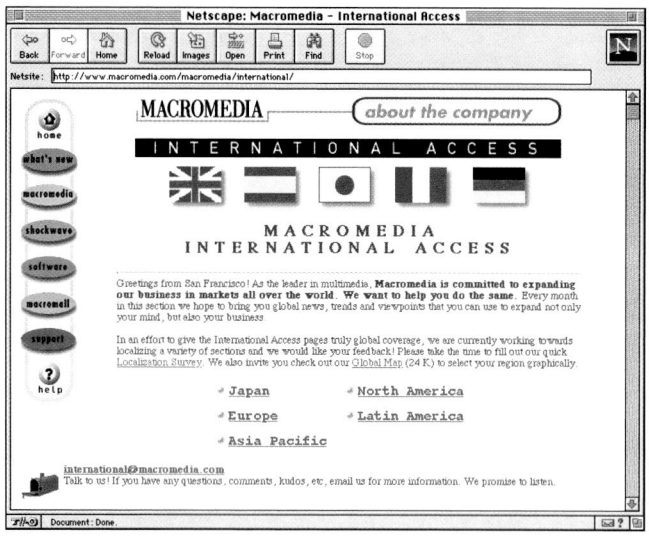

VARIATIONS

Create a more widely spaced, all-caps look with font size=5, bold. Add space between letters by inserting " where you want the spaces to appear.

Create navigational footers for Web pages. Such footers are typically displayed in a smaller type size than that used for running text, much like footnotes in traditional print books. For the footer on this Macromedia page, the font style code `"font size="-1"` was used. ■

Varying Font Colors

Use this technique to:

- **Emphasize words or letters.** Colorize important words, bodies of text, or individual letters for a special effect.

- **Stylize headers.** Colorful headers can complement the rest of your page.

Colors can say a lot to users; using the right color is just as important as selecting the right typeface.

Make sure the colors you choose to add complement the colors already on the page, and try to stay away from using too many colors. The "rainbow effect" can be detrimental because users might find it difficult to concentrate on the important information. Choosing a color palette for your Web site can help you choose the right font colors. The color palette lists hexcodes for most colors and names for the few colors that can be coded in HTML by name. Color swatches are also included to give you an idea what the color looks like onscreen.

Writing the HTML

In this section, you use the <FONT> tag's color attributes to make your typography a little more colorful. You can apply the tag with a variety of attribute settings to see how little changes can dramatically affect the look of your display type.

This is what the page you want to enhance, from Macromedia's 1996 Annual Report, looks like now:

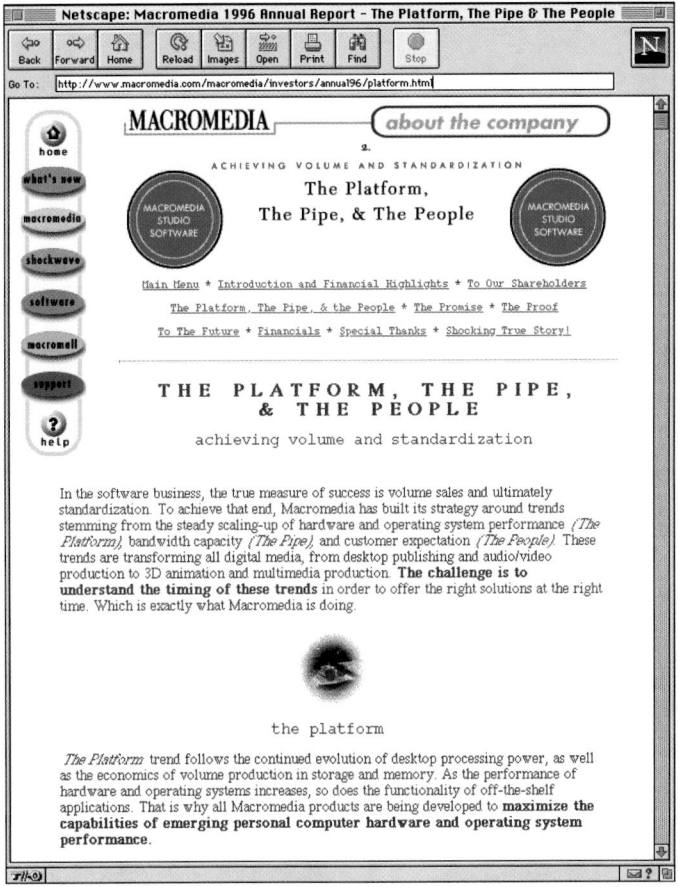

1 Open the HTML document and then color each of the sectional titles green. If you look on the HTML color chart, the shade of green you want in hexcode is 339966. Because there is already a font tag present (FONT SIZE=5), add the color element by typing <FONT SIZE=5 COLOR=#339966"> and close the header with </FONT>.

```
<CODE><FONT SIZE=5 COLOR="#339966>
achieving volume and standardization
</FONT>
</CODE>
.
.
.
<CODE><FONT SIZE=5 COLOR="#339966>
the platform
</FONT>
```

```
</CODE>

.

.

.

<CODE><FONT SIZE=5 COLOR="#339966>
the pipe
</FONT>
</CODE>
```

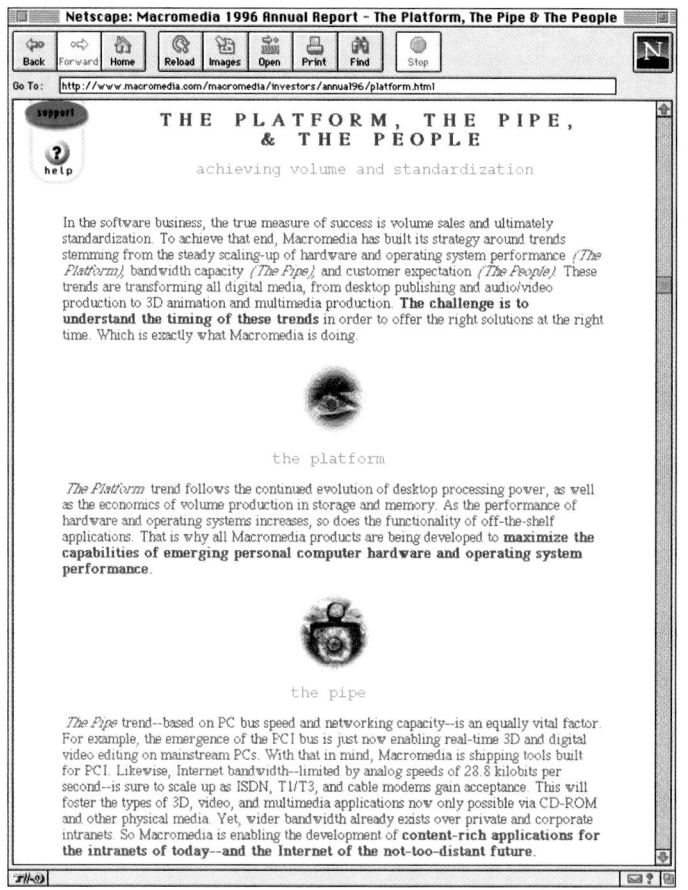

178

TIP It's a good idea to pick a different color for styling and emphasis than the one used for your link colors. Otherwise, users who have their URL underline default deselected will think the colored text items are links.

2 You want the bold text within the document to stand out, so color the text and increase the font size by 1. Add <FONT SIZE=+1 COLOR='#339966> to each of the phrases that are bold. Close the phrases with a </FONT> tag.

```
<FONT SIZE="+1" COLOR="#339966"><B>The challenge is to understand the
➡timing of these trends</B></FONT>
 .

 .

 .
<FONT SIZE="+1" COLOR="#339966"><B>maximize the
➡capabilities of emerging personal computer hardware and
➡operating system performance.</B></FONT>
 .

 .

 .
<FONT SIZE="+1" COLOR="#339966"><B>content-rich applications for the
➡intranets of today—and the Internet of the not-too-distant future.
➡.</B></FONT>
```

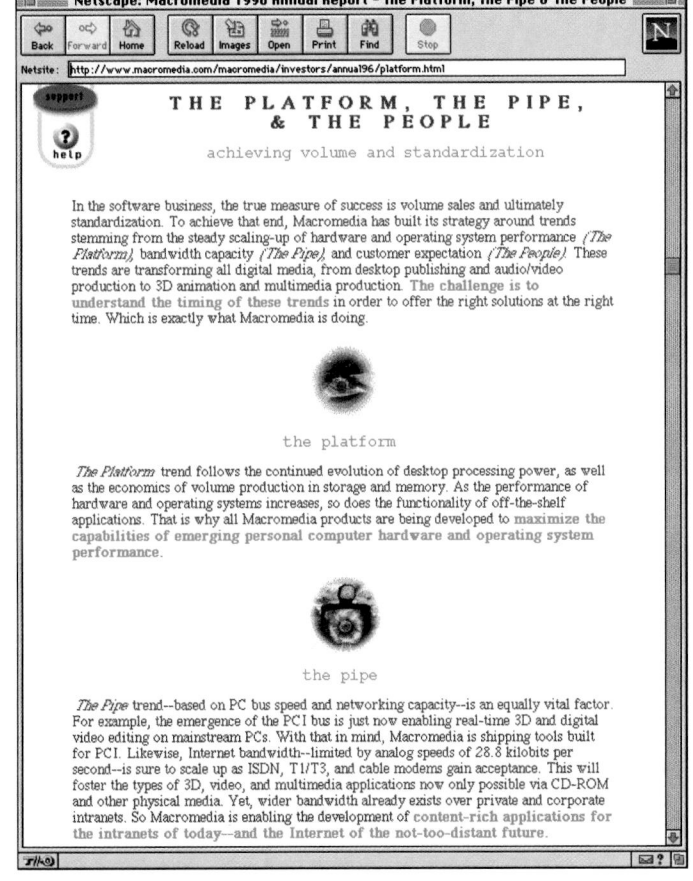

VARIATIONS

Paramount's *Mission: Impossible* Web site (`http://www.missionimpossible.com`) uses green text to replicate computer terminal settings.

Razorfish's Web site (`http://www.razorfish.com`) coordinates content colors on its Web page with header graphic colors, as shown. ■

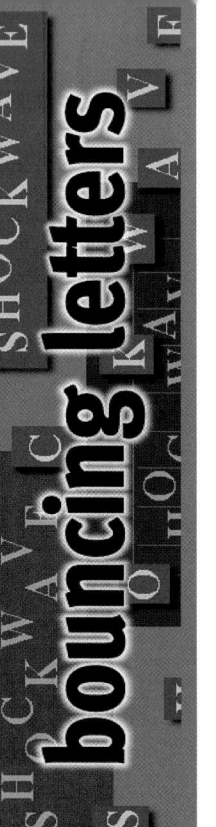

Bouncing Letter Effect

Use this technique to:

- **Create interesting typographic effects without using graphics.** If you want a playful look and feel, this is a great way to express the effect with individual letters in your HTML—without touching a graphics program.

- **Express yourself!** Many words lend themselves to more expressive typography to get their meaning across.

Any time is a good time to create a bouncing letter effect. The unusual shifts of individual letters in a line of text enhances the character and personality of your page.

Writing the HTML

Laying out your letters to create the bouncing effect involves creating tables. Instead of placing images or large chunks of text, you place individual letters within each table data cell. All you need is a basic table with one table row and a table data cell for each letter in your word.

To demonstrate this technique, I chose the word, "Shockwave." Look what happens when you shake up the letters to defy the normal, straight baseline.

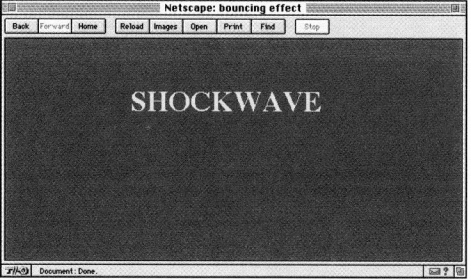

Alternating Bounce

The most basic example involves alternating the vertical alignment of every other letter.

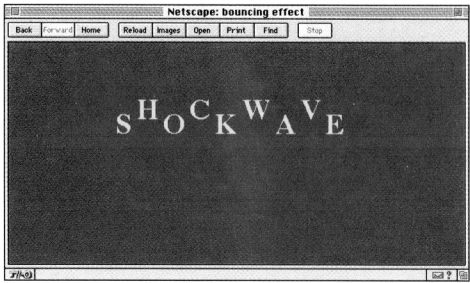

1 Set the vertical alignment within your first `<td>` tag to correspond with how you want to orient the first letter. I chose to start with the first letter down.

Here is the code:

```
<td valign=bottom>
```

If you want your letter to be up, here is the code example:

```
<td valign=top>
```

2 Alternate the vertical alignments for the subsequent `<td>` tags. Since I chose to have my first letter down, my next is up, the third letter is down, and so on.

3 Add spacing above and below letters. Setting the `<td>` tags is not enough. Because you are dealing with single letters, you need to give your table more information so that it aligns the data either to the top or bottom of the table data cells. Without the extra spacing, your letters show up as a regular word along a single line. When your letter is down, you must add space above it:

```
<td valign=bottom> <p>S</td>
```

When your letter is up, you must add space below it:

```
<td valign=top>S<p></td>
```

4 That's all there is to it! Here is an example of code where I added my own font preferences:

```
<center>
<table>
  <tr>
    <td align=bottom><p><b><font size="+5">S</font></b></td>
    <td align=top><b><font size="+5">H</font></b><p></td>
    <td align=bottom><p><b><font size="+5">O</font></b></td>
    <td align=top><b><font size="+5">C</font></b><p></td>
    <td align=bottom><p><b><font size="+5">K</font></b></td>
    <td <td align=top><b><font size="+5">W</font></b><p></td>
    <td <td align=bottom><p><b><font size="+5">A</font></b></td>
    <td <td align=top><b><font size="+5">V</font></b><p></td>
    <td <td align=bottom><p><b><font size="+5">E</font></b></td>
  </tr>
</table>
</center>
```

Bigger Peaks

If bouncing every other letter is too hyper for your taste, you can create bigger "peaks" by adding an intermediary center aligned letter between the up and down letters to create pronounced waves rather than quick ripples.

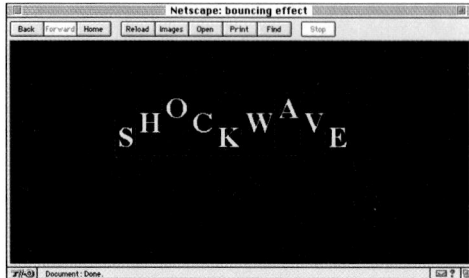

1 Select the alignment for your first letter. This time you have an added option to align your letter at the default center instead of just top and bottom. Again, I started with the first letter down.

2 Select the alignment of your second letter. Because I started with a down letter, my next letter is vertically aligned at the center of the table like this:

```
<td><b><font size="+5">H</font></b></td>
```

You don't need to do anything special to the `<td>` tag in this case. It automatically defaults to the center of the table data cell.

3 Select the alignment of your third letter. My third letter, which goes up, follows the same code as my up letters in the previous example.

4 Repeat the pattern for the rest of your letters.

5 Add the desired vertical spacing for your top and bottom letters just as you did in the previous example.

6 You may adjust the peaks by changing the height of the row.

7 Here is an example of my own code:

```
<center>
<table border="1">
  <tr>
    <td valign=bottom><br><p><b><font size="+5">S</font></b></td>
    <td><b><font size="+5">H</font></b></td>
    <td valign=top><b><font size="+5">O</font></b><br><p></td>
    <td><b><font size="+5">C</font></b></td>
    <td valign=bottom><br><p><b><font size="+5">K</font></b></td>
    <td><b><font size="+5">W</font></b></td>
    <td valign=top><b><font size="+5">A</font></b><br><p></td>
    <td><b><font size="+5">V</font></b></td>
    <td valign=bottom><br><p><b><font size="+5">E</font></b></td>
  </tr>
</table>
</center>
```

Subtle Bounce

If the first two examples overwhelm you, why not try a more subtle bouncing effect? This variation shifts the letters slightly from the baseline creating a gentle rocking motion between the letters.

To achieve this look, take the second variation and remove the extra spacing for all table data except for the first, using this code:

```
<center>
<table border="1">
  <tr>
    <td valign=bottom><br><p><b><font size="+5">S</font></b></td>
    <td><b><font size="+5">H</font></b></td>
    <td valign=top><b><font size="+5">O</font></b></td>
    <td><b><font size="+5">C</font></b></td>
    <td valign=bottom><b><font size="+5">K</font></b></td>
    <td><b><font size="+5">W</font></b></td>
    <td valign=top><b><font size="+5">A</font></b></td>
    <td><b><font size="+5">V</font></b></td>
    <td valign=bottom><b><font size="+5">E</font></b></td>
  </tr>
</table>
</center>
```

Eliminating the <p> tags enables the table to default as closely around the table data information as possible.

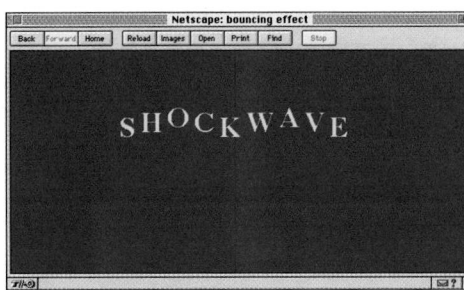

185

| TIP | Play with font size for perspective and shatter effects. The larger the font size the closer it appears, while smaller font sizes give the appearance of receding into the page. ∎ |

Placing Text Over Text

Use this technique to:

- **Create cool typographical effects.** Add drama and style to your words by overlaying text of different sizes, styles, and colors. Have fun with your text in HTML!

- **Create unique page or section headers with just HTML text.** You don't have to open a sophisticated graphics application to overlay your text. It all happens in HTML!

By overlaying text of different sizes, styles, color values, and hues, you can alter the depth of your image and therefore emphasize or de-emphasize certain groups of words or letters.

One long title—almost a topic sentence—does not impact a reader as strongly as a few well-chosen key words. You can add some pizzazz to your words by using an overlap effect.

Writing the HTML

Placing text over text follows the same principles as the other overlay sections dealing with graphics in compressed tables; however, this technique has more predictable and reliable results. You can display the technique onscreen with no problems.

Just as in the "Placing Graphics Over Graphics" and "Placing Text Over Graphics" examples, understanding the HTML code for this technique involves understanding the dynamics of a regular table. Remember each table consists of at least one table row containing at least one table data cell or column. You can manipulate the width and alignment of the `<td>` tag as well as adjust the cell padding, cell spacing, and border width of the entire table.

Regular Table

1 Create a normal table with the opening tag, `<table border="2" cellspacing="2">`, and closing tag, `</table>`. Setting a border and some cell spacing allows you to see the distinct table data.

2 Create one table row within the table tags with the opening `<tr>` and closing `</tr>`.

3 Create the first table data cell within the row tags with `<td bgcolor="white">`. Adding a background color helps you distinguish between the `<td>`s. After adding some text, close the data cell with a `</td>`.

4 Create the second table data within the row as you did the first. This time choose a different color for the background. Here is the complete code which incorporates the above steps:

```
<center>
<table border="2" cellspacing="2">
<tr>
<td bgcolor="white"><font size="+2">HTML Web Magic</font></td>
<td bgcolor="yellow"><font size="+2">your dream guide to designing cool
➥Web pages</font></td>
</tr>
</table>
</center>
```

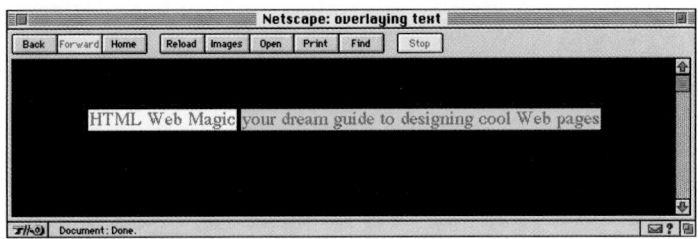

Compress the Table

With some adjustments to the `<td>` widths, you can compress your table to create the overlay effect.

1 All you need to do is compress the width of the first `<td>`. Set `width="5"`.

2 Because text normally wraps within a `<td>`, you must add a `<nobr>` or "no break" to force the text on one line and therefore allow the overhang. Without the `<nobr>`, the text would be compressed within the narrow `<td>`. Here is the proper code for the new first table data cell:

```
<td width="5" bgcolor="white"><nobr><font size="+2">HTML Web Magic</font>
➥</td>
```

187

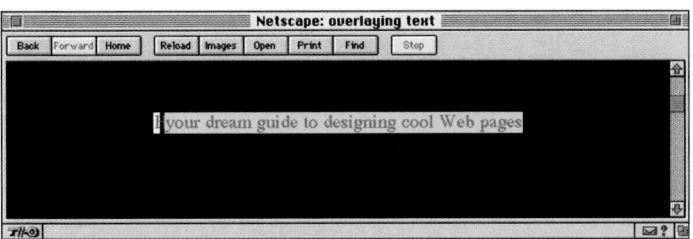

If you take off the table border and background colors, you can see how the overlapping text lies exactly on top of each other.

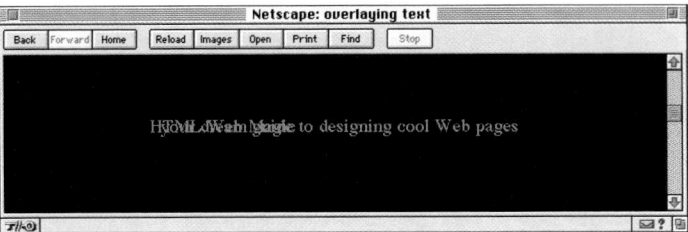

Adjust Alignment

Now let's play with alignment to orient the words properly. Remember that you can place the words horizontally and vertically within the <td> tags. Notice that overlapping text in this manner results in compressed leading or spaces between lines—something that is difficult to accomplish with straight text attributes in HTML, such as <br> or <p>, which create standard carriage returns.

The following steps describe how to deal with basic vertical alignment.

1 Adjust the vertical alignment for the first <td>. Simply add valign=top within the existing <td width="5"> tag to make its table data content align to the top of the <td>.

```
<td width="5" valign=top><nobr><font size="+2">HTML Web Magic
➥</font></td>
```

2 Adjust the vertical alignment for the second <td>. In addition to the valign=bottom attribute within the <td> tag, you must create some extra space above the text. Using the transparent GIF described in "Defining Space," you can set a specific amount of space just as you would set the dimensions of a regular graphic.

```
<td valign=bottom><img src="images/space.gif" width="1" height="10"
➥alt="This is a completely transparent graphic."><br><font
➥size="+2">your dream guide to designing ➥cool Web pages</font>
➥</td>
```

Modifying horizontal alignment follows the same ideas outlined above. Use align as you would valign except with the left, center, or right settings.

Sizes

A better way to see the overlapping effect in action is to adjust your font sizes. Enlarge the words that you want to emphasize and shrink the secondary details. Bigger objects seem to come forward, and smaller objects appear to recede.

1 Enlarge the text in the first `<td>`.

```
<td width="5" valign=top><nobr><font size="+5">HTML Web Magic</font></td>
```

2 Set the text in the second `<td>` to a smaller size and align it to the right.

```
<td width="325" align=right valign=bottom><img src="images/space.gif"
➥width="1" height="25" alt="This is a completely transparent
➥graphic."><br><font size=+1>your dream guide to designing  cool
➥Web pages</font></td>
```

After playing with the font sizes, you might need to re-adjust the alignment to create better results. As you can see from the figure, I had to adjust the vertical space above "your dream guide...," as well as set its `<td>` width so that the text extends further than the "HTML Web Magic" title.

Colors

Because the overlap effect necessarily brings text closer together than normal, how can you make sure that your ideas are still readable and emphasized? With font colors! This is an important option that can make your own example more of a success. Keep in mind that objects with warm or bright or dark colors seem to pop forward and approach the viewer whereas cool or dull or light colors seem to recede.

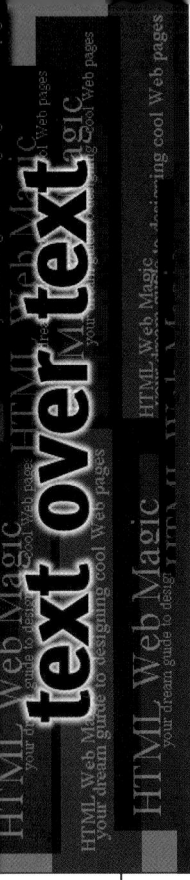

Here are two variations of the same code that includes color attributes. (See the "Varying Font Colors" technique (p.176) for more examples of text color variations.)

1 Change the color of the tagline that is located in the second `<td>` by adding the `color` attribute within the `<font>` tag like so:

```
<font size="+1" color="red">your dream guide to designing  
➥cool Web pages</font>
```

2 You can change the font color of the title text in the first `<td>` in the same way:

```
<font size="+5" color="red">HTML Web Magic</font>   ∎
```

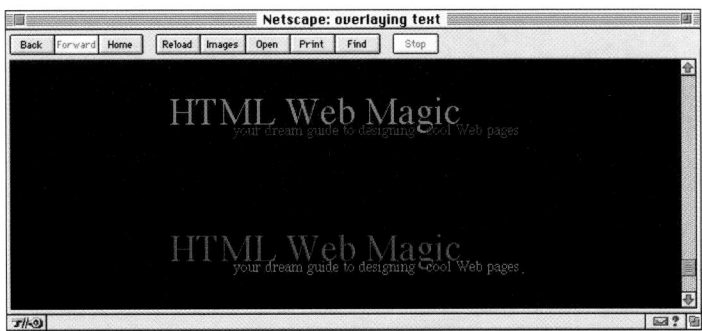

Fine-Tuning Header Typography

Use this technique to:

- **Stylize Headers.** Create customized headers in HTML by combining various techniques outlined in this book.

With one header, funkyWEBdesign, we'll outline various type, color, and size techniques you can use alone or together to create a unique look, all in HTML.

Writing the HTML

In this section, we'll dress up our headliness by varying different <FONT> tag attributes—all in the same head!

Emphasizing "Web"

1 Use the following example to emphasize the word WEB using color and all uppercase:

```
<FONT COLOR="white" FACE="courier" SIZE=7>funky</FONT>
<FONT COLOR="red" SIZE=7><b>WEB</b></FONT>
<FONT COLOR="white" FACE="courier" SIZE=7>design</FONT>
```

2 Use this example to emphasize the word WEB with color, larger type, and a different font:

```
<FONT COLOR=white FACE="courier" SIZE=6>f u n k y</FONT>
 
<FONT COLOR=darkturquoise FACE=Verdana, arial, helvetica
➡SIZE=7><b>WEB</b></FONT>
 
<FONT COLOR=white FACE="courier" SIZE=6>d e s i g n</FONT>
```

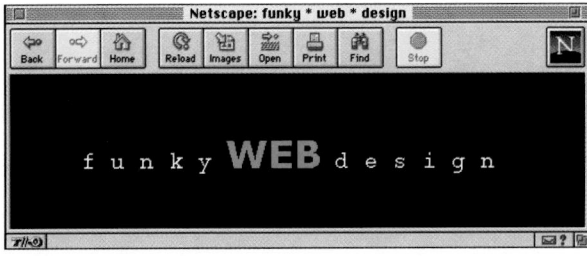

3 This code emphasizes the word web by color only:

```
<FONT COLOR=white FACE="helvetica" SIZE=7>funky</FONT>
<FONT COLOR=lime FACE="helvetica" SIZE=7>web</FONT>
<FONT COLOR=white FACE="helvetica" SIZE=7>design</FONT>
```

Emphasizing "Funky"

1 Use this example to emphasize the word funky using color, a different font, and all lowercase:

```
<FONT COLOR=tan FACE="arial black" SIZE=7><b>funky</b></FONT>
<FONT COLOR=maroon FACE="helvetica" SIZE=7>WEB</FONT>
<FONT COLOR=maroon FACE="helvetica" SIZE=7>DESIGN</FONT>
```

193

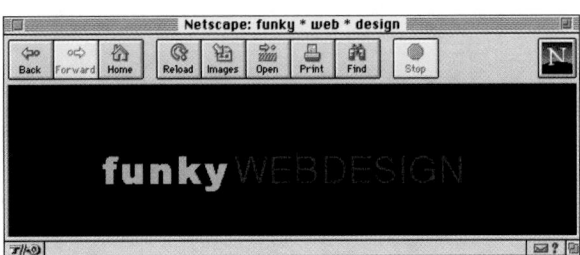

2 This code emphasizes the word funky by overlaying text, color, larger
size, and a different font:

```
<TABLE>
  <TR>
    <TD WIDTH=80>
      <FONT COLOR=gold FACE="courier" SIZE=7>funky</FONT></td>
    <TD><FONT COLOR=brown FACE="helvetica" SIZE=6>w e b</FONT>
     
      <FONT COLOR=brown FACE="helvetica" SIZE=6>d e s i g n</FONT>
    </TD>
  </TR>
</TABLE>
```

Emphasizing "Design"

1 This code uses color, a larger size, a different font, and a more widely
spaced look to distinguish the word "design":

```
<FONT COLOR=olive FACE="arial, helvetica" SIZE=6>funky * </FONT>
<FONT COLOR=olive FACE="arial, helvetica" SIZE=6>web</FONT>
<br>
<FONT COLOR=gold FACE="courier" SIZE=7><b> d e s i g n</b></FONT>
```

2 This code emphasizes the word design by making it white opposite colored words, and by using a more widely spaced presentation:

```
<FONT COLOR=tomato FACE="Verdana" SIZE=7>funky</FONT>
<FONT COLOR=tomato FACE="Verdana" SIZE=7>web</FONT>
<FONT COLOR=white FACE="Verdana" SIZE=7><b>d e s i g n</b></FONT>  ■
```

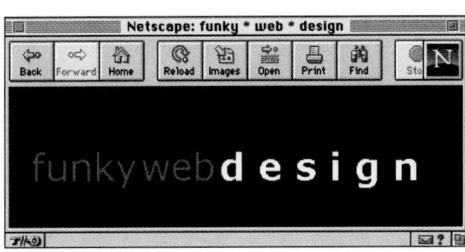

Text Leading

Use this technique to:

- **Create a double-spaced line effect.** Currently in HTML, formatting your pages to create text leading or double-spaced text is not possible. To solve this problem, Web designers are relying on one of the major tricks of the trade, the single pixel GIF. By making it transparent, you can have better control of layout and spacing of your pages by manipulating in HTML any one of four dimensions: height, width, vertical space, and horizontal space.

Writing the HTML

`<img src="pixel.gif" VSPACE="number" HSPACE="number">` transparent single pixel gif (adjust vertical and horizonal space as necessary)

Attributes

TYPE=horizontal or vertical

SIZE="number" (in pixels)

WIDTH="number"

HEIGHT="number"

ALIGN=left, right, center

We want to create a single pixel GIF and a text leading effect for this Web page.

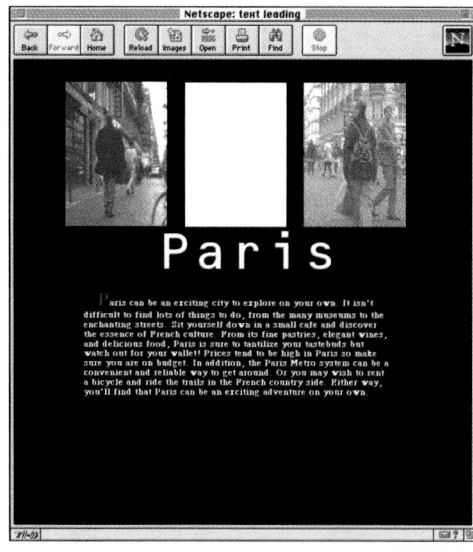

Creating Single Pixel GIF

1 Open any imaging software. (I used Adobe Photoshop 3.0 for this example.) Create a new document by selecting File➤New.

2 In the dialog box, enter 1 pixel for both the width and the height. Make sure the resolution is set at 72 pixels/inch (all Web graphics should be set at this number). The Mode is set to RGB Color and choose White in the Contents box. Click OK.

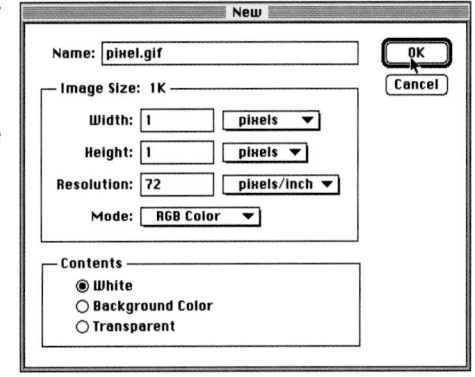

3 From the File menu choose Mode➤Index. The Resolution is automatically selected at Other: 2 colors and the Palette is Exact. Click OK.

4 Save as pixel.gif, select PhotoGIF, and make sure white is selected for transparency. Click OK to save the graphic.

Text Leading Effect

1 Open your HTML file. Add `<br>` line breaks to each line of text that may not be wrapping correctly.

```
&amp;&amp;&amp;<B><FONT SIZE=6 COLOR="#cc0000">P</FONT>aris can be an
➡exciting city to explore on your own. It isn't
<br><IMG SRC="images/pixel.gif" VSPACE=10>difficult to find lots of
➡things to do, from the many museums to the
<br>enchanting streets. Sit yourself down in a small cafe and dicover<br>
the essence of French culture. From its fine pastries, elegant wines,<br>
and delicious food, Paris is sure to tantalize your tastebuds but<br>
watch out for your wallet! Prices tend to be high in Paris so make<br>
```

2 Keep the text in a table because you have better control over layout.

```
<TABLE>
<TR>
<td>
&amp;&amp;&amp;<B><FONT SIZE=6 COLOR="#cc0000">P</FONT>aris can be an
➡exciting city to explore on your own. It isn't <br>
difficult to find lots of things to do, from the many museums to the<br>
enchanting streets. Sit yourself down in a small cafe and discover<br>
the essence of French culture. From its fine pastries, elegant wines,<br>
and delicious food, Paris is sure to tantalize your tastebuds but<br>
watch out for your wallet! Prices tend to be high in Paris so make <br>
```

```
sure you are on budget. In addition, the Paris Metro system can be
➥a<br>

convenient and reliable way to get around. Or you may wish to
➥rent<br>

a bicycle and ride the trails in the French country side. Either
➥way,<br>

you'll find that Paris can be an exciting adventure on your own.
</B>
</td>
</TR>
</TABLE>
```

TIP You can make the table a fixed width for better control of text flow, but keep in mind the different text and font display sizes on Macintosh and Windows. Windows browsers tend to display type a bit larger than that on a Macintosh.

3 Insert pixel.gif with a vertical space of 10 at the beginning of each line (after each <br>). Because this image is not supposed to be visible, do not enter an ALT tag for the pixel.gif.

```
<TABLE>
<TR>
<td>
<IMG SRC="images/pixel.gif" VSPACE=10>&amp;&amp;&amp;<B><FONT
➥SIZE=6 COLOR="#cc0000">P</FONT>aris can be an exciting city to
➥explore on your own. It isn't <br>

<IMG SRC="images/pixel.gif" VSPACE=10>difficult to find lots of
➥things to do, from the many museums to the <br>

<IMG SRC="images/pixel.gif" VSPACE=10>enchanting streets. Sit
➥yourself down in a small cafe and discover<br>

<IMG SRC="images/pixel.gif" VSPACE=10>the essence of French
➥culture. From its fine pastries, elegant wines,<br>

<IMG SRC="images/pixel.gif" VSPACE=10>and delicious food, Paris is
➥sure to tantalize your tastebuds but<br>

<IMG SRC="images/pixel.gif" VSPACE=10>watch out for your wallet!
➥Prices tend to be high in Paris so make <br>

<IMG SRC="images/pixel.gif" VSPACE=10>sure you are on budget. In
➥addition, the Paris Metro system can be a<br>

<IMG SRC="images/pixel.gif" VSPACE=10>convenient and reliable way
➥to get around. Or you may wish to rent<br>

<IMG SRC="images/pixel.gif" VSPACE=10>a bicycle and ride the trails
➥in the French country side. Either way,<br>

<IMG SRC="images/pixel.gif" VSPACE=10>you'll find that Paris can be
➥an exciting adventure on your own.
</B>
</td>
</TR>
</TABLE>
```

4 Save your HTML page and test the format in your browser.

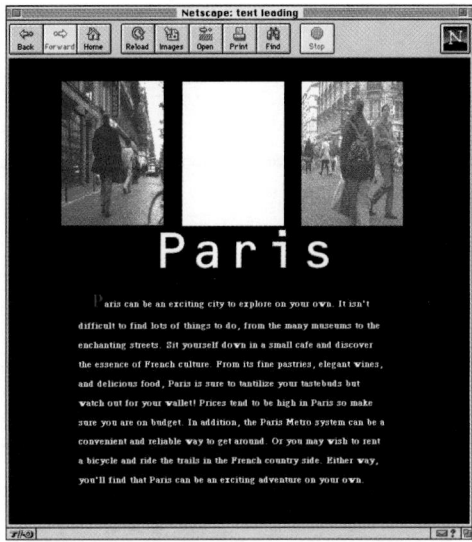

Browser Watch

Netscape 2.0 and higher

Internet Explorer 2.0 and higher

<SPACER> tag: Netscape 3.0 only ■

Determining Your Visitor's Browser and Platform

Use this technique to:

- **Tailor your site to the user's platform.** Something that looks perfect when you create it on the Macintosh usually looks skewed on a Windows machine. With some JavaScript, you can tailor your pages according to your user's platform.

- **Tailor your site to the user's browser.** By detecting which browser the client is using, you can give customized versions of your site to accommodate certain features enabled by the browser.

If you've found it virtually impossible to design one magic design that looks good on all Macintosh and Windows browsers, you can now write some JavaScript to adjust your HTML code according to certain conditions. You have a better chance to create a good first impression by only displaying pages relevant to a user's browser and platform.

Make your job easier by asking yourself who your audience is, and what hardware and software they use. You might have to make some tough choices and decisions. Remember that you can never please everyone.

Writing the HTML

After you write your HTML code as you normally would if you were addressing one specific audience, add the JavaScript functions described in the following steps to display pages specific to certain users.

Determining the Platform

One of the biggest differences between the Macintosh and Windows platforms is the way that they display fonts. Although a font size set to "2" may look beautiful on a Windows machine, it appears tiny and almost unreadable on a Macintosh. One solution to this problem is to set the font size at "2" if your visitor is using Windows and at "4" if your visitor is using a Macintosh. The code for the Macintosh example looks like this:

```
<font size="4">
This is some text on the page.
</font>
```

Insert the following code where you would normally put the opening <font size="4"> tag in order to use <font size="2"> if the visitor is using a Windows machine.

```
<SCRIPT LANGUAGE="JavaScript">
    if (navigator.appVersion.indexOf("Mac") > 1){
      document.write('<font size="4">');
    }else{
      document.write('<font size="2">');
    }
</SCRIPT>
```

In this example, you are working with the built in "appVersion" variable—a descriptive bit of text that comes built in to your browser. Although the PowerMac's appVersion looks like "3.0 (Macintosh; I; PPC)," on a Windows machine it looks like "3.0 (Win95; I)." The previous if statements determine whether the phrase "Mac" is found in the appVersion and set the font size to "4" by writing <font size="4">, otherwise; they write a tag that sets the font size to "2". Here is what the complete code looks like within the <body> tags:

```
<SCRIPT LANGUAGE="JavaScript">
    if (navigator.appVersion.indexOf("Mac") > 1){
      document.write('<font size="4">');
    }else{
          document.write('<font size="2">');
    }
</SCRIPT>
This text will be set at size 4 on the Mac and size 2 on the PC (and any
➥computer other than a Mac)
</font>
```

That's it! That simple. Of course, you can do all kinds of things in addition to setting the font size. For example, if you had a columns layout, you could stretch a one pixel GIF, as in "Manipulating Image Dimensions," a little more for the Windows version than on the Macintosh in order to create a vertical line that aligns to the bottom of the columns on both platforms. If you were dealing with advertising, you could write "BUY THESE MACINTOSH PRODUCTS" if the visitor is using a Macintosh or "BUY A PC UPGRADE" if the visitor is using a PC. The possibilities are endless!

201

Determining the Browser

Differences between browsers are even more extreme than between platforms. Microsoft Internet Explorer 3.0, for example, has the capability to display floating frames, whereas Netscape Navigator does not. You could detect which browser the visitor is using and route them to a page featuring floating frames if they are using MSIE 3.0 or to a page with regular frames if they are using Netscape. If you have a lot of time, you can make an entire site for one set of users and an another site for the other. Here are the steps that enable you to detect your user's browser and display a specific version of a page.

   1 **Create a welcome page with an entry button.** An easy way to create a button for your page is to use the standard button input type used in HTML forms. Set

the input value equal to the text that will be displayed on the button. Add the "onClick" event handler to call upon the function, "routeUser()," when the button is clicked.

```
<form>
<input type=button value="Enter My Site" onClick="routeUser()">
</form>
```

2 **Define the routing function.** When the user clicks the button, the function routeUser checks if the phrase "Explorer" is found within the built-in object called "appName." If the phrase is found, the location is set to "explorerSite.html," the Internet Explorer version of the page. Otherwise, the user is sent to "netscapeSite.html." Here is what the JavaScript looks like incorporated within the HTML code:

```
<html>
<head>
<scipt language="JavaScript">
function routeUser(){
    if (navigator.appName.indexOf("Explorer") > 1){
      location="explorerSite.html";
    }else{
      location="netscapeSite.html";
    }
}
</script>
<title>Browser Test</title>
</head>

<body>

<form>
<input type=button value="Enter My Site" onClick="routeUser()">
</form>

</body>
</html>
```

Advanced features in some browsers are unavailable in older versions. For the 1996 Macromedia International User Conference and Exhibition, the Macromedia site hosted a live Web broadcast of conference events. Programmer John Petersen wrote a simple code to check what version of browser visitors had in order to display a special floating navigational bar with JavaScript roll-overs in a pop-up window.

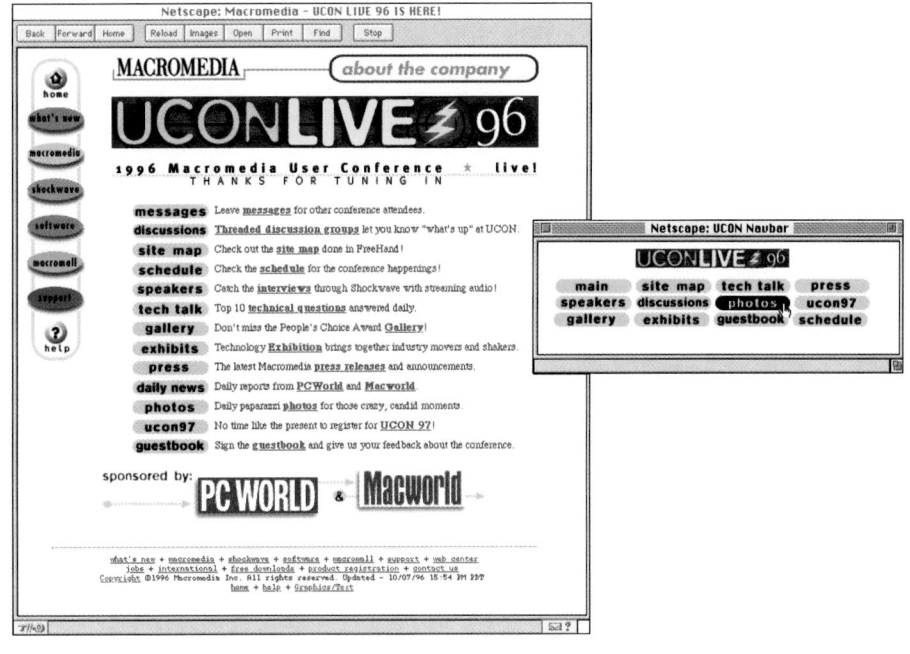

```
<html>
<head>
<script language="JavaScript">
var vers = navigator.appVersion.charAt(0);
if (vers >= 3) {
  window.name = "mywin";

newwin=open("index2.html","win","width=400,height=120,scrollbars=no,menubar=no");
}
</script>
<title>Macromedia - UCON LIVE 96 IS HERE!</title>
</head>
```

His script determined whether not a visitor had Netscape Navigator version 3.0 in order to display the special navigation. If a user had an older version of Netscape or an entirely different browser, then he or she saw only the main page in the original window.

You can help your users by making certain viewing choices for them. With JavaScript, you can tailor your pages to reflect cosmetic changes, as in the font size example, or to display user-specific content, as in the advertising and the routing examples. Your users can experience the best possible viewing conditions of your site based on their own browser and platform capabilities. ■

Detecting Specific Plug-Ins

Use this technique to:

■ **Check if a visitor's browser is enabled to view your site properly.** Hate broken icons? If your Web site requires a specific plug-in to view it, do your audience a favor by checking for them.

■ **Provide different versions of your home page (or entire Web site).** You will do favors for two types of viewers—those without the plug-in and those with it. Those without the plug-in get a page that recommends downloading it, and those already equipped with it get to go straight to the "plugged" version of your site.

You can minimize the chances for this broken icon situation by determining whether or not a visitor has the necessary plug-in(s) to view and experience your pages properly. If a visitor has the plug-in, great! If not, you can feed them a page with a static image, regular GIF or JPEG and direct your visitor to the appropriate place to get the download. Certain browsers are taking steps to bundle plug-ins automatically, but it might be a while until this option is available.

Writing the HTML

In this section, we'll write a simple JavaScript that tests for the QuickTime plug-in. If the plug-in is missing, we'll swap in a new page for the current page.

1 Create a backup version of your page that doesn't use the plug-in that you're seaching for. In this example, the backup page should be called "Backup.html" and should reside in the same folder as the page that contains the script.

2 Create a JavaScript function that tests to see if the plug-in is installed in the browser. The function below searches for any plug-in name passed to it as a parameter and returns a value of true if the plug-in is installed.

```
<html>
<head>
<title>plugin examples</title>
<script>
function plugdetect(plugName)
    {
        if (navigator.plugins[plugName]) return true;
        else return false;
    }
```

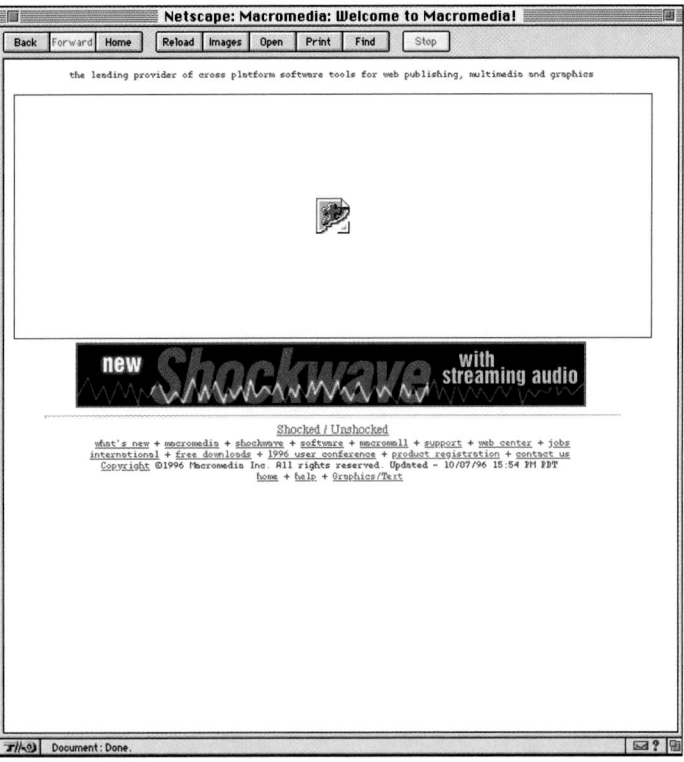

3 Call the plug-in. If the QuickTime plug-in isn't installed, the function returns a value of false, and the script replaces the current page with Backup.html. If the plug-in is installed, the current page does nothing. Here's the code:

```
if (!plugdetect("QuickTime Plugin"))
    {
        location.replace("Backup.html")
    }
</script>
</head>
```

4 Add whatever body section you like to the HTML document. ■

Using Form Input Without CGI Scripts

Use this technique to:

■ **Get information from your audience and respond according to their feedback.** You can orchestrate your pages to respond to user input. Feed specific pages to your users based upon the responses they give in HTML forms.

■ **Process information from forms without dealing with your server or server administrator.** Achieving interactivity with your visitors involves a certain amount of scripting—simple or sophisticated. You can sidestep the need for writing your own CGI scripts.

Using this technique is like playing a game with your audience. Implementing JavaScript in your HTML forms gets your audience more involved in their experience of your site. With a few simple commands, you can compile information from user input in a simple form to crank out pages that relate to the users' answers.

Writing the HTML

In this technique, we'll use a form to create navigation controls for the user. Rather than submitting the form to a CGI for processing, however, we'll use a JavaScript to process the user's form entries and (after a bit of calculation) direct the browser to load the appropriate URL.

We thought it would be fun to take the example of a "virtual restaurant" to demonstrate this technique. The home page of this site presents the user with a form asking two basic questions, "How hungry are you?" and "What type of meal would you like?" Each response has two radio button options. The user can either select "Starving!" or "Not that hungry" in combination with "Meat Entrées" or "Vegetarian Entrées." By responding to these questions, the user then receives a customized menu.

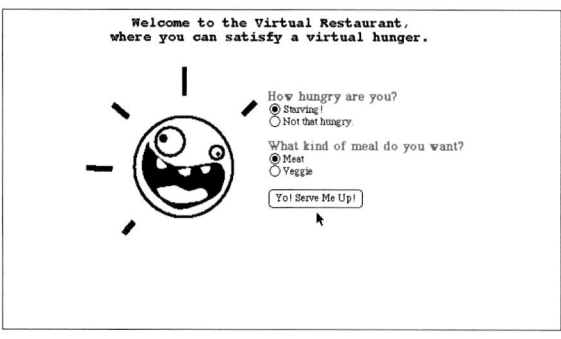

TIP Adding more questions and more options per question tailors the survey further to a customers needs but creates more work for you. Start with this example and add more questions as you see fit when you're more comfortable with the technique.

Creating the Form

In order to get user feedback, you must design a page with some sort of survey in the format of an HTML form. After the form, you must define a function within the <head> tags that processes the head information.

1 **Assign names to the radio buttons.** Name the radio buttons that indicate how hungry the user is, hungerRating. Name the radio buttons that indicate what kind of meal the user wants, mealType. The function that processes the form information uses these names later.

2 **Assign values to the radio buttons.** Give each radio button a specific value that represents the checked response. The different values for my "virtual restaurant" are starved, soso, meat, and veggie. Again, the function definition will use these values to process the form data.

3 **Add a button to call upon the processing function.** After the user fills out the form, he or she must click on a button in order to get to the customized menu. Behind the scenes, this button accesses a JavaScript function processForm by way of the onClick even handler. Here is the code for the entire form:

```
<form name="info">
<b><font color="red" size="+1">How hungry are you?</font></b><BR>
<input name="hungerRating" TYPE="radio" value="starved">Starving!<BR>
<input name="hungerRating" TYPE="radio" value="soso">Not that hungry.<P>
<b><font color="red" size=+1>What kind of meal do you want?</font></b>
➥<BR>
<input name="mealType" TYPE="radio" value="meat">Meat<BR>
<input name="mealType" TYPE="radio" value="veggie">Veggie<P>
<input type=button value="Yo! Serve Me Up!" onClick="processForm
➥(this.form)">
</form>
```

Defining the Function

The processForm function takes the data from the form and sorts which HTML page the user should get next. The definition of the function must incorporate checking the radio buttons with routing the user to pages related to these answers.

1 **Verify which buttons are checked.** Use for loops to scan through the radio buttons and determine what the user selected.

2 **Route the user to a specific page.** Use if-else statements that use combinations of input value pairs to test where a user should go. Here is the code for the entire function definition that lies between the <head> tags:

```
<head>
<script language="JavaScript">
//this function takes the data from the form and sorts out
//which html page they should get next
  function processForm(form){
      var hunger="", meal="";
      //loops through the radio buttons finding out which one is selected
      for (var i=0; i<2; i++){
        if (form.hungerRating[i].checked==1){
          hunger=form.hungerRating[i].value;
        }
      }
      for (var i=0; i<2; i++){
        if (form.mealType[i].checked==1){
          meal=form.mealType[i].value;
        }
      }
      //series of if else statements, sorts out where the user should be
➡routed
      if ((hunger == "starved") & (meal == "meat")){
        location="starvedMeat.html";
      }else if ((hunger == "starved") & (meal == "veggie")){
        location="starvedVeggie.html";
      }else if ((hunger == "soso") & (meal == "meat")){
        location="sosoMeat.html";
        }else if ((hunger == "soso") & (meal == "veggie")){
          location="sosoVeggie.html";
      }
  }
</script>
</head>
```

If a user is starving and wants to eat meat, he or she will see a different customized menu page than a vegetarian who is not so hungry.

That's all there is to it. This technique provides a way for your users to have fun and interact with you through your content. By creating an engaging survey with customized results, you could inspire your users to fill out the form again and again just to see the results of the answers. ■

Refresh Function

Use this technique to:

- **Create a front-door home page.** You can create a simple logo for your home page and have it automatically jump to your table of contents.

- **Cycle pages.** Create an automatic gallery that can cycle through different pages.

- **Make stylized animations.** Create thematically related Web pages and cycle through them to create a story or message.

- **Move to a new URL.** As your site grows, use the Refresh tag to "jump" users to the correct pages.

The Refresh function is an easy way to automate your HTML pages. You can time your pages to automatically "jump" users from one page to another.

Writing the HTML

```
<META HTTP-EQUIV="Refresh" CONTENT="numberofseconds; URL="page.html">
```

1 Create a simple, streamlined home page. In this example, we use the J. Crew site.

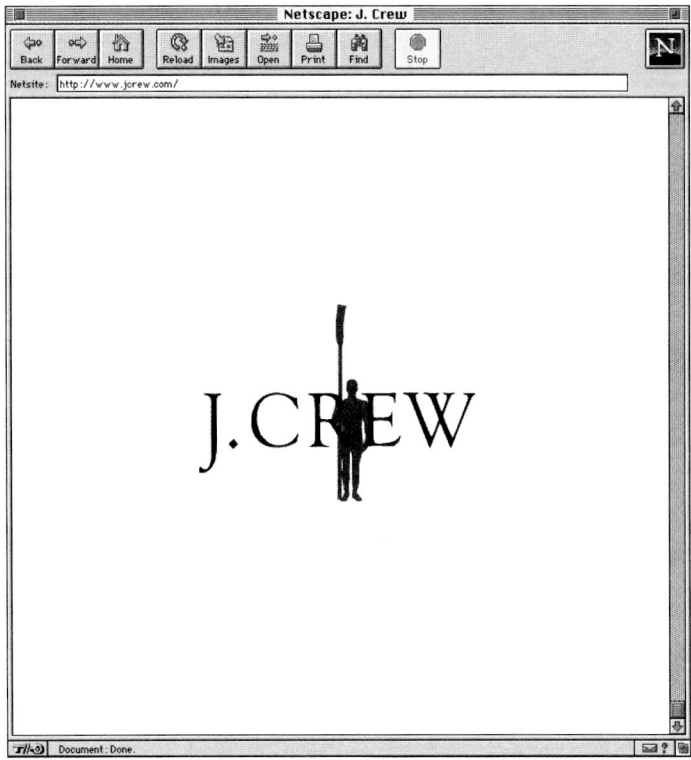

2 Add the following META Refresh tag before the closing </head> html tag:

```
<META HTTP-EQUIV="Refresh" CONTENT="20; URL="index2.html">
```

Content indicates the number of seconds idle and URL indicates which new page to jump to.

TIP Make sure you allow enough time for users to be on a page; usually somewhere between 15-30 seconds. Test on different modem speeds and browsers to make sure that your users have enough time to view the changing of the pages. Note that the timing starts as soon as the page starts to load, so allot enough time for the full page to load before it jumps to the next.

3 In addition to Refresh, you can also add the URL link to the graphic so that users have the choice to jump to the next page if they do not want to wait.

```
<A HREF="index2.html"> <IMG SRC="images/jcrew_title.gif" WIDTH=267
➥ALIGN=MIDDLE BORDER=0></A>
```

4 Save your HTML document, upload and test in your browser. Your main index page should jump after 20 seconds to index2.html.

211

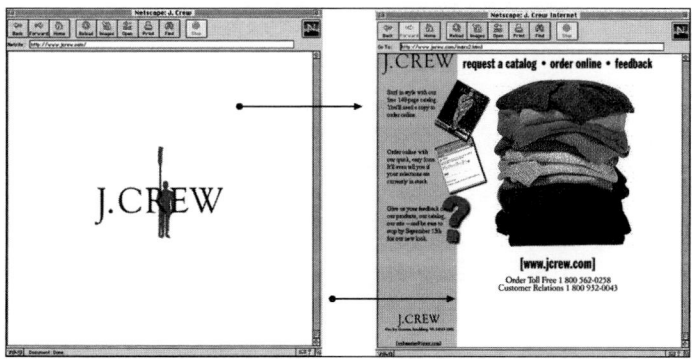

Using the Refresh function is good for opening pages where there isn't a lot of information. Perhaps the page is just a logo or a series of images for a gallery. Nonetheless, make sure that the function is useful and that it won't annoy users who want to remain on the page.

VARIATIONS

Another variation is automatic gallery display. You can create a "slide show" of different images by controlling the timing.

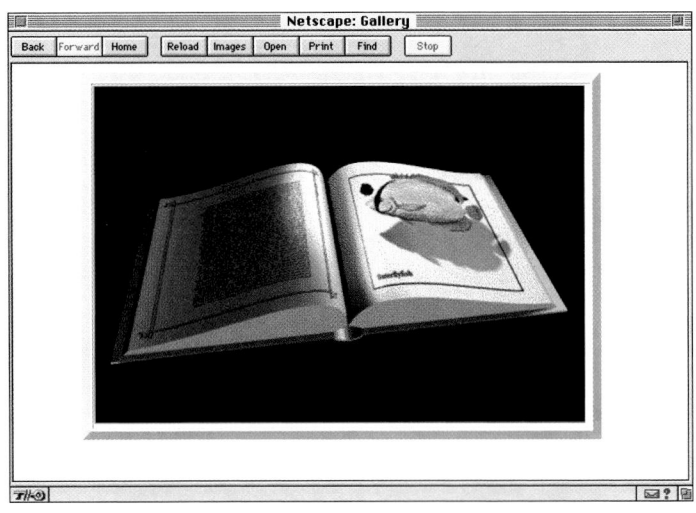

Browser Watch

Netscape 2.0 and higher

Internet Explorer 3.0 ◼

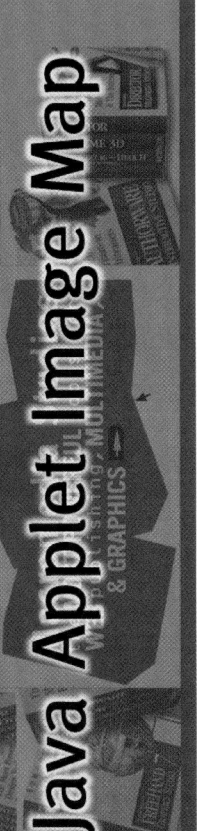

Creating Java Applet Image Maps

Use this technique to:

- **Create easy roll-over animations.** Roll-over animations (images that change when the mouse "rolls over" them) are a great way to grab the user's attention.

- **Add pop-up text that names each hot region as you roll-over.** If you use image maps to help users navigate your site, pop-up text can make your image maps even easier to use. When the user moves the mouse over an image map hot spot, the text can provide information about the destination URL, or any other information you'd like to provide.

- **Outline hot regions of any shape with any color.** You can stylize image maps by creating colored outlines that appear and disappear as the mouse moves through the image map.

- **Create interactive animation using multiple hot regions with replacement images.** For an interesting effect, you can set up your image map so that it changes as the user passes the mouse over the image map. You can use this effect to give the user visual feedback, or just to catch the user's eye.

- **Add dazzling effects using hot regions within hot regions.** Go beyond the basic HTML image map specification and make your image maps as flexible as you want them to be.

Image maps take on a new dimension with Macromedia Java PowerApplets. You can highlight, outline, replace graphics as roll-overs, add effects and more! The easiest way to create a PowerApplet image map is to use AppletAce. You can find it on the CD or download the most current version at `http://www.macrome-dia.com/software/powerapplets/`.

Writing the HTML

AppletAce writes your HTML for for you! All you need to do is design your image map with AppletAce's visual interface. When you've previewed your image map, cut and paste the script into your HTML.

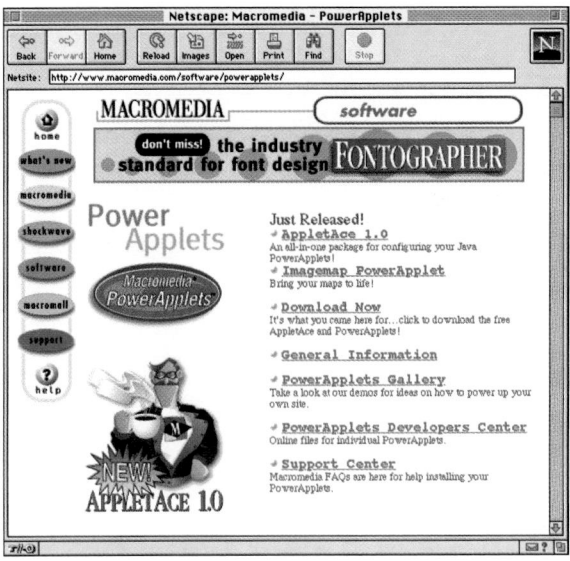

Creating a Replacement Graphic

1 Create your graphics. In this example, idle.gif is the graphic you want on the page and hot.gif is the graphic you want to replace it with when the mouse rolls over.

TIP Unlike using roll-overs in JavaScript or in a Shockwave movie, replacement graphics must have all the roll-overs in one graphic. You must select each area individually in order to "paste" in the correct roll-over. Therefore, if you create a bunch of different roll-overs for idle.gif, hot.gif has to contain all of the different roll-over replacement images.

2 Open AppletAce and select Image Map from the pull-down menu. Type in the width and height of idle.gif, choose alignment of the image map, and add the name of the directory where you want to place your image map. Do not enter anything in the "HTML Directory" or "Copy Applets To:" boxes. You will add these into the HTML manually.

215

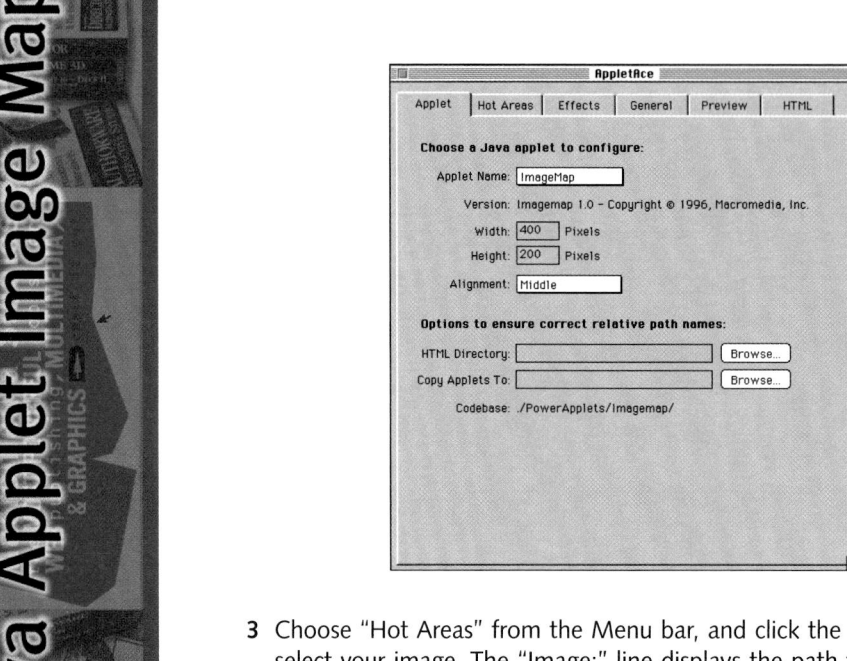

3 Choose "Hot Areas" from the Menu bar, and click the Browse button to select your image. The "Image:" line displays the path from your desktop. Keep this here so you can preview the image map in AppletAce.

4 For the Default Mouse Enter Effect, choose replaceImage. A dialog box appears asking you to locate your replacement image. Find hot.gif and choose OK.

5 Click the Box tool on the side bar next to the graphic and select the entire graphic. Type **studios** for the Hot Area Name and enter the Target URL as http://www.macromedia.com/software. (Target Frame is used when you want the URLs to appear in an adjoining frame or new browser window, and Pop-up Text is used for creating and naming small pop-up boxes that appear when you roll-over the hot area.)

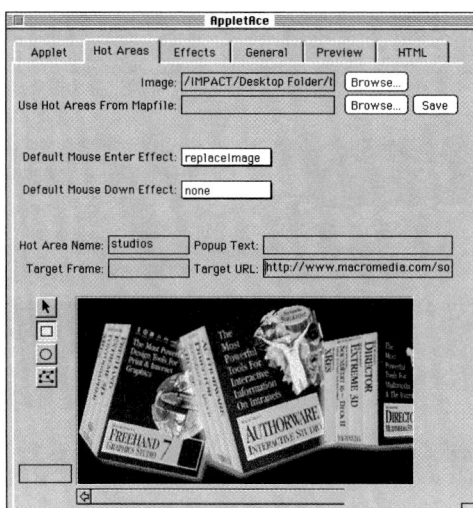

6 Go to Preview and roll-over the image. It should replace the image with hot.gif.

7 Choose HTML from the Menu bar and cut and paste the script from the window into your HTML document.

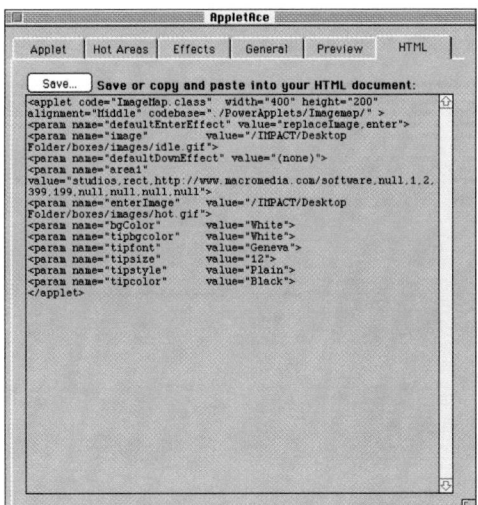

8 Go into the HTML document and fix the paths to the exact location in your directory structure. Add the following code where you would ordinarily add the `<IMG ISMAP>` tag:

```
<applet code="ImageMap.class" width="400" height="200"
➥alignment="Middle" codebase="Imagemap/" >
<param name="defaultEnterEffect" value="replaceImage,enter">
<param name="image"         value="boxes/images/idle.gif">
<param name="defaultDownEffect" value="(none)">
<param name="area1"
value="studios,rect,http://www.macromedia.com/software,null,1,2,399,
➥199,null,null,null,null">
<param name="enterImage" value="boxes/images/hot.gif">
<param name="bgColor"     value="White">
<param name="tipbgcolor"  value="White">
<param name="tipfont"     value="Geneva">
<param name="tipsize"     value="12">
<param name="tipstyle"    value="Plain">
<param name="tipcolor"    value="Black">
</applet>
```

9 Upload the image map classes taken from the PowerApplets folder located in your AppletAce folder. Upload all the contents of the image map directory.

The classes must live either in the same directory as the HTML file or in one directory below the HTML file.

10 Test the HTML document in your browser.

Here's what the image map looks like when it's first loaded:

Here's what the image map looks like after the user rolls the mouse over a hot spot:

Browser Watch

Netscape 3.0 (Macintosh)

Netscape 2.0 (Windows 95/NT)

Internet Explorer 3.0 (Windows only)

Other Java-compatible browsers, such as HotJava

 For security reasons, all Java-compatible browsers offer the user the option of disabling Java. Even the browsers listed in the Browser Watch section will not support this technique if Java has been turned off in the browser. ■

HTML Animation with Java Applet Banners

Use this technique to:

- **Create text-based animation with special effects.** Message animations include scroll, zoom, wipe, and fade.

- **Load messages from a URL, and reload often for fast-changing content.** A single banner applet can display any message you want. You can change the message without changing the applet or any HTML by editing a text file on your server.

A banner is a Java applet that provides text animation and effects geared toward displaying continuous, changing information on Web pages in eye-catching ways. You can animate any number of separately controllable messages by using banners.

Writing the HTML

All of the hard work in this technique—writing the applet and HTML code to add it to your page—is done by Applet Ace. You need to cut and paste the automatically generated HTML into your own page...that's it!

Creating the Banner

In this example, you are going to create an ad banner that displays text in different effects.

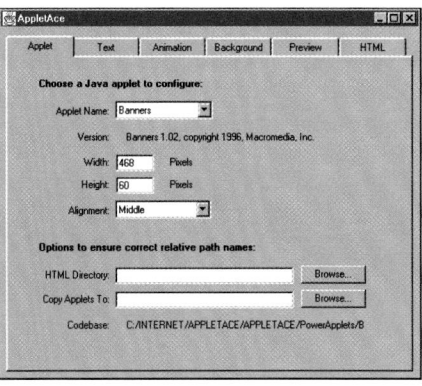

1 Open AppletAce and choose Banners from the Applet Name pull-down menu. To set the size of your banner, enter Width=468 and Height=60. From the Alignment pull-down menu choose Middle.

2 To create text, click the Text tab at the top of the window. Type **welcome** in the Text of Message dialog box. Choose the font attributes using the pull-down menus. For this example Font: Courier, Style: Bold, Effect: None, Size: 36, and Color: White were used.

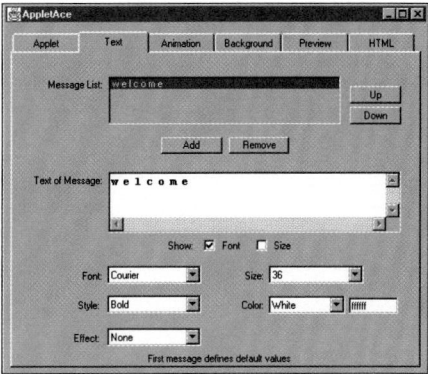

3 Click on the Animation tab. Use the pull-down menus to choose the Entrance and Exit properties. (Your choices in the pull-down menu include: None, ScrollLeft, ScrollRight, ScrollUp, ScrollDown, ZoomIn, ZoomOut, WipeLeft, WipeRight, WipeUp, WipeDown, and Fade.) For this example, ZoomIn for the entrance and fade for the exit were used.

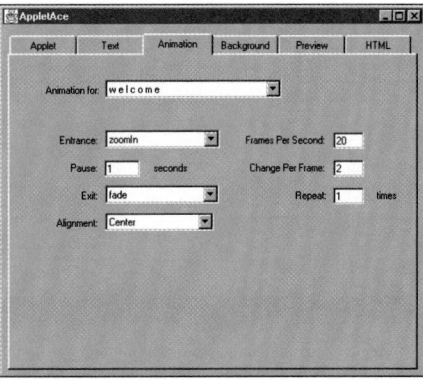

4 Choose your background by clicking on the Background tab. Highlight the Solid Color button and choose Black from the Background pull-down menu. In this example, black with a white border of value 3 was used. This menu also enables you to add URLs to link text.

221

5 Go back to the Text tab and add the content of your banner. Choose different fonts if you want and repeat Steps 2 and 3.

Creating the HTML

1 Click on the HTML tab. Cut the applet code from the AppletAce window and paste it into your HTML document.

2 Double-check the codebase attribute in the HTML. If you have copied the applets to a directory called "Banners" inside the directory that contains your HTML page, the codebase attribute should read:

```
codebase = "/banners"
```

In general, the codebase specifies the directory where the applets are stored, and is required *only* if the applets are not in the same directory as the HTML file that references them.

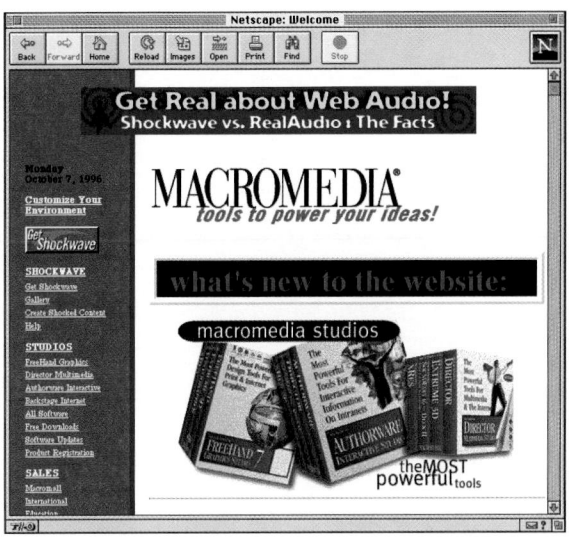

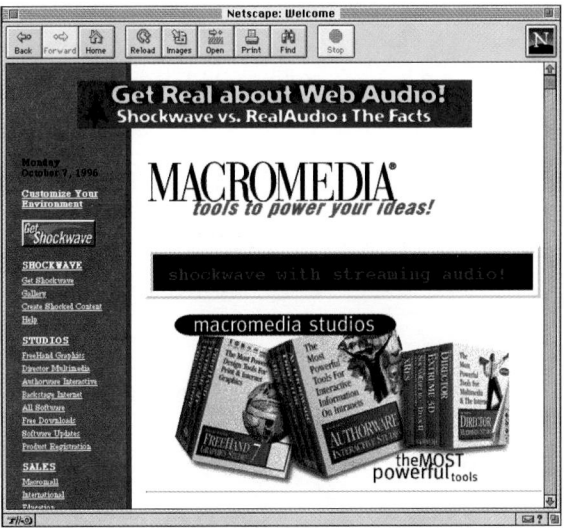

223

Browser Watch

Netscape 2.0 and higher for Windows

Netscape 3.0 for Macintosh

Internet Explorer 3.0

 NOTE For security reasons, all Java-compatible browsers offer the user the option of disabling Java. Even the browsers listed in the Browser Watch section will not support this technique if Java has been turned off in the browser. ■

Customizing Alert Boxes

Use this technique to:

■ **Provide specific instructions or directions.** This is your way to provide a customized message to your users instead of letting them get a default error message.

■ **Provide a tip.** If you have a cool tip, service, or product to offer your users, you can give them a surprise each time they click on a certain button.

Customizing alert boxes for your site enables you to have fun with your audience. Many people are intimidated by alert boxes because they automatically assume that something is wrong. Unfortunately, you can't change that exclamation point graphic that contributes to this impression. Use your sense of humor and surprise your audience with a joke. They will notice and appreciate your efforts and come back for more.

Writing the HTML

Alert boxes serve as reminders associated with form input. Using a series of `"if-else"` statements in Java Script, you can test to see if a user has left input fields blank or has typed data incorrectly into your HTML form. Alert boxes can also confirm that the user is about to execute a certain function with the given parameters.

The Main Quad provides some fun alternatives to the standard alert box text. Their "Flash Card" service enables users to send Web greeting cards to anyone with an email address. The service requires that you fill out a form to send the card.

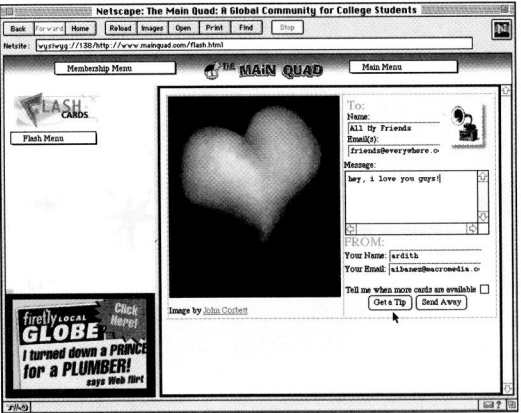

Because leaving certain fields empty makes it impossible to send the card, Ben Rigby programmed customized alert boxes to display certain messages according to the missing data. Some examples are quite funny.

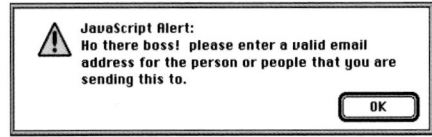

Creating the Form

In this example, you want to use an abbreviated version of the form used to send a "Flash Card." You need entry fields for a name and email address, and a button to process the data.

1 Create the input field for the recipient's name. Within the `<form>` tags, use the `<input>` tag and assign it a name:

```
Name: <input name="recipientName">
```

2 Create the input field for the recipient's email address. Use the same format that you used for the name, but be sure to assign a unique name to this input field:

```
Email(s): <input name="recipientEmail">
```

3 Create the button to send the card. Use the button input type with the "`onClick`" event handler that calls upon the function "`prepareAndSend`."

```
<input type=button value="Send Away" onClick="prepareAndSend(form)">
```

Defining the Function

Within the `<head>` tags of the HTML lies the definition for the "`preapreAndSend`" function that checks the form data.

1 Create the alert box for an empty field for the recipient's name. Use an "`if`" statement to verify whether or not the input field was left empty. Then, add "`alert`" followed by your customized message contained in parentheses and quotes.

```
if (form.recipientName.value == ""){
alert ("Hey, who you sending this to? Please enter their name.");
return;
}
```

2 Create the alert box for an invalid email address. Use another "`if`" statement that checks to see if the email input field is entered and if the "@" character is missing.

```
if ((form.recipientEmail.value == "" || form.recipientEmail.value.
➥indexOf ('@',0)==-1)){
    alert ("Ho there boss! please enter a valid email address for the
➥person or people that you are sending this to.");
```

225

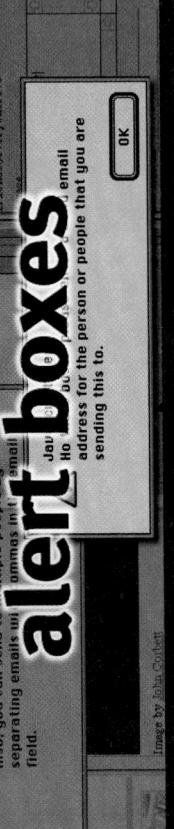

```
        return;
    }
```

3 Only after the user fulfills these criteria can the function successfully send the form data. Here is the the the code for the function, "prepareAndSend:"

```
<script language="JavaScript">
 function prepareAndSend(form){
   if (form.recipientName.value == ""){
     alert ("Hey, who you sending this to? Please enter their
 ➥name.");
     return;
   }
   if ((form.recipientEmail.value == "" ¦¦ form.recipientEmail.
 ➥value.indexOf ('@',0)==-1)){
     alert ("Ho there boss! please enter a valid email address for
 ➥the person or people that you are sending this to.");
     return;
   }
   form.submit();
   }
</script>
```

Creating an Alert Box to Share a Tip

Alert boxes do not always have to signify errors. Use this form of communication to provide tips or to promote a special service or product. The same "Flash Card" example also utilizes the alert box feature to display a helpful hint in sending a card when the user clicks on the "Get a Tip" button.

This button depends on a different function to execute its task. By defining the "tip" function within the <head> tags, you can edit the tip text easily, even if the body of the page changes drastically.

1 Create the "Get a Tip" button. As with the "Send Away" button of the previous example, use the button input type within a form with the "onClick" event handler. This time it should call upon the "tip" function.

```
<input type=button value="Get a Tip" onClick="tip()">
```

2 Define the "`tip`" function. Again, set up your definition within the `<head>` tags. The function requires no "`if-else`" tests. It creates an alert box with the `alert` command followed by the customized message:

```
function tip(){

   alert('You can write HTML code in the message box. Also, you can ↦send
to multiple people by separating emails with commas in the email
↦field.');

   }
```

As you can see, your options are limited only by your imagination! ∎

227

Appendix

Browser Capabilities and Comparison Chart

Windows

Browsers	Supporting Elements
Netscape Navigator 3.0	Java, frames, tables, plug-ins, font size, font color, font face, colored table data cells, columns, compacted lists, JavaScript, animated GIFs
Netscape Navigator 2.0	Java, frames, tables, plug-ins, font size, font color, compacted lists, JavaScript, animated GIFs
Netscape Navigator 1.1	Tables, font size
Microsoft Internet Explorer 3.0	Java, frames, tables, plug-ins, font size, font color, font face, colored table data cells, compacted lists, JavaScript, animated GIFs, style sheets
Microsoft Internet Explorer 2.0	Tables, font size, font color
Microsoft Internet Explorer 1.0	Tables, font size, font color
Mosaic 2.1.1	Tables
Mosaic 1.0	None
AOL Browser 3.0	Frames, tables, font size, font color
AOL Browser 1.0	None

Macintosh

Browsers	Supporting Elements
Netscape Navigator 3.0	Java, frames, tables, plug-ins, font size, font color, JavaScript, animated GIFs
Netscape Navigator 2.0	Frames, tables, plug-ins, font size, font color, JavaScript, animated GIFs
Netscape Navigator 1.1	Tables, font size
Microsoft Internet Explorer 2.1b1	Tables, plug-ins, font size, font color
Mosaic 3.0b4	Frames, tables, font size, font color
Mosaic 2.0	Tables
Mosaic 1.0	None
AOL Browser 2.7	None
AOL Browser 1.0	None

 NOTE Data obtained from Webmonkey Browser Kit, October, 1996. For more up-to-date browser capabilities see http://www.webmonkey.com/browserkit/. ■